THE BEST OF WOOLDRIDGE

THE BEST OF WOOLDRIDGE

EVEREST BOOKS LTD
4 Valentine Place, London SE1 8QH

Published in Great Britain by Everest Books Ltd, 1978
ISBN 0905018 737

Designed by: GWA Ltd, Strand, W.C.2.
Typeset by: BSC Graphics Ltd.
Printed in Great Britain by The Anchor Press Ltd.,
and bound by Wm Brendon & Sons Ltd., both of Tiptree, Essex.

Introduction

Far from being a collected works this is a confusion of newspaper columns originally written in hotel rooms, stadium press boxes, bars and, failing all else, the friendly and invigorating lunatic asylum more formally known as the open-plan newsroom of the Daily Mail, *London.*

A few were written at leisure, most with one eye on the clock. All of them were written for money, sportswriting being a marvellously equable arrangement by which a newspaper actually pays you for doing what you were going to do anyway.

The intimidating idea of laying them end to end in book form was not mine. It originated with a Daily Mail *reader, Col Steve Purcell, who contacted the publisher. I hope they knew what they were doing.*

The selection of pieces is mine, however, and their arrangement less arbitrary than sheerly high-handed. They do not appear chronologically and only in a few instances are they linked together by subject. The only motive was to suggest that, contrary to East German methodism, sport is still about people and places and losers and friendships and style.

There are many people I now have a chance to thank. They include:
The sportsmen and sportswomen who actually do it; my sportswriting colleagues in Fleet Street without whom it wouldn't be worth doing it; the sports sub-editors on the Daily Mail *who have kept the lawyers at bay; my proprietor, Vere Harmsworth, for footing the bills; my editor, David English, and my sports editor, Tom Clarke, for their enthusiasm, encouragement and occasional indulgence; three former sports editors, Bill Hicks, Bob Findlay and late J.L. Manning for years of experience generously offered; and, above all, my wife, Veronica, who has kept the home fires burning and both feet firmly on the ground.*

Four months before the Raid on Entebbe a somewhat less imposing commando, similarly uninvited, arrived in Uganda at dawn. My companion, uniformly crumpled after an overnight flight from Rome, was Monty Fresco, a Cockney Jewish photographer with the resilience and resource of all three of those races. It was a period in Ugandan history when foreign journalists were particularly unwelcome, a reality proved by my Daily Mail *colleague Leslie Watkins the previous year when he was transported directly from Entebbe Airport to jail without passing go. While our real motive was to see how a nation was faring under the patronage of a bloodstained maniac we at least had the spurious excuse of arriving to cover a major boxing match which, predictably, never took place.*

At the immigration barrier we were immediately invited to leave. "S'orright, dawling," said Fresco, waving a glossy photograph of President Amin under the eyes of a bemused man in uniform, "yer guvnor's a personal mate of mine." He started walking and thus we entered that satanic dictatorship.

For five days we were required to report each morning to the Ministry of Information. For five days Fresco was forbidden to take pictures. For five days he bewildered Ministers and Permanent Secretaries with a galaxy of outrageous lies, Kosher jokes, inquiries about their pension schemes, cackling laughs, dismissive waves, solicitous concern for their children and repeated reminders that to offend us would be to imprecate the wrath of our close friend, the President. On the sixth morning we flew 200 miles west by private plane to Semliki where we were granted an interview.

President Amin was childishly flattered to be questioned about his boxing career. He was more reluctant to demonstrate his sparring style. Even this failed to defeat Fresco's ingenuity. "My friend 'ere," he said, referring to an apprehensive reporter whose pugilistic career was as brief as it was abysmal, "is a very fine boxah. Go'orn, sir, whack 'im." Fresco got his pictures. Next morning we courageously caught the first plane out of Entebbe to Kenya.

There is a distressing postscript. The Minister of Culture and Sport, referred to in this column, was Major-General Francis Nyangweso. Eleven months later he was posted missing, presumed assassinated.

‘I am still heavyweight champion of Uganda. Nobody is willing to fight me’

Semliki, Uganda. — As befits any humanitarian who only that morning had stepped straight from the breakfast table to save seven men from the firing squad, His Excellency Field-Marshal Doctor Idi Amin Dada, VC, DSO, MC, was in benevolent mood.

The blades of his armour-plated helicopter had barely stopped spraying dust in our faces before he lumbered forward, hand extended, and said: ‘My aides tell me you have come from London to discuss my boxing career.’

This was not necessarily the whole truth but one does not readily contradict a 19-stone statesman with a gun at his hip even though he has recently been cleared of an allegation of murdering not fewer than 25,000 of his brother Ugandans.

‘That is correct, sir’ I said.

Respectfully, his large entourage of Ministers, Permanent Secretaries and some unspecified gentlemen whose perspiration-flow appeared to be impeded by shoulder-holsters fell silent as President Amin began to recall his days as a pugilist.

In some respects they were more remarkable than Muhammad Ali’s.

‘I first won the heavyweight championship of Uganda in 1951,’ he said. ‘Then in 1952 I became champion of all East Africa. I used to train with heavyweights, middleweights and lightweights so that I was always ready to fight short or long men.’

His aides murmured approval at their leader’s sagacity.

The President then added that he held both titles until 1962, which seemed a fairly safe cue to ask the name of the man who had the presumption to beat him.

‘Nobody beat me,’ the Field-Marshal replied.

‘You retired, then?’

‘No, I did not retire. I am still heavyweight champion of Uganda. Nobody is willing to fight me.’

At this the 48-year-old reigning champ shoved both thumbs behind a belt threaded with 36 bullets and the ribbons of the VC, DSO, MC and 12 other decorations heaved on his massive chest as he bellowed with laughter.

His entourage were silent for perhaps half a second before breaking up. They slapped their thighs, as well as each other, and shrieked their appreciation of the President’s wit so purposefully that two vile-looking birds rose almost vertically from a distant tree and fled towards the Sudan.

Understandably for a man who is now spokesman for about nine-tenths of Africa as well as heavy-weight champion of Uganda, Doctor Amin — he conferred the academic title upon himself quite some while after awarding himself the VC—does not like squandering his *bon mots* in private discussion.

That morning, for example, he had invited a film crew from the government-owned Ugandan Television Service to accompany him into the yard of Kampala's Luzira Upper Prison, where seven convicted black-marketeers shivered in the sweltering heat.

They had been sentenced to death by an Economic Crimes Tribunal and were waiting to be shot.

President Amin, legs astride, planted himself in front of both them and the cameras and proceeded, with much finger-wagging, to denounce their wickedness in over-charging, hoarding and smuggling.

Then, first in English and then Swahili, he not only commuted their death sentences but set them free. One man collapsed. Another slid to his knees in gratitude.

All this was introduced on that evening's TV by a girl who, if anything, looked even less emotionally affected by news of any sort than Miss Angela Rippon.

At the time the President was performing his good deed for the day, we were flying 6,000 feet above Lake Idi Amin Dada (formerly Lake Edward) to a point 200 miles west of Kampala famous for the ferocity of its pigmies and its breathtaking views of the Mountains of the Moon.

It was here, during the afternoon, that the President was due to take a break from urging Mozambique into full-scale war with Rhodesia by opening the new Idi Amin Wing of the Semliki Safari Lodge. In view of our interest in Uganda's forthcoming world-title boxing promotion he might, we were informed, be prepared to discuss aspects of his distinguished sporting life.

In fact, due to an administrative hitch, the President had been informed only the previous evening that he was hosting a light-heavy-weight world boxing championship planned for next Sunday week.

Heads, metaphorically speaking of course, will probably roll when he discovers that his Minister for Culture and Sports has pledged £250,000 to overseas white boxing promoters at a time when Uganda's sugar industry is dying because its refinery is broken, most of Kampala's buses are off the road for want of spare parts, and that among the commodities you could not get all on the same day in Kampala's ritziest hotel last week were: bread, water, salt, eggs or beer.

In short, for a man who'd never

heard of either John Conteh or Alvaro Lopez and clearly had not the remotest idea of what weights they boxed, President Amin demonstrated his undoubted powers of magnetism by convincing the 300-strong audience who listened in to our interview that he's the Third World's Nat Fleischer.

'The fight will bring more world attention to Uganda' he said. 'Already we are preparing 30,000 hotel beds for visitors from Britain.'

The fact that Kampala doesn't have 30,000 hotel beds and that getting into Uganda requires more persistence than getting out of Dartmoor should not be misinterpreted. The Field-Marshal was having one of his love Britain days.

'Next year,' he declared, sidetracking from sport for a moment, 'is the silver jubilee of her Majesty the Queen and I intend to come to London to take part in the celebrations. I respect her as my former Commander-in-Chief. Please pass that message to Her Majesty.'

Expanding on his own sporting achievements, President Amin briefly recalled his early days as a champion soccer and rugger player, marvelled at the way in which he had become a champion swimmer since he had had to train in a river, modestly conceded that he had driven in an East African Safari car rally and revealed to the world for the first time that he has recently taken up squash.

'According to affairs of state, I play either one or four times a week,' he said. 'It makes you sweat in five minutes.'

He also revealed, to his stunned Cabinet, that he intended to stage the Commonwealth Games in Uganda as soon as he had built the largest sports stadium in Africa.

His main sporting intention this year is to attend the Olympics in Montreal. When I pointed out that, like Uganda, Canada's Olympic stadium was not yet complete,the President thundered 'Why?'

'Union troubles,' I said.

It was a foolish remark. It triggered, right there in the green hills of Africa, a political harangue which embraced the iniquity of all unions, the flaccid weakness of all non-socialist states and ended with the bellowed words: 'Everybody must obey the system.'

The President's aides nodded vigorous agreement.

Unfortunately, the Minister of Culture and Sport was not present. He was back in Kampala learning how to bounce a live televised picture of a boxing match off a piece of metal in the sky so that it comes down in London and New York simultaneously.

You may well wish to join me in wishing him luck.

Three months after our flight from Uganda I was watching a cricket match at The Oval in London. There was an intriguing advertisement along the boundary fence to the left of the Vauxhall End sightscreen. In large letters it bore the words MikroPul Ducon. In smaller letters it said Environmental Protection. By the end of the day I had once again learned the lesson that preconceived outrage has no place in investigative journalism.

'Do you sell anything in packets of three?'

London. — The only problem about MikroPul Ducon, as advertised at The Oval cricket ground and therefore on BBC television, is whether you purchase it by the quart, the yard, the kilo or in packets of three?

'No doubt about it' said my informant. 'It's the most brilliant coup of the year. It's a Greek firm, you know. Trust the Greeks to think up that "environmental protection" line.'

The implications, of course, were huge. If the BBC have banned Grand Prix motor-racing from their screens because some of the cars roar around with Durex written all over them, how could they conceivably televise the fifth Test from The Oval with MikroPul Ducon staring you in the face every time the ball ran down to the Vauxhall Stand boundary?

Well, millions of bewildered televiewers *did* see it on Wednesday when BBC screened the one-day Surrey-Essex match. So, bristling with puritanical outrage, one felt it only right to telephone the Surrey County Cricket Club and castigate them for the offensive tastelessness of their boundary advertising.

'Oh my God,' said a Surrey spokesman. 'Is *that* what they are? It never occurred to us. I say, you're not going to print this, are you? You realise that the fifth Test will be blacked out on television?'

'It is the duty of a free Press to protect young children and elderly ladies from being affronted by this kind of nauseating advertising,' we boomed. 'Motor racing? Cricket? What's the difference?'

A low moan from The Oval indicated they knew all was lost.

To conclude our inquiries we called at a chemist's in London, EC4, waited until two lady typists had bought some shampoo, gestured a male assistant to the end of the counter and whispered: 'Three MikroPul Ducons, please.'

'I'm afraid I've never heard of the products, sir.' said the assistant.

'Really,' we replied nastily, 'of course, they *are* the very latest and presumably only very *up-to-date* stores stock them for really *discerning* clients.'

'Possibly, sir,' said the assistant.

So the search widened.

'Awfully sorry,' said a worthy-sounding man at the Family Planning Association, 'we don't seem to have them on our recommended list.'

'What on earth,' demanded a businesslike lady at the Association of British Pharmaceutical Industry, 'are you talking about?'

'Very sorry old boy,' said a jolly chap at the Ann Summers Establishment up near Marble Arch, 'can't help you out at all.'

'If they're rivals of ours,' said a big wheel at the London Rubber Company somewhat brusquely, 'we've never heard of them.'

'I've just searched through all our reference books,' said an infinitely helpful secretary on the *Chemist and Druggist Directory*, 'and they don't appear to be here. A Greek firm, you say?'

'Yes, a Greek firm,' we replied testily and promptly rang our correspondent in Athens to track down, once and for all, these Hellenic environmental protectionists whose cunning advertising was about to wipe cricket off the English television screens.

He drew a blank.

It was fast approaching teatime on the cricket grounds of England when we received a telephone call from a man in Shoeburyness, Essex.

'I understand from Surrey County Cricket Club,' he said pleasantly, 'that you wish to buy an air-conditioning unit?'

'Are you some kind of nutcase?' we demanded. 'Get off the line.'

'No,' he replied, 'I am the managing director of MikroPul Ducon, manufacturers of filters for cleaning dirty industrial and domestic air.'

'Do you sell *anything* in packets of three which have to be sent out under plain cover?' we asked weakly.

'Certainly not,' he retorted, 'air filters is our business and we are cricket fans to a man.'

'Thank you for calling,' we said. 'Forgive us our trespassing.'

'Not at all' said Mr MikroPul Ducon. 'I'll send you a price list.'

An infallible ploy to provoke a large and hostile correspondence to a British newspaper is to write about bullfighting in terms which imply you do not regard matadors as men who should be emasculated on sight without anaesthetic, a risk which they happen to take every time they enter the ring. The letters mostly arrive, unstamped, from readers who saw nothing wrong in Vietnam, are bored with Belfast and hold no views on apartheid. While never advocating that anyone else should attend the bullfights, I go as frequently as possible and am thus confronted with the minimal problem of having to find some other subject to write about. The Horses of Andaluzia seemed a good idea at the time.

'They are driven and ridden by men with faces straight off Roman coins and ladies with names like Consuela and Immaculata'

Jerez, Spain. — Those wrestling with the social problems of hooliganism at soccer matches may be intrigued by the psychological deterrent employed here to maintain something resembling law and order at the 692nd annual Jerez Horse Fair.

It was demonstrated most effectively the other afternoon when four members of the American armed forces determined to disrupt an electrifying display of bullfighting by El Viti by yelling such Texan epigrams as 'Go screw him, toro' and 'Who's the broad in the fancy suit?'

This was observed quite dispassionately for around five minutes by an employee of the Spanish police. When it became clear that the noise would never abate, the policeman moved calmly along the row behind the ring leader, raised his truncheon and struck him a terrifying blow on the left shoulder.

This caused the Texan humorist to forget his lines as he slumped forward on to my neighbour. It was then suggested to his three companions that they might care to carry him out, a request with which they complied at approximately the same speed most of us would leave a blazing arsenal.

The Feria of Jerez then proceeded as peacefully as it has every year since 1284.

While unlikely to win over any

followers of Jung and Freud, it had to be admitted that the tactic was effective. It also confirmed that there are still areas in post-Franco Spain as yet untouched by the shock waves of the new democracy.

Indeed, what we have been watching here these past few days is one of Europe's effective aristocracies whooping it up as though there's no tomorrow which, for them, may be less a cliché than a fact of life.

It's quite some scene. They have the same obsession with horses as two-thirds of the British Royal Family and so much money they still dress up their regiments of coachmen and grooms in Ruritanian livery.

Most of their wealth, these past 200 years, has come from producing sherry and much of it has been spent breeding a strain of Carthusian horses that can dance to martial music, stroll around on their hind legs, turn carriages on a tighter lock than a London taxi, goose-step, perform feats of dressage so dramatically beautiful that they don't even bother to enter the Olympics and genuinely make you feel intellectually moribund.

They are driven and ridden by men with faces straight off Roman coins and ladies with names like Consuela and Immaculata who have jet black hair, high cheekbones, olive skin and all look alike. This is probably because the rich families keep on marrying one another to stop the hoi-polloi getting their hands on the readies.

They live in palaces with grey walls and things like Persian carpets hanging out of the windows and they have a dignity which exists nowhere else on the face of the earth. It doesn't worry them whether anyone comes to see their horse show or not and the fact that a drunken Texan bore was whacked by one of their policemen is unlikely to cause anxiety to a caste which has probably never heard of Henry Kissinger.

In fact, 300,000 people turned up this year to watch the dressage, the polo, the carriage driving, the bull-fighting and listen to the flamenco.

Oddly enough, the most awesome experience for me was drinking a glass of sherry kindly offered by Don Thomas Terry, who is distinctly not to be confused with the comedian. It had been waiting in the barrel since the very year Napoleon retreated from Moscow.

As Spanish fiestas go, the Jerez Feria is a restrained affair, which means that all the taxi drivers are sober and about one person in three retreats to bed around 5 a.m. to snatch four hours' sleep.

All this has been watched with some amusement by Miss Sally Mapleson, 19, from Billericay, Essex, and Master Nick Skelton, 18, from Coventry, who rode so well at last year's Horse of the Year Show in London that they won scholarships from a Spanish sherry family to come here and further their equestrian education.

Since my knowledge of equestrianism extends no further than having once played golf with Geoff Lewis, I have to rely on their judgment. Here, they agree, they have seen horsemanship at its most supreme.

They are super kids and it is touching to see Miss Mapleson moved almost to tears on being introduced to Descarado II, the all-white stallion who is the most famous horse produced in Spain this century. He's 27 now and was lying down in a stable not unlike a suite at the Dorchester. Apparently all is not lost. We were informed that he is still shown to a mare three times a year, whatever that means.

Another highlight was meeting the goat who can get all four hooves onto an upturned log the size of a soup plate and balance there for about 20 seconds before falling over.

But these are all side-shows. The real stars of Spain's greatest horse show are the owners whose pedigrees are faithfully recorded in the *Almanac de Gotha* and whose attitudes to encroaching democracy are not conspicuously different from those of Marie Antoinette.

There is a famous story of one of them on a visit to Washington who became so snarled in a traffic jam that he was an hour adrift for dinner with one of that city's most celebrated hostesses.

'Ah Duke,' she sniped when he eventually arrived, 'I notice you continue to exercise your nation's prerogative for being perpetually late.'

'I am filled with remorse, senora,' replied the Duke. 'I fear the last time we were early was when we discovered America.'

Horse traders still rule, OK?

We left Jerez on a Sunday morning of such unbetrayable beauty that there was never a chance we would arrive at our intended destination, which was dinner with our families in London. On the road to Seville Airport Stephen Danos, husband of the Daily Mail's *Travel Editor, Jill Crawshaw, suddenly remembered an urgent business conference in Madrid. Peter Hardy, foreign correspondent with the* Daily Express, *rightly concluded that Madrid was an ideal place from which to inform his readers more about the liberalising intentions of the young Juan Carlos. The Duke of Alburquerque, who lives only 30 miles from the capital, immediately assumed an even greater fascination for me than he had had an hour before. We switched our tickets to*

Madrid and were thus able to witness the first four days of bullfighting at the San Isidro feria. Newspapers are generally malleable to these kind of coincidences provided you come up with a column.

The Duke's private secretary arranged our meeting and confirmed it on an embossed card inviting us to be at the Finca Soto Mozanaque at 11.30 a.m. precisely. Elementary protocol demanded punctuality. Our taxi arrived 20 minutes early so we waited, diplomatically, at the Duke's gates. At 11.29 exactly I determined that our taxi-driver, my American photographer and I could proceed to make an entrance of impressive precision. Alas, the lack of acceleration in Spanish taxis combined with my ignorance of the continued lifestyle of the Spanish aristocracy, meant that at the appointed moment we were still floundering around the perimeter of his vast estates.

Nine months after this piece was written the Duke of Alburquerque, having willed his bones to knit, applied to ride as usual in the Aintree Grand National. The Jockey Club politely refused his request. Nereo, ridden by Robert Kingston, fell at the 22nd fence.

'She smiled the hopeless smile of a woman married to a man of iron will and lifelong obsession'

Madrid. — For a man whose 16th-century front porch is separated from his monogrammed wrought-iron front gates by 1½ miles of private estates, the Duke of Alburquerque may strike you as an unlikely defence witness for what goes on in public wards in British National Health Service hospitals.

In fact, he is less effusive than positively emotional about the efficiency of our breadline doctors and the warm charm of our underpaid nurses.

'It would be most kind of you,' he said, accepting a glass of 50-year-old amontillado from a silver salver, deferentially proffered by Pedro the second footman, 'if you would publicly extend my personal gratitude to Doctor Little and Sister Heywood and Sister Willis and everyone else in the Sherrington Ward at Walton Hospital in Liverpool.'

It was a curious setting to hear what sounded like a record dedication on *Family Favourites.*

The orchards and vineyards of the Finca Soto Mozanaque lay in the shadow of the Sierra de Malagon and their owner, the umpteenth in a line of blue-blood Dukes to whom the Spanish Armada seems only like yesterday, was propped up at the far end of a lawn large enough to accommodate two Cup Finals and a polo match.

He apologised for not receiving us standing up.

This, his elegant Duchess explained in Roedean English, was because while his seven broken ribs have healed and his shattered femur is knitting together quite nicely, the broken vertebrae low down in the spine are still giving him hell and his surgeons some cause for concern.

Each morning he has to be pushed down to inspect his horses in a bathchair.

Despite his efforts at concealment his great El Greco face contorts with pain whenever he tries to lever his tall gaunt frame on to an elbow-crutch.

His admiration for British hospitals stems from 56 hours after that gruesome moment 48 afternoons ago when some 20 million of us, crouching over our television sets, saw him part company with Nereo at the 13th fence in the Grand National and fall headlong under a stampede of hooves and loose horses.

That was when he came to in the intensive care unit at Walton General Hospital just down the road from Aintree, and was declared well enough to be moved to the Sherrington Ward.

'I received care and kindness there that could not have been surpassed in any of the clinics of the world,' he said.

'I have also received more than 350 letters from people in England wishing me well. Some are from friends. Most come from people I have never met.

'Many do not even bear addresses, so I cannot observe the courtesy of replying. Again, I would be grateful if you thank them for me in your newspaper.'

The Duke of Alburquerque was visibly moved.

What is more, at the age of 57 years and five months, he has every intention of riding in the Grand National again. And again. And possibly again after that.

'If I were not fully recovered by next year, then I wouldn't think of competing,' he said, 'but that would not prevent me taking part the following year.

'I would like to go on to complete the course on a Spanish horse. I would like to win, of course, but perhaps that is now not possible.

'I do not regard age as something which automatically eliminates a man from doing anything.'

It was a very Spanish observation and, at his side, the Duchess of Alburquerque reacted in a very Spanish way. Not a muscle moved in her handsome face.

She is aware, anyway, that neither violent tantrum nor gentle reproach would make the slightest difference.

Only later, privately, she smiled the hopeless smile of a woman married to a man of iron will and lifelong obsession and said quietly 'Perhaps one day he will stop. He is not too young, you know.'

As she spoke she took their one-year-old daughter, Maria-Christina, from her nanny and held her up to nuzzle against a shining mare which turned out to be the mother of Nereo, the very horse from which the Duke crashed at Aintree.

The Duchess is the Duke's second wife. His first wife died early one morning in 1968 as she was driving into Madrid and was in head-on collision with a party of young bloods returning from an all-night party.

She left three children and the Duke of Alburquerque's sorrow was such that his friends delight in the visible happiness of his second marriage.

He is a stunningly impressive man, hugely formal and charming and wholly bereft of the bravado of the jet-set sportsmen who spend half their lives searching out death.

He has broken virtually every bone in his body in riding falls and dismisses requests for precise statistics with the sort of glance which tells you you've just asked an extremely vulgar question.

'I do not record such things,' he said. 'For example, on one occasion I broke my femur in 15 places. Does that count as 15 fractures or one? It doesn't interest me. I don't like breaking bones.'

Nor does he like the adjective 'fearless' when applied to himself.

'It is not exactly fear, perhaps, that I feel on the morning of a Grand National. It is a certain excitement, and there is also apprehension. But it is wrong for one man to assume that another man does not know fear. I knew fear very greatly when I was 17. I have known it since on horses.'

The fear he felt at 17 came from being shot at during the bloody fratricide of the Spanish Civil War.

He was so young he volunteered without military training and fought in vicious actions in northern and central Spain as an infantry private. Only later was he commissioned in the cavalry.

He was fighting, of course, for the Spain of his inheritance, which adds up to land and wealth and privilege on a scale now being questioned.

You feel he would still die for a cause other than winning the Grand National but it is an assumption he is not prepared to discuss.

His public world begins and ends with horses. He has 19 of them in his stables and corrals and there is not a table in his lovely home not covered with silver-framed pictures of them, some of which he is in the familiar process of falling off.

There is one of him leaping a fence in the 1952 Grand National alongside a horse bearing the No. 13. 'That was my downfall that year,' said the Duke.

'I have been superstitious of the number 13 all my life and when I saw that I lost my concentration and fell.'

It was his fall at the 13th fence at Aintree this year which caused him this week to be sitting under the trees on his lawn and waiting for the next six weeks to pass swiftly.

'My doctors tell me that by then I may be able to put my right foot to the ground,' he said.

The Duchess smiled in anticipation. 'He is not,' she explained quietly, 'the world's most equable patient.'

ITEM: In a wet December rush-hour during his Premiership Mr Edward Heath was in some haste to return to No 10, Downing Street from the House of Commons. Between these two privileged places the long-suffering British public were ensnarled in an inevitable traffic jam. Even the Prime Minister's car couldn't move. Mr Heath decided to walk. He got wet. He complained.

'At a stroke, so to speak...'

Our Leader's fury at being forced by adverse traffic conditions to negotiate the 457 yards from the House of Commons to No. 10 on foot has caused a certain perplexity in sporting circles.

Admittedly, there is a tricky left-hand turn before coming into the 132-yard home straight. Nevertheless, with the Home Office buildings reducing wind-resistance to a minimum, it is felt that the course falls somewhat short of the ultimate endurance test.

The following statistics, calculated on personal-best performances or Olympic medal-winning times, tend to support that view:

British athlete David Jenkins could have run it in 47.32sec. Ugandan Gold Medalist John Akii-Bua could have hurdled it in 49.95sec. In tidal conditions America's Mark Spitz could have swum it in 3min. 57.1sec.

British racehorse Golden Miller (who carried 12 stone averaging 31.15 m.p.h. in the 1935 Cheltenham Gold Cup) could have been there in 29.82sec. and British greyhound Beef Cutlet (clocked at 39.13 m.p.h. in 1933) would have chased a hare there in 23.38sec.

Italian roller-skater Guiseppe Cantarello would have required a surprising 33.61sec. but French cyclist Jose Meiffret (who once topped 127 m.p.h.) would have accomplished it in 7.35sec.

And what of Jack Nicklaus, the great American golfer? By taking the direct route, 349 yards over the Ministry of the Environment, he could have reached No. 10 with a two-wood. At a stroke, so to speak.

In the span of three months and the space of some 6,000 miles I ran across two old friends. One was black, one white but they had much in common. They had both known the world's acclamation and its cold rejection for they were the real life versions of recurrent figures in sporting fiction, the Fallen Idols.

'It's too late to argue the finer points: they've smashed him into oblivion'

Los Angeles.—If you want to know how to get yourself reclassified from a national idol to no-star bum in the time it takes to play The Star Spangled Banner, here, with no feelings spared, is how it's done.

First, you smash every world sprint record in sight and establish yourself as the fastest foot-runner since electronic timing devices were invented. Then, surreptitiously, you go out and buy yourself a black golf glove.

Next you run for America in the Mexico Olympics, win an inevitable medal and stride out brazenly to the victory rostrum in the arena spotlight.

What follows, depending on how you look at these things, requires either stupendous moral courage, drunken bravado or inestimable idiocy. You simply pull on the golf glove, clench your fist, raise it in defiance and lower your head in humiliation as the first bars of the American national anthem blare out on the cool evening air.

Hold that pose long enough, inspired by the certainty that 400 million television viewers are watching, and you have committed social, professional and national suicide.

The only reason I know this is that I spent an hour here on Saturday evening with the man who did all this, in exactly that sequence, in

Mexico City three years ago last autumn.

At 26, at what should be the shimmering zenith of his track career, Tommie Smith has been broken on the wheel of American patriotism.

Amateur status compromised, professional football career ruined, marriage finished, socially ostracised, he is now teaching 14-year-olds in a Blackboard Jungle school and, without admitting it, cursing the day when his conscience told him to make the pathetically ineffectual gesture which became known as the notorious Black Power Demonstration.

Tommie Smith is to Black Power what I am to the Angry Brigade. Nothing.

But it's too late to argue the finer points: they've smashed him into oblivion, to the point where he now says: 'I've kept myself in pretty good shape. If you could spare a paragraph or two in your newspaper to say that I'm available to run in open races in London or Stockholm or Sydney, anywhere, I'd be very grateful.'

When Tommie Smith was asked to pack his bags and stop polluting the American Olympic quarters in Mexico, he knew his amateur track days were over. He turned to American professional football where his phenomenal acceleration as a wide-receiver — a position requiring more speed but even less skill than a rugger wing-threequarter — had undoubted value.

He spent two seasons with the Cincinnati Bengals and 12 months with a team in Canada. In those three years he played precisely one first team game, received more than 50 threats of death, was spat upon in the street and reviled at public social functions.

To the promoters he became box office poison.

Tommie Smith happens to be one of the most gentle, courteous, articulate, university-educated star sportsmen I have ever met. He has great dignity, charm and intelligence. At 6ft. 5in., with an almost unimpaired sense of humour and invariably beautifully dressed, he still makes heads turn wherever he walks.

He is — or was — the American champion who dared to imply criticism of his country for the way it treated his race.

Tommie Smith is still very much alive in the record books. So far as contemporary American sport goes he may be officially posted as dead.

‘You could tell from his eyes that the small room was filled with the roar of the crowd’

Nottingham. — The Lawton family received six phone calls over the weekend. One was from a newspaper, three were from sympathisers, two were anonymous and vilely abusive.

The head of the house, Tommy Lawton, answered none of them. He sat, beaten, in a fireside chair. He looked thin and ill and shook slightly.

At 52, only the famous hair-style remained of my first sporting idol. The long strands are still slicked back from the left-centre parting.

Just occasionally, when he roused himself to re-enact some stirring goal from The Forties, his head triggered back like a striking cobra's and you could tell from his eyes that the small room was filled with the roar of the crowd.

But it's not football memories that are sustaining Tommy Lawton just now. It is his family, the kind of family any man would pray for if he fell on hard times.

There is Carol, his step-daughter, who flew down from Scotland to organise the house with brisk efficiency.

There is young Tom, his son, who started his O-levels yesterday and told his dad to stop worrying because he had a pair of good fists waiting for anyone who made any cracks.

And there is Gay, his wife, who remains proud and fiercely protective.

It was Gay who told me the story that sounded more like the script of some social-predicament play than something that actually happens to people you know.

It was of how her husband had for seven months concealed from her and the children the fact that he had lost his job as the sales representative of a furniture firm.

Throughout all those weeks he had caught the bus daily into the centre of Nottingham, wandered the streets, sat in Market Square, bought the odd half-pint of bitter in pubs and read the sports pages in the public library until sufficient hours had dragged past for him to go home and talk vaguely about a fairly hard day at the office.

An ironic non-event took place one morning when Lawton was waiting at the bus-stop at the bottom of his road in Woodthorpe. A Mercedes flashed past, driven by a footballer named Tony Hateley who, at a rough guess, has made £24,000 alone out of legal cuts from his many transfers.

Hateley is a good header of the ball. He learned much of the art from Lawton who, in the great days, could head a ball harder than most men could kick it. 'He didn't see me,' said Lawton, 'though I'm sure he would have given me a lift if he had.'

What really hurt the Lawtons was a reference in court to the 'glamour' of the days when heads turned when Tommy walked down a street. It seemed to imply a life-style latterly enjoyed by George Best, or Bobby Moore, of Geoff Hurst. It was, of course, not quite so.

When Tommy Lawton played his last game for England he was paid £20. His top wage with a club was £17 a week plus £2 for a win and £1 for a draw.

'The glamour,' said Gay Lawton, 'was going out for a Chinese meal on a Saturday night or eating at The Orchard in Ruislip. Tommy and I have never been to a night-club together in our lives.'

With the same ability 25 years later Tommy Lawton would at this moment be bronzing himself on a Barbados beach with perhaps three businesses, two newspaper columns, one agent, one accountant and a couple of ghost writers going for him.

Lawton was in the waning years of his career when Jimmy Guthrie began to make militant noises about the professional footballer's lot and when Jimmy Hill finally smashed the iniquity of the maximum wage.

'In my time,' said Lawton, 'we had no figurehead. We played football because we loved it and we thought of nothing else.'

You can say, with some justification, that Lawton had the weapons of his own supreme talent and immense professional standing to have led the fight himself. But to do so now is to evade a subtle issue: whether today's young footballing tycoons have any responsibility to the giants who made their game.

I would like to think that the matter may be worth a few moments' discussion at the next meeting of the Professional Footballers' Association, the players' trade union.

They may feel that it would leave them as a soft touch for a legion of yesterday's men. They may also feel that to make no reference to this distressing story would be roughly the modern equivalent of passing by on the other side of the road.

Apart from the occasional libel writ, the average response ratio to an opinionated column is one letter of support to four expressing anything from courteous disagreement to disgust. I would like to think this is because those in agreement see no reason to write, but I am probably wrong. The curious sequel to the piece about Dr J.A. Harrington's views on sex in sport is that it is the only opinion I have ever had published which won 100 per cent approval. This only proves, of course, that there is no animal so dangerous as the sportsman whose masculinity has just been impugned.

'Now they take their wives and lose the Ashes. In the old days they won the Ashes and lost their wives'

London.— The sex life of Dr J.A. Harrington, be it prolific, bizarre, hetaerismic, erratic, monogamistic, on the wane or already extinct, is not normally a subject I would bore you with on a Tuesday morning in spring.

Unfortunately he has just been so gratuitously insulting to some mates of mine that I am impelled to load both barrels and discharge them in the direction of Birmingham, where he appears to run a clinic when he is not talking nonsense in London.

On his latest visit, to address members of the Institute of Sports Medicine, Dr Harrington insisted that sport had become such a tense, all-demanding rat-race that it was reducing many men's sex lives to cold ashes and breaking up a generation of marriages.

From his rostrum as professional voyeur he said things as profound as 'Sport is now rivalling sex as a leading topic of conversation' and 'Not a few homes have been broken up on the playing fields of Eton.'

Admittedly Dr Harrington has the makings of a nice racy style which will serve him well when *Kitchen and Crochet Weekly* offer him £10,000 to lay bare the case histories of Olympic javelin-throwers, Test match wicket-keepers and relegation-haunted goalkeepers who are so knackered every night that they can barely wind up the alarm clock before passing out.

However, his dazzling grasp of the obvious is matched only by his tenuous comprehension of what's happening elsewhere in the world.

Of course, there are plenty of sportsmen with frayed nerve-ends and power-cut sex drives. But that also applies to overworked atom scientists, bank tellers, electrical and heating contractors, tea planters, signwriters, operatic baritones and Hansard stenographers.

Of course sport is directly responsible for breaking up marriages. But so is commercial travelling, piloting Jumbo-jets, presenting religious programmes for BBC television, directing plays for amateur dramatic societies and working on newspapers.

Some doctors even have been divorced.

Why Dr Harrington should single out sportsmen as people expected to keep their marriage vows when all around them are breaking theirs is beyond me.

In any case to imply near impotence in one breath and allege mass philandering in the next is about as helpful to the human predicament as voting Tory and Labour on the same voting paper.

Dr Harrington's pronouncements strike me as owing more to guesswork than fieldwork. I do not recall meeting him, for example, on one of England's overseas cricket tours during the past 15 years. This is a pity because had he been on one he would have learned something to both his and sport's advantage.

Minimal research would have proved that the incidence of broken and distraught marriages in the world of cricket in much lower now than it has been for many years. Now they take their wives and lose the Ashes. In the old days they won the Ashes and lost their wives.

Before he jettisons any further rumours on learned sports medicine symposia I do wish he would talk to Dr Brian Corrigan, who travels the world as medical adviser to almost every Australian sports team. Or, failing that, he might care to accompany any member of the *Daily Mail's* sportswriting staff on his next long-term overseas assignment.

He will discover that while a huge majority of married sportsmen stay happily married the single ones are still keeping the Union Jack flying, so to speak.

Of course, by taking sex as his subject and provocatively writing off many sportsmen as a 'psychological mess' the good doctor annexed the headlines and appropriated much air-time.

He is not alone in that. Ever since Premier P. Clemenceau assured the French parliament that sport is too important to be left to sportsmen, every goddam expert in anything has been telling us how to run our lives, mend our ways, resolve our problems or make ends meet.

It is not so much that we are embarrassed by it as tired of seeing sport used as a barn-door target. Dr Harrington's package tour of sporting boudoirs is about as amusing to us as he might find a midnight visit from a team of Olympic long-jumpers. Exhausted ones, of course.

Cricket-watching remains the supreme pleasure. It is about sunshine and eternal friendships and great artistry, even if the age spanning the next two pieces may hardly be described as a golden one. Both Sabina Park, Jamaica, and Sydney Cricket Ground, Australia, were being revisited after absences of more than four years. They are thrilling arenas when the heat is on.

'A test it obviously is. A match it is most certainly not'

Kingston, Jamaica. — There have been a number of outstandingly lopsided contests since Herod took on those babies and it would be idle to pretend we're not watching one of them here.

Should West Indies now take it into their heads to go for a record, instead of a win, there is no logical or technical reason why they shouldn't score between 1,100 and 1,400 runs in their first innings of this second international collision.

I avoid the billing of 'Test Match' out of concern for prosecution under the Trade Descriptions Act. A test it obviously is. A match it is most certainly not.

That, now, is the measure of how good they are, how bad we are and how this state of affairs couldn't be hushed up any longer because of mutual exposure on a wicket as true as the nave of St. Paul's.

There is no point regretting it, bemoaning it, decrying it, debating it, investigating it or, above all, attempting to repudiate it. That's how it is.

Having failed to qualify for the World Cup at soccer we've now come up with a cricket team which, on an average day, is just about a match for New Zealand.

These words are not written in passion. I feel no sense of shame whatsoever at being an Englishman watching his compatriot mates get whacked out of sight. If it's got to be, let it be mid-February in some place where the sun is blazing, the bougainvillea is blooming, the palms are swaying, the natives are friendly and opinion polls are concerned with such really fundamental problems as whether Kanhai is a better captain than Sobers.

Sabina Park, which shortly, alas, is to be developed into another stadium with all the character of a Ford assembly plant, is just such a place.

Watching cricket here, amid the fervour and noise and primary colours, is not far from what it must have been like to attend a Shakespeare first night at The Globe or be there when Gutsy Moran came out fighting for the 22nd round against Mauler Pearson at the old Blackfriars Ring. 'It lives, man,' as a gentleman without shoes remarked yesterday from the top branches of an overhanging tree.

When the local boy, Lawrence Rowe, hits a four it sounds like Sunderland scoring the goal against Leeds all over again. When an England wicket falls the earth moves. What is more, when Sobers suddenly slips in the googly the whole crowd recognises it for what it is, and that doesn't even happen at Lord's.

They know a very great deal here about the supreme and complex and lovely game called cricket. Enough, anyway, to acknowledge that great teams rise and wane, that superstars are as unpredictable as the harvest, that supremacy and abject failure are not permanent conditions and that some day, within our lifetimes, some Englishman bearing a wooden Excalibur, will come here and exact a terrible vengeance.

Just for the moment, though, the whole place is a bloody slaughterhouse.

England's 353 in the first innings may have inspired some misunderstanding 4,000 miles away back home. It wasn't good at all. Its intrinsic value was probably equal to 180 on an overcast day at Lord's.

The Sabina wicket is so true and slow that a genius like Sir Len Hutton would have made a century on it with a baseball bat and Lady Hutton would probably have been good for 40.

Its true character became apparent when Rowe and Roy Fredericks got going on it for West Indies. It was like watching Bradman batting with Bradman with eight more Bradmans still to come in. Only Lance Gibbs, out of the entire West Indies team, is positively incapable of scoring a century.

Denigrating our bowlers is useless. They have lacked nothing in courage or assiduousness. The paceman have hurled themselves at the fortress walls until their mouths have sagged open in the search for oxygen and their eyelids have drooped in frustration. Of the others, Underwood, particularly, has spun his brains out. But this wicket is built for batsmen.

Batsmen so dictate everything by tradition that this is the banker draw ground of world sport. No Test match has produced a result here in the past nine years and there is no reason why England, second time round, shouldn't yet achieve a draw as well.

Not that that would paper over the canyon that divides the two teams. West Indies are on the march again and England confirm every rumour that they've actually sent their second eleven.

Any day now, back in England, somebody is going to come up with the idea that we should sack the selectors and hang the hierarchy at Lord's. In the absence of any progenital miracle by which we could mate one body with the other and rear a new generation of thoroughbreds such recrimination is futile.

It is by no means impossible to discern how we've come to this all-time low in yet another game we invented.

Firstly we have strangled indigenous talent at birth by flooding English cricket with overseas players to the point where ten of the eleven West Indians involved in the contest either are, or recently have been, full-time professionals in our own county championship.

Secondly the huge proliferation of one-day cricket at home has weakened the strain to the point where big-innings batsmen are about as two-a-penny as Whig parliamentarians. The whole, grim irony of England's batting at Sabina Park is that man after man played himself in only to fall with a collapse of concentration after one hour instead of six.

Why, then, did England pursue such a suicidal policy? The answer is that they had no alternative. Without star overseas players at a critical time the English professional game would have collapsed. And without the vast infusion or sponsorship money for 'instant' cricket the game would have gone bankrupt and died.

What we are witnessing at Sabina Park, in short, is English cricket paying the price of continued survival at home.

This, to a degree, may make you feel somewhat better about all those depressing dispatches coming nightly from here.

Remember, anyway, that England still lead the world at trout-fishing, cutting suits, trooping the colour, exposing charlatans and making marmalade.

Cricket is as English as any of those and a new dawn may confidently be expected to follow the darkness. Even if it doesn't there's still heart to be taken from the simple inscription which Mr W.C. Fields left to be engraved on his tombstone: 'It's better than playing Philadelphia.'

Watching cricket, any sort of cricket, at Sabina Park is still better than most things on earth.

‘England exchanged bouncer for bouncer, curse for curse and dissent for dissent’

Sydney.— Coming fresh to this Test series is like walking into a pitched battle between the Mafia and the IRA. You knew they'd been at each others' throats but you couldn't believe it was this uncompromising, this violent or this uncouth. Practically none of the traditional courtesies of cricket survived the second day of this fourth Test.

Bats were thrown, oaths exchanged, umpires abused, obscene gestures made and, for much of the time, batsmen were subjected to some of the most viciously intimidatory bowling witnessed since the dark ages of bodyline.

All of it was enacted before a packed crowd, one-eyed in its allegiance, one-voiced in its prejudice and motivated less by the normal patriotisms aroused by international sport than the bloodlust you feel in the bullrings of Spain. The hostility came off The Hill like a heat haze.

Three points are worth making.

It was a thrilling and unforgettable spectacle, as war often is. Sydney cricket ground, with its Baroque architecture and domed pavilions, is the Grand Opera House of the game and the cast in this Test are almost all prima donnas.

There is no innocent party. England, released from the restraining influence of Mike Denness's diplomatic leadership, exchanged bouncer for bouncer, curse for curse and dissent for dissent.

There is, I believe, no lasting enmity off the field between the two teams. It is merely in public and before huge television audiences that they are indulging in a game which now has all the makings of a martial art. They appear, most of the time, to enjoy it.

This will make sad reading to those born to the literature of Blunden and de Selincourt and reared to believe that cricket is a synonym for words like honour, etiquette and nobility.

They will probably ascribe it to the age of long hair — half the Australian team, it must be admitted, wear Mexican desperado moustaches — and see it as another sign of moral decay. This would be coming it a bit strong.

In a somewhat embarrassed appearance before the Press, England's manager, Alec Bedser, conceded it had been an ill-tempered day but added that he'd seen a few of those in his playing era. Of course, he is right.

On this same ground, 43 years ago, diplomatic relations were almost broken off between our two countries because of the violence of the cricket exchanges and in those days England had an amateur, a gentleman and Wykehamist as captain.

This is not to condone the loutishness we have seen in this Test but to remind the new middleclass militants that good manners have never been exclusive to any one generation.

The new element now, I suspect, is a crowd, unfettered from an Empire and disenchanted with a Commonwealth, exhorting its young tigers to tear the old lion's tail out by the roots.

They bayed for blood yesterday and both teams did their damndest to spill it.

Thomson's mere emergence through the swing gate to start bowling was greeted by a roar barely gentler than the one which accompanied Foreman to the canvas in Kinshasa.

Lillee, with The Hill at his back, was swept in to bowl on soundwaves of soccer-style chanting.

It could have been any old Sunday afternoon in the Rome Colosseum, and England, tired of the taunts and the humiliations and an Australian Press patronising them as overweight geriatrics, retaliated. Only the 12 Apostles or the late Albert Schweitzer wouldn't have done so.

These remarks, I fear, apply only to England's bowlers. When we batted we did so with something less than conviction.

It reminded you of a remark by Mr E. Hemingway, who thrived on blood and thunder. 'They fought' he wrote of contestants in another sport altogether 'as though they were condemned to it rather than if they had chosen it.'

They could have been England's batsmen at the end of a remarkable day.

Whoever claimed there is drama behind every drawn blind in the suburbs may well have had the room above Burton's in mind. I would certainly have remained unaware of it had it not been for Jeffrey Powell, football correspondent of the Daily Mail, *whose interests may be described as catholic. At closing time one evening he said "Come on, I've got something to show you."*

'He stared at the table cloth and raised no objection when his backer said 'You played like a bum''

London.— The way they kept looking at one another you would have thought it was Carson City, 1880, with one contestant about to growl the immortal line: 'This town ain't big enough for the both of us.'

That, as it happens, was the size of it but both the weapons and the venue were absurdly different. It was snooker cues at midnight in a room above Burton's the Tailors in that most suburban of all London suburbs, Southgate.

The match — D. Elrick v. R. Gross, best of 11 frames for £100 sidestakes — wasn't advertised which explains why only about 40 of us slipped up the stairs after closing time. The place was a solid cube of Embassy smoke and the hardest drink you could buy was instant coffee. For all that, no more bitter sporting battle was fought anywhere in Britain over the weekend.

Des Elrick swaggered straight in from a bar with his backers. He wore flared trousers, a skin-tight shirt open down to his navel, a medallion on a chain round his neck, a chain bracelet on his right wrist, a gaudy ring on his left little finger and an unmistakable let-me-get-at-the bum kind of smile.

Ronnie Gross, if he'll forgive the comparison, looked more like one of those gentlemen who carried out an awful lot of hypodermic experiments during World War Two.

He wore menacingly-glinting rimless glasses, blue trousers with turn-ups, kept his waistcoat on and limped heavily round the table, the result of paralysis when he fell and hit his head on a rocking-horse at the age of seven. His face wore an I-hope-you-know-what-you're-doing -sonny expression.

The nicety that made their confrontation worth staying out of bed for was this: Gross, three times English champion between 1957 and 1962, represented the Establishment. Elrick, by his own admission, has been a snooker hall hustler all over Britain for the past 12 years. He's still only 26.

You could feel the needle as they switched all the lights out except over Table Two. Gross pressed his lips tight, broke and dragged the cue-ball right back to the bottom cush. But first, more about Elrick, who has a wife and two kids.

'Sure they've gone hungry,' he said. 'Hustling isn't exactly a steady profession. You go to a hall, pick out the best player, let him win a couple and then take him for the lot.

'Scotland's the place for the easiest pickings. The worst is Weston-super-Mare. They're canny bastards all right. It took me a week to make 20 quid down there.

'When times were bad, though, there was always this guy in London. He had a death-wish about losing money. I'd clean him out time and again until he was crying for me to give him a quid back for a drink. No deal. 'Go and get some more money' I'd say and he would. He went right through his wife's bank-book and I took the lot.

'But it's an up-and-down job. One night I won £1,300 in a private club. Another time I played straight through three days and nights without going to bed.'

It explains Des Elrick's complexion, which is a perfect match for a parchment lampshade. It also explains why he came to be playing Ronnie Gross, for Elrick came to the profound decision a fortnight ago to pack in hustling and make his claim for national recognition as a straight upstanding professional.

What promoted this conversion was less some bright light on the road to Damascus than the economic boom which snooker is now enjoying.

In the decade between the retirement of the dignified Joe Davis and the emergence of the flamboyant Alex 'Hurricane' Higgins the game nearly died. Now, with sponsors fighting to put up prize-money and *Pot Black* on TV growing into a cult programme for bishops, actresses and strike-weary captains of industry who can't face the Nine O'Clock News, the star player can make up to £25,000 a year. Elrick simply wants to swap the shadows for a slice of the legitimate action. But to do that, of course, he has to start mowing down some of the big names in the game.

He started very well 11 nights ago when, to the chagrin of the Establishment, he inflicted a severe defeat upon another former English champion, Paddy Houlihan. This, of course, is why the knives were out for him this time.

Ronnie Gross, who once picked up £1,000 in a week gambling on the two tables in the Red Cow, Hammersmith, was wary and already warmed up when Elrick arrived. He took the first frame, lost the second and narrowly won the third without once changing his bleak expression.

What happened next, I am obliged to report, may well bring a certain smile to those who play snooker for money with strangers and lose.

Gross massacred his man in the fourth game, just won the fifth, took the sixth with a series of diabolical snookers, conceded the seventh with all the colours still up and came back to win the eighth by rattling down a volley of blacks that must have sounded like a firing-squad to Elrick.

It was all over. The hustler had been hustled to a 6—2 defeat and he was still within earshot when Gross announced: 'Ah well, it was useful practice for the World Championships next month. The lad has a certain potential.'

Desmond Elrick was so sick that he couldn't eat his dinner in the Greek restaurant up the road. He stared at the table cloth, cursed himself and raised no objection at all when his chief backer said 'You played like a bum.'

In fact he's a very fine player indeed and I have little doubt that we shall see him some day on the official circuit. It was just that the road to righteousness didn't start over Montague Burton's, that's all.

The next three pieces were written in the space of a fortnight in the late summer of 1972. The first, which I find somewhat laboured now, at least reveals the euphoric mood of any reporter off to the Olympic Games. David Bedford had just broken the world 10,000-metres record in London and we were in high spirits. The Munich Games were a disaster and the mood, for me, changed on the very eve of the opening ceremony during a visit to Dachau Concentration Camp.

I should have known better. Eleven years earlier, while kicking my heels between an athletics match in Warsaw and a soccer game in Katowice, a Polish newspaper editor took me to Auschwitz, still preserved almost as it was in 1945. I remain grateful to the Daily Mail *for destroying the words I attempted to write about that horrendous experience. Dachau, therefore, was probably a mistake. But, of course, it also proved to be the first link in a terrible chain of events that are now all too familiar history.*

The memorial service to the murdered Israelis remains as sickening in retrospect as it was when I wrote the third of these pieces in hot blood.

There is another memorial service I recall without much affection. On the first anniversary of the Olympic killings I travelled from Tel Aviv back to Munich with Ilana Romano, widow of the second Israeli athlete to be murdered by Black September. She was received with much ceremony and moved not a muscle when shown the exact spot in the first floor apartment at 31, Connollystrasse, in the Olympic Village, where her husband died.

Later we sat outside the apartment in the early evening sunshine for the service. Certainly no fewer than 500 uniformed security guards were in attendance. "I presume," said Mrs Romano with understandable bitterness, "that if only two of these guards had been here this time last year my husband would now still be alive."

'I have a few drachmae on Hill, a slender apothecary from Northern Britannicus'

London.— The Olympic Games were merely revived in 1895. They were born 2,672 years earlier, at the time of the full Moon in the month of Apollonius, in a meadow near the temple of Zeus. The men ran and wrestled naked and the women did not run at all.

The first winner of the first Olympic final was Coroebus, who won not money but a wreath. Little has changed, least of all the style of those who sit and watch and report.

So here is a report from BERT SOCRATES in OLYMPIA.

It came to pass here last night that Bedfordogenes, a curious youth of unkempt countenance, did win the 10,000-pace foot race at a speed like the wind. 'It doth afford me great satisfaction,' he cried, 'because there are certain scribes in Londonium who can now go and get stuffed.'

I had not myself heard this strange mode of speech before but assume that Bedfordogenes was preparing much feasting and drinking for these friends when he returns to his city.

It was a truly famous victory that brought him his laurel-wreath, the more so because soothsayers had given him not a dove's chance in Hades.

His demeanour before the contest — including firing an arrow at a compatriot and lurking like a wolf in the mountain-tops — convinced many academics that he was either mad or had partaken liberally of wine.

This first triumph for Britannicus has greatly inspired a team which, until then had been dispirited by the events of last week when three handsome youths were expelled from the Games for sipping popy-juice with much, but not enough, furtiveness.

'We are under fearsome pressure,' they explained, but it saved them not and they were sent to the wilderness.

Now the Britannicus team and their physicians, who outnumber the foot-runners by two to one, are pacing the athletes' encampment at night with the chests expanded with pride and crying such strange oaths as 'Hemery will have your guts for hose-strings.'

This Hemery is a flaxen-haired man of great beauty and is known to be a diligent follower of Zeus.

Those not engaged in this nocturnal ritual were congregated before the gates of the female quarters, housing as it does four-and-twenty virgins down from Macedonia.

Their presence here has led to much poetry being composed in their honour, some of which may survive for 2,000 years.

Females do not partake in the racing and this has led to much wrath from one Greer, a lady who adorns herself in men's vestments and blows smoke from her nose in her anger.

No one is acquainted with from whence she comes but there is much talk here that she will be put to death.

There is also talk that the Emperor Brundagus, a fierce man reputedly 200 years old, is so displeasured by much of the conduct here that he will summon a council and disband the Games.

Tomorrow, as the sun cools over Mount Olympus, we shall witness the climax of the Games, the marathon. A local boy named Achilles is greatly favoured by Ladbrokes, but there is suspicion that he is troubled by a heel injury and I have a few drachmae that say the victor will be Hill, a slender apothecary from Northern Britannicus.

Hill, like Bedfordogenes, is an uncommunicative man crying to all scribes who seek conversation with him: 'Approach me not, I am exclusive to the sun.' I am unable to fathom the import of this mystical remark.

If Hill wins, messengers will doubtless carry tidings swiftly to all corners of Britannicus.

If he fails to outstrip his rivals I can already hear his compatriots at the wailing wall, proclaiming: 'Alas, we are undone. Sack Hill. Sack the Senator for Sport. We are disgraced in the eyes of civilisation.'

Nothing at the Olympic Games will ever change.

‘The last rising note of the 121st Psalm hung in the still mid-day air’

Munich. — The fanfares will blare out here today, and the massed choirs will sing, but it is another sound altogether that will continue to haunt me, long after these Olympics are over and done with.

It was the last rising note of the 121st Psalm, sung in Hebrew by a Rabbi, which hung in the still mid-day air, as if reluctant to die.

Eventually it did, and the only sound which followed was that of perhaps 4,000 feet rustling through gravel.

There were young athletes in gay track-suits or blazers, aged Jews all in black, tourists festooned with expensive cameras, and what appeared to be the entire Russian track and field team in identical grey lightweight suits.

Some wept, many looked shocked, and very few spoke, until they were outside the awful gates of Dachau concentration camp and heading back in a flotilla of buses to the space-age city they have built for the Games.

As they left, the Israeli team stood motionless before a memorial. They wore blue and white skull-caps, bearing the Olympic emblem.

Yesterday was the day Germany laid out her conscience, and almost insisted that the world should trample all over it. The Germans provided free transport, told every runner and writer here about the hour-long service that was to be conducted at Dachau, and hid nothing when we got there.

According to official statistics, 31,951 of Dachau's 206,000 prisoners, mostly Jews, died there between 1933 and 1945, not counting the 6,000 Russians, who were shot in a field down the road.

I could tell you none of these things had the facts not been forced upon me like some commercial handout.

Dachau is so close to the centre of Munich that it cannot be hidden, but yesterday one could only get the impression that Germany was almost masochistically purging itself of its past, before the Games open today.

It may have been a courageous decision, but it is possible to question its wisdom. Two hours within those walls, with its hideous instruments of torture and genocide, leave the mind in turmoil, and there were many young minds there yesterday which will reel from the experience for days to come.

The service, with an address given by an archbishop, who was once a prisoner there, was broadcast and televised. It roused many deep emotions, which, on the eve of an Olympics which threaten to be as nationalistic as these, might have been better left undisturbed.

This is hardly a happy preface to the most expensive, the most spectacular, the most computerised and probably the most efficient sports event yet staged on this earth, but there is no point pretending it didn't happen.

We stood in the centre of Dachau, at Germany's invitation, so presumably they were expecting it to be written about.

So far as I am concerned, it has been. For the last time.

Today, at 3 p.m., the first athlete will enter the stadium, and while it may be too much to expect that anyone still believes it is greater to take part than to win, may we just hope that this time nation will get along with nation.

'He hurled himself at the microphone and used the bodies of 11 dead Jews to beat the drum of his ideology'

Munich. — The XXth Olympic Games broke stride in Munich yesterday just long enough to pay tribute to the massacred Israelis. By teatime they'd carried out the dead and the show was on the road again.

Mr Avery Brundage's unilateral declaration that the Games must continue was not the only piece of showbiz fortitude to offend many thousands of people who took their grief to the Olympic Stadium.

In fierce mid-morning heat, they witnessed a memorial service so precisely staged for world television that it was more like a Hollywood Bowl spectacular. You found yourself looking for the drum majorettes.

What started as a solemn act of remembrance turned into a political rally and ended as a symphony concert.

When it was over the bewildered survivors of Israel's Olympic team straggled out of the stadium to search for a bus to carry them on the first leg of their sorrowful journey home. They had to watch out they didn't get knocked over by attendants officiously marshalling limousines for the VIP mourners.

They must have found the seating plan at the service ironic. They were placed centre-front of a mass block of chairs, symbolically protected from the world's chill winds by athletes from other nations.

The West German Olympic team, fetchingly attired in pale blue blazers which must have shown up well on colour television, stood round three sides of the square like guards in a lavish Wagnerian production.

One tenth of that protection 30 hours earlier might have been more appropriate.

All most people wanted to do in the Olympic Stadium yesterday was to howl their eyes out in private at the horrors of the night. Instead, they found themselves cast as extras in a world telly-cast of stage-directed sympathy.

All the right, trite things were said. Until, that is, Mr Avery Brundage rose to speak.

He is in his last week of office as president of the International Olympic Committee, and thank God for that, for his insensitivity to the occasion was beyond credulity.

He hurled himself at the microphone and used the bodies of 11 dead Jews to beat the drum of his ideology.

It was his cue to attack the commercialism which has increasingly infected the Olympic Games . . . then he could not resist the opportunity to go further: 'We lost the Rhodesians to naked political blackmail,' he rasped.

It was no spur-of-the-moment remark because he was reading his speech.

Mr Brundage may well be right. But it is unlikely that the Israelis, with 11 of their closest friends in a Munich morgue, found it an academic point.

Their dignity under stress was noble. The most emotional remark of Mr Samuel Lalkin, *chef de mission* of their team, was that 11 of his charges had died 'in the bloom of their lives'.

There was no criticism, direct or implied, of the circumstances which had permitted it to happen.

The real anger here comes from the sideline nations who witnessed the day-long cops-and-robbers show between German police and the desperate men of Black September only to wake up stunned by the news that every hostage had been murdered.

There is equally justifiable anger at the colossal bureaucratic blunder which permitted the unfortunate German Minister of the Interior to announce in public that the men's lives had been saved. Newspapers round the world published the escape story in good faith.

Opinion is divided in Munich, as everywhere, about the decision to allow the Olympics to continue. My own view is they should have been abandoned.

If you question that, I would only ask what your reaction would have been if gunmen had burst into the British headquarters in the Olympic Village and murdered Mary Peters, David Jenkins, Harvey Smith, David Hemery, Alan Pascoe, Ron Hill, Lynn Davies, Precious

McKenzie, Andy Carter and Anne Moore?

It may be unforgiveably cynical to suggest that it would have caused considerable office work to handle the ticket refunds, but the way the Israeli team left Munich yesterday to an almost audible sigh of relief from those passionate for the Games to continue was not an ennobling moment.

Israel's anguish, and indeed Germany's as the hosts who failed where they most wanted to succeed, should be shared by the world.

The competing Arab nations, as expected, did not turn up for the memorial service. They remained in the Olympic Village where they will continue to live. Nor did Tunisia carry it on television.

They are due to show themselves on the track today, and I can only wonder about the reception they will receive in such an atmosphere.

Montreal and Moscow, the next hosts for the Olympics in 1976 and 1980, must be watching it all with apprehension.

They may even be wondering whether the Munich Olympics, where the crowd will now think twice about raising its voice, are the last in the line.

ITEM: From time to time it is publicly lamented that sport is losing its 'characters'. I have not found this so. There are more conformists now because there are more professional sportsmen, but eccentricity lives.

'The Nawab of Pataudi told them he would like to be known as Mr Smith'

As befits a team which once numbered Rudyard Kipling among its supporters, Sussex County Cricket Club are to ignore the Indian Government's decision to demote their princes to mere misters.

Next season as for the past decade the Nawab of Pataudi will appear on their scorecards as the Nawab of Pataudi. This will be in regal contrast to the Indian newspapers who are already referring to their Test captain by his commoner's name of Mansoor Ali Khan.

Sussex officially consulted the Nawab before they made their decision and then predictably regretted it. He told them he would like to be known as Mr Smith.

This is reasonably typical of Pataudi's outlook on life. On one occasion he recorded a long, sound radio interview for the BBC in pure Peter Sellers Hindi without ever hinting that he in fact speaks the kind of beautifully modulated English which takes six years at Winchester and three at Oxford to instil.

On another occasion while driving an English journalist to a match in India he suddenly apologised for the fact that his car radio was broken. He then snapped his fingers.

At this signal a hired minstrel appeared from the back floor of the car and proceeded to strum frantically on a guitar.

Pataudi's last gesture before returning to India in August to be present at the birth of his first child was to stride into Harrods and order 48 feeding bottles.

The astonished assistant asked 'Are you expecting quads, sir?' 'No,' replied yesterday's prince, 'I've got four wives.'

Cartoonists are the heroes of the newspaper trade. Their talents for drawing and caricature are invariably taken for granted. Their daily Waterloo is The Idea which, on non-inspirational days, is occasionally obtained by the expedient of smashing the forehead against the nearest brick wall at five-second intervals. Column-writing also depends on ideas but there is always a congenial escape route. When all else fails you simply pick up your golf clubs and go and do something ridiculous.

'She is to female golf what Master W. A. Mozart once was to the music industry'

Killarney.—Getting massacred on the golf course is no new experience to this 18-handicap column with its built-in slice and permanent putting twitch.

Stricken by nerves we've lost at the 11th to Gary Player in Johannesburg and decimated by dry Martinis we've gone down 4 and 3 to Richie Benaud in Sydney. Still name-dropping we've even been thrashed by Laurie Pignon, the *Daily Mail's* monocled lawn tennis correspondent, and he's got a swing like Sir Adrian Boult.

Losing to Miss Bridget Josephine Gleeson, however, was an altogether novel sensation. It felt like being sand-bagged by a leprechaun or karate-chopped by a nun.

She splashed out of a canyon-sized bunker at the 13th, stroked down the subsequent four-foot putt, extended one diminutive hand and offered falsetto condolences for having won our match 6 and 5.

If you are not conversant with golf mensurations, 6 and 5 is what the Washington Post did to Nixon or the likeliest result if the Soviet Union declared war on Free Cornwall. In short, obliteration.

What really hurt, though, may be conveyed by a somewhat more alarming set of statistics: Miss Gleeson, who stands 4ft 9¾in., weighs fractionally under five stone and has a 40 per cent. loss of vision in one eye, is 11 years and four months of age.

She is to female golf what Master W.A. Mozart once was to the music industry and if you suspect that's hyperbole I suggest you go to Killarney, County Kerry, and take her on for yourself. It will cost you a quid. She likes a side-bet to sustain her concentration.

This was not necessary against me. Five up after five holes she had it so buttoned up that she observed new-born lambs, picked spring flowers, discussed her maths homework with her Daddy and, at one totally demoralising juncture, climbed a tree.

Between times she had five single putts in 13 holes, hit both par-five greens against the wind in four shots, struck her drives a consistent 135 yards, her three-woods an equally consistent 120 yards and strayed from the fairway only once. Off her 18 handicap she finished three shots over regulation figures and that was wholly attributable to a sudden hail storm which shrieked in off the Atlantic.

It would be quite impertinent of this column to claim Bridget Gleeson as a discovery. She's been an Irish tourist attraction since she was 3ft. high and an established starlet since she mistressed Killarney's monstrous par-74 course in 87 shots for a net 69.

She has been playing golf since she was two and apart from a fleeting and now abandoned ambition to be a nun has never wanted to do much else. This is just as well. Under the vigilant eye of her father, who has jettisoned his own golf career to mastermind hers, she practises four hours a day. Last Christmas Day she practised for six.

When you hear facts like that you begin to wonder what sadistic forms of child-cruelty they are getting up to out on the west coast of Ireland these days.

Reassurance comes in the size of Bridget Gleeson's smile, her absolute unprecociousness and her naughty little confession that the only boring thing in the whole wide world is having to go to school when she could be hitting ten million chip shots up to the pin.

Impervious to all the acclaim, unaffected by much publicity and utterly unspoiled by her triumphal exhibition tour of North America last year, her only non-golfing interest is to play with her two pet cats. These are named Lee Trevino and Gary Player. What else?

'You're not the first chap to come here suspecting we're manufacturing some sort of golfing monster,' said Bridget's dad, who has been greenkeeper at the Killarney club all his working life and himself plays to scratch.

'We've had to examine our own motives very carefully. Of course we want her to succeed. Of course we'd love her to become the greatest woman golfer in the world. But the real ambition is Bridget's. That's what she wants for herself and so long as she goes on wanting it we'll give up everything for her career.'

Already the Gleesons drive her all over Ireland in their ten-year-old car to play on new courses and toughen her up competitively against big, busty girls of 18 and 19 who'd skin her alive if they could. Most of them can't.

They live in a lodge with leaded windows in a village so quiet that two cars are a traffic jam and three add up to a fuel crisis. Its geographic position is the secret of Bridget Gleeson's prodigious talent.

Fifty yards from the door are Killarney's 15th green and 16th tee, and it was between the two, as soon as she could stand, that she started hitting golf shots with a club 12in. long.

'I honestly can't remember a time when I *didn't* play golf,' said Bridget. Then she was playing with cut-down clubs. Today she carries specially manufactured woods and irons in a bag almost as big as she is. John and Mary Gleeson are far from rich but they are prepared to stake their last penny on their only child's golfing development.

Before we drove off in what must be embarrassingly dismissed as our non-contest, Miss Gleeson and her dad took me out to the 15th where it all began.

It was less practice than a Palladium act.

She placed 30 balls in a bunker slightly deeper than her own height. She hit ten one-handed with her right hand, ten one-handed with her left hand and ten conventionally two-handed. She hit 29 of those balls cleanly out of the trap and left 26 of them clustered within four yards of the flagstick.

For her next trick, still hitting half the shots one-handed, she struck 30 chip-shots from behind the bunker to the green. Of these 18 finished within two yards of the hole and a further eight within six yards. Of 30 drives, also hit one- and two-handed, she pitched 24 in an eight-yard circle over a distance of 130 yards.

She used to perform these feats blindfolded but her father has stopped all that. 'She was in danger of becoming a circus,' he said, 'and what we are trying to make is a very good golfer.'

What any sane challenger would have done, of course, was leap in his car and rush back to Barley Cove with such real characters as the Japanese singer who specialises in Irish folk songs and the barman whose aunt's first husband, second husband, eldest son and only cousin all dedicatedly drank themselves to death.

But we had to go through with it and what I must say for the gorgeous, cherubic Miss Gleeson is that she drove me into the green turf of Killarney as swiftly and painlessly as possible.

What I meanly never let on was that I'd played just about as well as I damned well can. It just never looked like being enough against a child I must rate as the finest 11-year-old player of any ball game I have ever seen.

'His putt travelled 5,111 feet, a range from which even the immortal Jack Nicklaus has occasionally been known to miss'

Washington. — Since Mr Trevor Nash is to big-time golf roughly what Mrs Margaret Thatcher is to the Kremlin netball team, there will be those who resent the fact that he commemorated the dawn of 1977 by achieving The Most Remarkable Putt in History.

Mr Nash, I should explain, is a buddy of mine with a 22 handicap, a swing like a Klondike lumberjack and a philosophy which maintains you might as well do it today because tomorrow you're more than likely to be struck by a Green Line bus.

To be truthful it was at his third attempt — a deviation from the rigid code of rules laid down by the Royal and Ancient which I shall have to explain later—that Mr Nash holed out.

Overcome by euphoric emotion he immediately called for several glasses of Dom Perignon '69 which were instantly served by a lady with good legs and a nice blue uniform. And really there *was* something to celebrate.

For one thing, his putt travelled 5,111 feet, a range from which even the immortal Jack Nicklaus has occasionally been known to miss.

For another, it sped along at almost 1½ times the speed of the average high velocity rifle bullet.

Thirdly, it was accomplished 2,000 miles out over the Atlantic at an altitude approximately twice the height of Mount Everest.

Some explanations are in order and the first is that with most of Britain greeting the New Year with an attack of almost terminal lethargy Mr Nash and I contracted to relieve the boredom by playing a golf match with a small difference.

The difference was that the first nine holes were to be played in Great Britain, the second nine holes were to be played in the United States of America and all 18 holes were to be negotiated in the same day.

While this, during the brief dark days of a Northern Hemisphere mid-winter, may appear to present certain logistical problems, nothing in fact could be more childishly simple.

All you have to do is play the 2,992 yards that comprise the front nine holes at the Royal Mid-Surrey Club on the outskirts of London, hail a taxi to take you the nine miles between there and Heathrow, hop on a plane for the 3,778-mile ride to Dulles International Airport in Washington DC, hire a car for the 25-mile run to the military suburb of Arlington and then hack your way round the 3,356-yard back nine holes of America's Army-Navy Country Club.

By the time you're through, you will have played 18 holes, par 70, over a course measuring 3,812 miles 1,068 yards from first tee to last green.

You will also have accomplished it in a single span of daylight, which may just add up to the most meaningless record in the annals of mediocre amateur sport.

Anyway, it was one way to start the year and the contestants are mutually grateful to the man who made it work: Captain Keith Myers, who belted British Airways' fourth and newest Concorde, Alpha Delta, through head winds to cross the Atlantic in three hours 56 minutes.

Concorde's speed, in conjunction with the five-hour time difference between Greenwich and Washington, actually meant that we were landing 64 minutes before we were due to take off.

It also permitted us, in one day, to hit shots out of some pretty big-shot footprints.

At 8.50 a.m., London time, we were driving off at Royal Mid-Surrey, which is bounded by Kew Gardens on one side and some distinctly plebeian municipal planning on the other, on the very terrain where the late Edward VIII took his problems when he was trying to grapple with the constitutional impasse which decreed he could have the Throne *or* Mrs Simpson but definitely not both.

At 3.58 p.m., Washington time, we were hitting off at the Army-Navy Country Club, which is within mortar range of The Pentagon and just down the hill from John F. Kennedy's grave, at a course whose membership in recent years has numbered such contrasting luminaries as Richard M. Nixon, Lyndon B. Johnson and JFK himself.

Unfortunately, the world being the shambles it is, none of them was permitted to play there during his Presidential term since one corner of the course is overshadowed by high-rise buildings from which even the most astigmatic assassin could not have missed a man stooped in concentration over a putt.

Its most famous Old Boy, therefore, remains Dwight D. Eisenhower who played there as cadet, General, Supreme Commander and President, and bequeathed to the club his gaudy old red and blue golf bag and a full set of irons.

These are impaled on a wall and testify to Dwight D.'s eternal self-effacement. The five stars of his military rank are not only plastered in gold all over the golf bag but engraved on the heads of each of the clubs as well.

However, the Eisenhower spirit prevails. With Washington white-faced and shivering at 27 deg. F. all the golf courses were closed except the Army-Navy Club where words like defeat, withdrawal and adversity are unknown. 'It's our pleasure,' said Mr Steve Tobash, professional, as he directed us to the 10th tee.

Since tactics on both sides of the Atlantic were never to hit the ball out of sight on fairways patch-worked with snow, frost and ice, the hole-by-hole scores will be treated as classified information for the next 30 years.

It is sufficient to record that we stood all-square on the ninth green at Royal Mid-Surrey, measured out the lengths of our respective putts, measured out the same distance in Concorde when it reached level flight at 59,000 ft. and proceeded to complete the hole by putting up the gangway into a champagne glass.

This was how Trevor Nash, at the third attempt, achieved The Most Remarkable Putt in History.

In the 2½ seconds it took his ball to travel along 45 feet of red carpet, Concorde itself, travelling at slightly more than 1,300 miles an hour, had rolled a further 5,066 feet towards Washington.

Mr Nash, as it happens, lost the match two-and-one but that was the least of his setbacks.

In the extremely expensive bar of an extremely expensive hotel that evening an American lady of indeterminate vintage but claiming to be a Basque whose many marriages had included one to the Count von Essen, asked him how he'd spent the day.

'Playing golf,' said my mate.

'Oh,' huffed the Countess. 'How stupendously boring.'

It is hard to recall now what trauma prompted the following rush of blood to the head. It would appear, from the opening paragraph, to have been a traffic jam. Inevitably it did no good. London still has traffic jams and there are still sportsmen and sports administrators who will look you straight in the eye and tell you exactly the opposite of what you know they are thinking.

'We are now on the receiving end of so many double-think clichés in sport that an examination may not be out of order'

London. — It was not so much the breakneck two-mile-an-hour car chase into Central London that set my pulse racing yesterday as the blood-curdling threat that came in by radio-telegraph from Dunedin, New Zealand.

In a statement that sounded like Blondin drumming up the crowds for his next Niagara walk, New Zealand's new cricket captain pledged his team to 'attractive, aggressive, crowd-pulling play in England this summer'.

Confronted by a Reuter representative, Mr Bevan Congdon was unwise enough to go on: 'This will mean declarations and the setting of targets. To win a few you've got to lose a few.'

Let us now rack our brains and consider where we've heard *that* before. Ah yes. From almost every Test captain prior to virtually every cricket tour of the modern era.

The last one who didn't say anything of the sort was probably Douglas Jardine who went down to Australia forty-one years ago with a sublime indifference about whether any spectators turned up or not.

His only distinguishable motive was to get Don Bradman hit between the eyes with the ball and, as a result, the grounds were constantly packed to the rafters.

Jardine, anyway, didn't speak to the Press. For one thing he regarded even its highest-paid practitioners as unspeakable errand boys. For another he had no intention of saying one thing while actually meaning another.

This second point has somewhat changed down four decades. Apart from a few startlingly original minds — such as Derek Dougan talking about Ulster, Jack Nicklaus discussing modern art or Brian Clough declaiming on any subject from contraception to euthanasia — we are now on the receiving end of so many double-think clichés in sport that an examination of some of them may not be out of order.

'We intend to play attractive, aggressive cricket, regardless of results in the Tests.' Actually means: *They'll only win over our dead bodies. If we declare setting them to make 240 in 110 minutes maybe they'll just be daft enough to have a go for it.*

'Rovers are a great club but now that I've been dropped into the reserves I must consider my future.' Actually means: *I hope the bastards lose on Saturday. Anyway I'll be on 5 p.c. of the transfer fee if I can stir it enough to make them sell.*

'Our manager has the complete confidence and full support of the board.' Actually means: *What did we see in him in the first place? If the twit loses once more at home this season he'll be out on his ear.*

'My consortium and I are all experienced businessmen and our takeover bid for Argyle, whom we've supported since boyhood is out of genuine concern for the future of the club.' Actually means: *One or two of us have even seen them play and, anyway, it's a good way of getting our names in the newspapers.*

'I am extremely proud of my players. To lose only 2—0 against a team dedicated to provocation and defensive tactics convinces me that England will qualify comfortably for the World Cup.' Actually means: *How dare these reporters ask me questions like that when I feel as sick as a pig?*

'Our decision to send our first XV to South Africa is because of our deep conviction that bridge-building is the best method of breaking down the evils of apartheid.' Actually means: *With those luscious, available birds and all that free booze, we'd have to be daft to turn down an expenses-paid trip to the sunshine at this time of year.*

'And now, gennulmen, introducin', in the red corner, from Chltembo, Angola, the new middleweight sensation of the entire African continent, Simon Ngombe.' Actually means: *If he gets knocked out I suppose we'll have to pay his bleedin' taxi fare back to Brixton.*

These are all songs our mothers taught us, and there are those still around, I suppose, who believe the lyrics.

Curiously, the track record for New Zealand cricket captains thinking before they speak is a good one. It surprises me, therefore, that so down-to-earth a man as Bevan Congdon should have put his head in the noose.

For one thing he doesn't yet even know who his opposing Test captain will be. For another you won't find too many pages in Wisden scorched by statistics of their combustible cricket. We await developments with particular interest.

The 1976 Olympic equestrian events were staged at Bromont, 50 miles south of Montreal. We were invited there one morning, ostensibly to interview the British team but primarily to interview Princess Anne. It was a Press conference of engaging banality, largely dominated by Canadian and American women reporters asking the Princess questions of a nature that may be described as domestic-familiar. In fact I can recall only one intelligent question all morning and it came from Hugh McIlvanney of the London Observer. *Pointing out that in a world of poverty and strife the Olympic Games were costing the earth and required 16,000 troops to protect them from terrorist attack, McIlvanney asked the princess whether she regarded the continued celebration of the Games as morally justified. Apparently outraged at a question which required reasoning and thought, Princess Anne replied in her tinniest voice "Are you trying to make a speech or something?"*

This capacity for instant hauteur has not totally endeared Princess Anne to Fleet Street, to whom interviewing Royals is just another day's work. The tone of the following three columns may therefore be surprising. They were written over five years, from the Princess's abortive attempt to win a place in the 1972 British team via her cross-country ride in the 1976 Olympics to a subsequent attack on her manners.

'It would all be easier if she were the daughter of Mr and Mrs P. Windsor, of London and Norfolk'

Rushall, Wiltshire.— For one naive moment at the weekend I leaped to the delusion that Mr Raymond Bellisario had upped with his shutters and quit.

Mr Bellisario is, of course, the man least likely to be knighted for his services to the photographic arts. The little chap who keeps leaping out of the bushes to take candid camera shots of British royalty and then flogging them to foreign magazines.

But there he was, with his attractive Girl Friday, strolling past the late Norman church of St Matthew in the Wiltshire village of Rushall, heading down to the meadows through which the River Avon takes its own good time about getting down to the sea.

Birds sang, crocuses peeped, last year's rooks' nests were sharply etched against a dove-grey sky and a westerly breeze ruffled the hair just like it used to in those groovy ads for menthol cigarettes. Nature was winning 5—0 at half time.

Alas, all was not as it seemed. Ten minutes later Mr Bellisario and assistant had set up their cameras at a point on the river, known locally as The Cattle Drinker, with one unmistakable intention in mind.

Namely, to snap Her Royal Highness Princess Anne Elizabeth Alice Louise, fourth in succession to the British throne, as she was flung headlong from one of her mum's horses into the freezing water.

Princess Anne, who 16 days from now either will or will not be chosen for Britain's equestrian team for the Munich Olympics, did not co-operate.

Riding the two-mile cross-country in the Rushall Horse Trials she retired on Collingwood long before The Cattle Drinker came in sight and later on Columbus, cleared the river with all the panache of Fred Winter belting Sundew home in The National.

She didn't smile much, which was probably wise because Mr Bellisario was also leaping about trying to establish her in the same shot as Competitor No. 190. Competitor No. 190 was Richard Meade, who was once idiotic enough to challenge Harvey Smith to a duel in his self-appointed role as the Princess's Champion.

The photographs — if any — are due to appear in a Swiss publication.

What, you will be asking by now, has all this dolce vita drivel got to do with sport? Quite a bit, as it happens.

You could easily run away with the idea that pressure in sport is a cross to be borne almost exclusively by such as Frank McLintock, Virginia Wade, Tony Jacklin, David Bedford, Bert Head and John Snow. Indeed only the other day Don Revie was talking about 'the pressures that tear your guts out', and he's not a man given to hysterical complaint.

My submission, after a day amid the hacking macks and hip flasks of the horse world, is that no sportsman or woman on the face of the earth is currently under such intolerable pressure as Princess Anne.

Her dilemma is obvious. The world, literally, waits to see if she's just good enough to make the Olympics. If she does there will be millions who'll nod knowingly and mutter darkly about Republicanism. If she doesn't, a thousand old ladies in Cheltenham will reach for the poisoned ink and fire off terrible Letters to the Editor and Willie Hamilton.

If in these last tense days leading up to next week's final selection at Badminton Anne shows the strain

ANOTHER MOTHER: *The Queen watching Princess Anne ride cross-country in the Olympic equestrian three-day event at the Montreal Olympics. Her anxiety was justified. Anne was thrown, concussed and recalled nothing of the last stage of the ride.*

BASQUE MORNING: *Running with the bulls at Pamplona, an activity not to be undertaken without brandy for breakfast. The author is judiciously close to the gutter.*

BULLS 2, HUMAN RACE 0: *Occasionally the bulls win, though in neither of these instances was a runner killed. The runs take place at 8 a.m. each morning from July 7 to 13. Entry is free.*

LONELY JOURNEY: *Alaska's annual sled-dog race across the 1,100-mile Iditarod Trail requires clothing not normally seen in Oxford Street. Before setting off Mr Lloyd Haessler kindly loaned us three wild dogs of the north to discover what husky-power feels like.*

by so much as a frown she'll be described as the petulant Princess. If she stares straight ahead she'll be written off, by others, as a haughty piece.

The dear girl can't win. I watched it all with ghoulish fascination at Rushall and I wouldn't be in her riding boots for all the sparklers in the Imperial Crown.

It wasn't only trial by Bellisario. It was persecution by Box Brownie, Instamatic, binoculars, hand-held television cameras appearing out of hedgerows, rifle-microphones which can pick up intimate conversations over huge distances, officials dry-throated with protocol, detectives failing to disguise themselves as elm trees and, worst of all, hundreds of people just like you and me who pressed as close to her as they could and simply stared.

''Ere, look,' shrieked a woman who could have reached out and touched the Princess's shoulder, 'she's got 'er ears pierced.'

It's all very well, I suppose, when Princess Anne is opening some Unmarried Mothers' Wing in Lanarkshire. I can tell you that in darkest Wiltshire on Saturday it was sheer bloody murder.

Princess Anne's mistake, of course, was in admitting in that marvellous *Blue Peter* programme, first shown more than a year ago, that it was her *ambition* to ride in the Olympics.

With that remark she tossed her coronet into the public arena. Quite rightly, when it comes to Olympic selection, even a palatial address in London, S.W.1. is no credential. You have to be good. You also have to be seen to be good.

But how you can *prove* yourself good from the inside of a magnifying goldfish bowl is beyond my simple comprehension.

It would all be so much easier if she were merely Anne Windsor, only daughter of Mr and Mrs P. Windsor, of London and Norfolk.

But she's not and never can be. Not when, as at Rushall, the waiting ambulancemen were genned up to the eyebrows with special instructions about what to do in the event of an accident.

Commoners were to be taken to the civil hospital in Swindon, Princess Anne was to be taken to the RAF Hospital at Wroughton, where a medical team was on red alert for just such an eventuality.

That, of course, is privilege. It is also part of the incredible pressure that this cool young girl must withstand for another 11 days until the last huge fence at Badminton has been cleared or demolished.

I do not mock Don Revie's remark about the pressures on his nervous system. I merely point out that Princess Anne isn't exactly swanning around these days in glass slippers.

‘The remote figure was the Queen who remained there, deep in the private world of maternal concern’

Bromont, Quebec.— With the profane optimism that hallmarks their profession, the Press photographers, almost to a man, tramped miles out into the sodden woods of Brome County to range themselves around the water hazards.

It is not every day that they can capture the fourth in succession to the British throne spinning royal head over riding boots into a Canadian brook. And, if anything, they were more edgy than the rider.

They had come from Sydney, Washington and London and all those glossy European magazines that treat royalty like film stars, and for once collusion was as rife as rivalry.

‘If you get any luck, let us know,’ they were yelling.

Well, most of them got drenched with nothing to show for it. HRH Princess Anne, as wilful as her strong handsome horse, came to grief at the undermanned 19th fence precisely where the equestrian cognoscenti least expected it.

It was almost like tripping over a mole hill after coming down from the Eiger north wall. For the 19th, a zig-zag fence that any respectable hunter should take in its stride, would have presented few problems had the rain not started belting down on the Olympic eventing cross-country course just before dawn.

The British team, inspecting the course earlier in the week, determined that the safest and fastest line was to clear it at the extreme right-hand end.

So it would have been had the 13 horses that preceded Princess Anne’s Goodwill not churned the take-off area into a swamp.

When it was seen what was happening an urgent message was sent back from that far-flung outpost for the Princess to go over from the firm ground in front of the exact centre of the obstacle.

It wasn’t urgent enough. It never reached her.

She obeyed the original instructions, and when Goodwill got his hind leg tangled in the spars she crashed, collected 60 penalty points, a critical mass of time faults, several bruises and mild concussion.

When they brought the news to the Queen she nodded curtly, said nothing and went on watching the other riders tackling the second fence. It was almost as though she had expected as much. Like any other mother, she had been unable to conceal her anxiety all the morning.

She looked as stern as when her own mount plays up while she is sitting side-saddle to review her soldiers on Horse Guards.

Her hands revealed her concern, and had they not done so, she would not have been human. There is no Olympic discipline more dangerous than the equestrian cross-country.

No one had more blood support than Princess Anne. Prince Philip was there, striding around with a massive lack of concern. Prince Charles was cheerfully chatting up people. Prince Andrew was again pretending not to know that all the girls couldn't take their eyes off him, and Prince Edward, caught yawning a couple of times, looked as though he could have done with another few hours' sleep.

Captain Mark Phillips, consort of Britain's first royal Olympian, was visibly more tense than his wife at the start line. Mr and Mrs Peter Phillips, Anne's in-laws, immediately went back to busy themselves around the stables.

Anne herself was still dismounted 30 seconds before her starting time.

'That was a very cool performance indeed,' said Jackie Stewart, ex-world motor racing champion, a man who knows something about pre-race tension and a commentator here for America's ABC television network. 'You could see she was uptight but she controlled it marvellously.'

The confusion, as the news of her fall crackled in on the short wave radios, matched almost everything else that was going on at this shambles of a race.

The thousands of spectators who had paid £3 for admission tickets were joined by thousands of others, mostly day trippers from across the nearby American border, who swarmed over the course for free.

Armed guards blocked the entrance to the start-and-finish enclosure, but all you had to do to mingle with royals and riders alike was stroll through a neighbouring barnyard and step over 18 inches of broken fence.

Reporters hot-lining the news to all points of the earth kept interviewing one another. It was a couple of hours before most of them found anyone who had seen the fall. The cameramen flooded back, cursing the loss of a prize-winning picture.

Eventually she came into sight round a spinney and up the long last rise, well out of her saddle. She slid off Goodwill, and was escorted to the back seat of a car and whisked away.

Dr Rob Kennedy, a British team official, announced that she was perfectly all right. Another British team man inexplicably said: 'It's the horse we're more concerned about.'

It was left to Mrs Anne Phillips to break the news of the concussion which left her daughter-in-law with no recollection of what had happened between remounting and the finish line.

The remote figure throughout had been the Queen, who trudged through mud to the second fence and remained there, deep in the private world of maternal concern.

Richard Meade, classically British, rode fast and beautifully round the course in the wake of Princess Anne but by the time he returned and learned of her massive penalty marks — and the lameness afflicting two of Britain's four horses—he knew that the team gold medal, almost the prerogative of Britain at recent Olympics, was lost.

Princesses, too, it seems need to take comfort from the Olympic notion that merely competing is a reward as rich as winning.

From the look of Anne yesterday that will be scant consolation.

'She's all woman, that one, and that's nine out of ten for a start'

London. — Mrs Phillips, a £2,916-a-month Camberley housewife, has been copping it all week from that bulwark of public propriety, the *Daily Mirror.*

It's tut-tutting executives decided to publish an earwitness report concerning Mrs Phillips's colourful vocabulary while witnessing the Burghley Horse Trials.

Presumably the evidence was obtained by the traditional method of disguising a reporter as a Dutch Elm and planting him in the paddock. What he heard may have been naughty but it was never obscene. Just two bastards and a bugger off.

These were apparently provoked by (a) the sight of Captain Phillips coming off his mount like a stricken Apache; (b) the intrusion of a TV cameraman and (c) some child careering out of parental control and treading on one of Mrs Phillip's feet.

Anyway it was all published as a matter of public concern, thus provoking puritanical outrage among those readers with outside lavatories and republican leanings.

What intrigues me about these outbreaks of Lutheranism is that if it had been Harvey Smith or Freddie Trueman sounding off they would have been congratulated in the public prints for their restraint in the face of intense provocation. Harvey's V-sign, after all, is now accepted as a rustic mannerism and Fred's language is regarded as equal in importance to English folklore as the May morning singing from Magdalen College.

Not so, it would seem, if Mrs Phillips blows her top in what she assumes to be a private place at a sport renowned for the vigour of its invective.

She is portrayed as a haughty witch with her hand in the public till who ought to have more respect for her mother's subjects.

Well, as one of her mother's subjects I find it odd that there should be one law for the poor and an altogether harsher one for the rich and that's quite apart from the fact that I reckon Mrs Phillips has actually earned dispensation from the very boring business of being born royal.

This view comes entirely from having watched her ride for Britain round those murderous cross-country courses where one minute you're clawing up the side of Fort Knox and the next you're standing almost vertically in the irons as your horse plunges headlong into a river. In between there are up to 36 fences where, from time to time, riders break their necks.

Apart from Grand Prix driving, fighting Miura bulls and ski-jumping it is the most vertiginous little caper I have ever watched and Princess Anne, who smashed her head on the ground and then rode on for another 17 fences at Bromont the other day, is pretty good at it.

This does not necessarily give her licence to turn the air blue when she cuts her hand on a can of baked beans but you don't just get off one of those things when you've risked your neck and say 'Fiddlesticks'.

It depends, I suppose, how you like your princesses.

We could easily have inherited some vapid young lady whose most strenuous activity was to go round laying foundation stones for new Inland Revenue offices and bashing vintage champagne against the hulls of battleships.

We could easily be paying out for some shrieking young super-deb whose closest brush with physical danger would be to negotiate the three-inch pavement outside the Odeon, Leicester Square, on royal film night.

Instead we have a girl who rides horses like the wind and when you know what we are paying out in other areas to restore the image of tired, lazy, listless Britain abroad, I don't even think she's dear at the price.

Anyway she had a go and if, from time to time, her renowned spirit gets the better of her mother's English it is probably because paragons don't often distinguish themselves in international sport. You will hear much, much worse at Lord's, the Wimbledon Centre

Court and in any of the Fleet Street watering holes where the literati assemble to decide how the rest of the world should conduct itself.

Among those who have expressed other views, ranging from distress to disgust, are Mrs Mary Whitehouse, whose Olympic record remains a mystery, and Miss Barbara Cartland, last pictured dictating another of those incredible novels to two secretaries while stroking a white cat in a drawing room absolutely strewn with delphiniums.

Well, by thy critics shall thee be known and while not wishing to advocate that the language of sport from now on should be pure Anglo-Saxon, I do reckon that Mrs Phillips has been harshly handled.

She's all woman, that one, and that's nine out of ten for a start.

The journey to New Orleans was kindly subsidised by the BBC for whom we were making a sports documentary on George Foreman, then still a challenger for the world heavyweight title. Foreman, like so many large boxers, turned out to be a gentle, generous man trapped in the vicious and often deceitful world of a dying business. We sat together at the ringside to watch what I think was the least noble physical contest I have ever seen.

'I have rarely witnessed a more phoney, tawdry, degrading or even disgusting spectacle'

New Orleans.— Massa Frazier has kept his world heavyweight title, the Dallas Cowboys have drowned the Miami Dolphins in the Super Bowl football match, the hot trumpets have blared out down Bourbon Street for 36 hours solid and, according to a radio news bulletin, eight people have been murdered since Saturday lunchtime.

America's greatest sporting weekend of the year is over and the voice of New Orleans is now so hoarse that it truly sounds like a scratched old 78. The nation has watched it all live on television — 65 million tuned into the Super Bowl final, 25 million to see Frazier dump Terry Daniels through the ropes like a sack of white trash and all that's left is a ghost city with a damp towel wrapped around a monumental municipal hangover.

At 4 a.m. here yesterday you could buy anything from a quarter-pint dry martini to a Louis Quatorze antique. You could also pay up to £120 for a black-market football ticket; get thumped over the head if you strayed down a dark side street; hear Kid Thomas, now 76, play the kind of jazz you only read about in books; or land yourself in an old fashioned fist fight if you ventured a single opinion about boxing, football, the slave trade or President Nixon's coming visit to China.

If I had a pound for every ten-galloned fan stumbling through the streets of the French quarter after mid-night with a charged glass in his hand, or a fiver for every drunk sleeping on his elbows at a bar, I need never write another word in my life. The American sports enthusiast, en fete, makes the Scots who invade Wembley every two years appear the epitome of social discretion.

Flying down the Mississippi to Dixie at the calmest of times must rank among the last of the great romantic journeys. When there is a world heavyweight title fight at the end of it the prospect is like basking for an hour at the end of a rainbow.

I have to confess to shattering disappointment. I have rarely witnessed a more phoney, tawdry, degrading or even disgusting spectacle than the three and a half rounds of sadism promoted to make a few hundred thousand fast bucks and, bewilderingly, permitted by the Louisiana State Athletic Commission, between Frazier and Daniels.

There was no need for the fight to be fixed. It was all summed up by the story of the one and only bookmaker to offer odds on the contest. He quoted 1,000—1 against Daniels.

It was never a contest. Daniels looked like a choirboy thrown to the lions. He was knocked down four times and got up three, thus earning nationwide acclamation for 'courage' and 'guts'. Rubbish. He earned more in ten minutes than Edward Heath makes in three years merely because he happened to be the man lucky enough to be chosen by the Frazier camp as the 'selected opponent'.

At the nauseating Press conference which followed, Frazier paid the traditional tributes to fallen opponents . . . 'He sure hurt me a time or two . . . .' 'Some day he could be champion of the world.' To my astonishment grown reporters wrote it down in their notebooks and to my greater astonishment it is printed today in a large number of American newspapers.

If Terence Daniels, scion of a middle-class family, ever becomes world champion I will cheerfully donate a year's salary to charity.

Boxing, meanwhile, goes from

bad to banal. The Frazier-Daniels fight was nothing more than a legalised hoax, heavily subsidised by television, cornily presented and tastelessly stage managed.

At one point, would you believe, the audience was invited to rise to its feet for ten seconds by way of tribute to the late Martin Luther King on the anniversary of his violent death. Half the audience stood, the other half pointedly stayed seated. It was the nearest thing we saw to a contest all night.

Not that many cared. Two men close to me in the $40 seats slept noisily throughout the evening's proceedings. It's been that kind of weekend in New Orleans.

Before the big fight we had dinner with Mr George Foreman, who would have been better coupled in the ring with Frazier instead of eating a surprising diet of cheeseburgers and a mound of French fries.

Foreman, who is a heavyweight of class, is dying to come to England and is quite hurt that he has never been asked. In due course he will be extremely well known, though never so voluble a character as his manager, Dick Sadler, who is small, fat, very black and possesses the most unique vocabulary I have ever heard. If you can imagine Freddie Trueman doing his stuff with Al Jolson's hand signals, that's Sadler.

His dinner consisted entirely of apple tart, stories of the late Sonny Liston, and horrifying warnings about the fate awaiting anyone foolish enough to stray downtown in search of local colour. 'Mah friend,' he said, 'they are down theah now, bowin' down and thainkin' the good Lawd for the blessin's they are about to receive.'

If either Parkinson or Frost can persuade Mr Sadler to eliminate a few of his favourite epithets for 30 minutes or so they could have a magical guest on their show. If they try it and fail the interview will consist entirely of bleeps.

One of the emancipations of column-writing is the freedom it affords to watch the trivial, the absurd, the also-rans and the no-hopers. You have the chance to learn what it feels like to be the first man knocked out of a tournament or the last man riding in the Tour de France. You can hang around the unlikeliest places.

'You don't get assigned to Court 14. You get excommunicated there'

Wimbledon.— Court 14 at Wimbledon is so far from the Centre Court that it's damned nearly in the Old Bailey. It is the end of the line, the last stop before outer space.

People have been coming to Wimbledon since the days of Tilden and Cochet and never even noticed Court 14. This is understandable. It lies in the same latitudes as the lavatories, tucked away between two neatly clipped hedgerows.

You don't get assigned to Court 14. You get excommunicated there.

On the way down there this week I passed Hombergen playing N'Godrella on Court 7 and Bleckinger and Holecek fighting it out on Court 11. None the wiser I pressed on but Court 14 failed to yield any sudden flash of enlightenment.

A Mr Jiri Hrebec, from Teplice, was playing a Mr Szabolis Baranyi, from Nagyvarad, under the intense scrutiny of an Indian umpire and an English line judge who kept shrieking 'out' when the ball overshot the baseline by as much as five yards.

Hrebec and Baranyi took it pretty well. They swore only softly in what sounded like Serbo-Croat out of deference to their audience. This comprised me, a giggle of schoolgirls in candy-striped uniforms and a couple of smart middle-aged ladies with wedding rings and roving eyes. Hrebec and Baranyi are very good looking in a sort of Central European way.

There were no commentators, no cameras, no reporters, no electronic figures flashing on scoreboards and when we all applauded a particularly good shot it sounded like a couple of dice rattling around in a bucket.

Just occasionally, to heighten our isolation, the tailend of a vast human roar would float down from the ivy-clad temple up on the hill: Billie-Jean must have missed an overhead smash on the Centre Court.

The roar testifies to the fact that more people than ever are watching Wimbledon this year but, for all that, Court 14, where no one knows anyone, is the symbolic site of the 1972 championships. Take Smith, Nastase, Goolagong, King and Evert out of the catalogue and what you have is a country fair tournament.

I do not speak, of course, on behalf of the cognescenti who can rattle off Goolagong's career record like the creed. I speak with the tongue of 50 million others who are missing Newcombe and Laver and Rosewall and even Roger Taylor's annual sensation, and find this a non-vintage year.

What it has gone a long way to proving is something I've suspected for years. This is that you could dress up a couple of chimpanzees in sneakers and tennis shorts and still pack the Centre Court to the rafters.

Wimbledon, with its well-pressed suits, picture hats, modulated voices, exemplary manners, courteous officials, machine-turned efficiency and inescapable strawberries-and-cream, could almost function without any tennis at all. It is the last of the great middleclass festivals and nearly 30,000 people a day are clinging on to it as though it is their last stand against anarchy.

They will look you straight in the eye and tell you that, if anything, this year's Wimbledon is even better than the last.

It isn't of course. The politics of tennis have for one year reduced Wimbledon to below the credibility rating as a world championship, and to believe anything else is self-delusion.

The spirit of this year's Wimbledon is out on Court 14 where, incidentally, Mr Hrebec dusted down Mr Baranyi in three straight sets. It was a very nice tennis match.

The following piece, which may loosely be described as a book review, had a charming sequel. The author, John Toshack, wrote a kindly letter of thanks pointing out that the review contained 11 words of which he had never heard. One could only write back and point out that the majority of sportswriters are only failed sportsmen anyway.

'No book since Genesis has been so sensitively titled'

London. — Those familiar with The Tay Bridge Disaster and other masterworks by William McGonagall, the famed Scottish poet and tragedian, will be stricken to learn that his once imperishable place in what at a dangerous stretch of the imagination might be described as English literature, was severely challenged, if not actually usurped, on Tuesday this week.

Tuesday saw the long-awaited publication of *Gosh It's Tosh*, an anthology of poems by Mr John Toshack who, when not wrestling with the muse, would appear to do something vaguely athletic with Liverpool Football Club.

It is for this tenuous reason that his works are being reviewed in the sports pages and I must say, at the outset, that no book since Genesis has been so sensitively titled.

Mr Toshack's command of the English language evokes so many of the finer sensibilities of British sporting life — Dunn's performance against Bugner, Sir Alf Ramsey's oratory, Harry Secombe's golf swing are but three examples that spring instantly to mind — that at a mere £2.25 for fully 95 pages it is like stumbling over a Picasso in a junk shop in Workington.

The astonishing fecundity of Mr Toshack's work stems, of course, from the fact that he is from time to time compelled to accompany Liverpool FC to foreign climes.

Tiresome though this must obviously be to one of such sensitive and perceptive disposition, it inspires in him, as it did in Rupert Brooke, a nostalgia so haunting and powerful that one wonders whether it would not be beneficial to British art if Mr Toshack were not to emigrate permanently.

Take this example, entitled *Zagreb Blues:*

We went to Zagreb full of pride,
To try and stop the deep blue tide,
But sixty seconds from the start,
All our plans were ripped apart,
Our players looked in disbelief,
In their faces, hidden grief,
The Yugoslavs have found the net,

And now the stage is really set,
Now, unless we settle down,
I'm sure they'll really go to town.

In contrast to this inner cry of pain, Mr Toshack's emotions upon returning to British soil (Speke being an airport somewhere north of London) are, in just four lines, an evocation of joy and reunion so powerful that one gropes vainly for any comparable example in English writing but is drawn inescapably, to the painting of L.S. Lowry, whose pin-head millworkers always preferred an afternoon at the Salford Public Baths to, say, a fortnight on the French Riviera:

We're coming in to land at Speke,
My legs are feeling very weak.
We've just returned from Barcelona,
And now I'm going for a sauna.

Those critics who have suggested that the metronomic metre is derivative — indeed there are those who have implied plagarism and drawn comparisons with the Rupert Bear captions — are ignoring the simplistic genre of Mr Toshack's chosen subjects.

For example, has the deep uncertainty, the lifelong insecurity of the professional athlete ever been more movingly expressed than in this at once sombre but defiant stanza:

One thing we can say for sure,
We'll do our utmost just to score,
We'll do our fair share of attacking,
If effort counts, we won't be lacking,
I hope and pray that all goes well,
But at this stage, we just can't tell.

That Mr Toshack has been concealing talent beneath a track suit and soccer shirt for so long must be a matter of regret to us all. What's more his book has got lots of nice pictures.

Gosh it's Tosh (Duckworth/Elmswood) £2.25.

Apart from the mass production of baseballs, which appears to be one of its major industries, Haiti's impact on sport was so minimal for so long that there seemed little chance of dropping in on the country immortalised by Graham Greene in The Comedians. *The opportunity came when, in circumstances alluded to in this piece, Haiti's football team surprisingly qualified for a place in the World Cup Finals. Although Papa Doc was dead Port au Prince had lost little of its atmosphere of menace. White English reporters were regarded with extreme suspicion and the four days I spent tramping from Ministry to Ministry in pursuit of an audience with Papa Doc's heir were utterly wasted. Haiti did not win the World Cup and, predictably, Antoine Tassy was invited to seek alternative employment somewhat more swiftly than the speed of light.*

'His father's marksmen used to drive around in 1956 Chevrolets using real live people for target practice'

Port au Prince, Haiti.— The one man above all others who got the old rum republic of Haiti through to the World Cup football finals would look nothing short of bizarre in a track suit.

In fact he sleeps most nights in silk pyjamas behind the Toytown protection of one war-surplus tank and two antique Bofors guns which, at a pinch, might delay a concerted cavalry charge on his resplendent, white-domed presidential palace.

His name is Jean-Claude Duvalier — otherwise known, behind his back, as Baby Doc. This is to distinguish him from his Dad, the late and widely unlamented Papa Doc, who now rests permanently six feet under an eternal flame.

Jean-Claude is far from being a chip off the old block dictator. He is 22, built like Colin Cowdrey, beams at his subjects through bulletproof glass and has some radically different ideas about the definition of sport.

His father, you will recall, was a shooting enthusiast who raised this team of marksmen called the Ton Ton Macoute who used to drive around in 1956 Chevrolets using real live people for target practice.

Not so Jean-Claude. He's a soccer man. This, admittedly, is insufficient evidence to proclaim him as one of the world's young liberals. You can still see things here, aside from the bone-jutting poverty, which span the whole history of evil from Al Capone's Chicago right back to the Old Testament.

Still, soccer must be a step in the right direction. It isn't merely that the boy President or his skewer-eyed Ministers see football as something to divert the nation's attention from its grim condition. His Excellency is as genuinely crazy about the game as any English lad who hangs around dressing-room doors for autographs and can reel off the names of all 22 contestants in the 1908 Cup Final without drawing breath.

The difference, when you're top man of a one-party Caribbean republic, is that you can collect living players and reel off directives to your Chancellor to start shelling out. It is under the personal patronage of Jean-Claude Duvalier that Haiti — unlike England — have got to Munich.

For example when they qualified by beating Trinidad 2-1 — a match believed to be unique in that the referee disallowed four Trinidad goals then immediately announced his retirement — Baby Doc personally awarded each of his players a 30 by 30-metre parcel of land.

This may sound modest enough to the likes of George Best but in a country where the average income is £65 a year and the average life expectancy 40, it's rather like being elevated to Burke's Landed Gentry.

Then there was the moment yesterday, while I was zig-zagging between pot-hole and beggar down the Boulevard Harry Truman, when three official cars blared past at 50 mph, which is almost impossible.

It was neither the Ton Tons riding again nor Graham Greene being arrested. It was Antoine Tassy, national soccer coach, being conveyed to the palace to make his weekly report to the head of state.

The audience lasted two hours. 'The President,' said the coach, 'is very knowledgeable about soccer.'

Mr Tassy is a really nice man. He's the same size and shape as Sir Alf Ramsey but you could definitely tell them apart because he's black and wears glasses. Also, at $ 550 a month, he's on less than half Ramsey's salary.

This money comes directly from the Haitian Government as do all the broken-time payments made to the international players, who are mostly minor civil servants or gym masters.

From next week, when Operation Munich starts in earnest, Tassy will have them full-time. He knows what he's about. He has played or coached in Cuba, Venezuela, Mexico and France and has attended every World Cup since Brazil raised soccer to an art-form in Stockholm in 1958.

Three of his stars were on show last night when he invited me to sit at his side in the President's box at the Stade Sylvio Cator to watch Haiti Racing Club play a team of self-exiled Haitians down from New York.

Leeds could have given either side a six-goal start and caught them by half-time. For all that, a combination of Latin-American shooting, Italian opera temperament, acrobatic overhead kicking and a warm purple night made it far more enjoyable than the Calvinistic attrition which is what now seems to pass for soccer whenever I go to Arsenal. In the second half the home-team reserve goalkeeper sprang off his bench and knocked the visiting right-winger cold.

The President didn't come to the match because of affairs of state, but Haiti's remaining intelligentsia were there in force.

I sat directly behind the Chief of Police, who takes 19in. collars and never moved once. On his right, the Minister of Tourism ate peanuts and drank Heineken straight from the bottle. On his left was a gentleman in white slacks and shirt with yachts and anchors all over it. He looked like Joe Frazier's twin and had a large revolver casually stuck in his belt.

He is the President's hit-man.

Later, at a small reception in the board-room, another gentleman reputedly close to the President was measuring Haiti's internationals for their World Cup track suits.

In pursuit of my duties I asked the hit-man in third-form French for the gentleman's name. He replied in post-graduate Harlem. 'That gennulman,' he suggested, 'ain't got no name.'

There are, you will gather, certain aspects about Haiti soccer which prevent it being confused with the game as played by Corinthian Casuals. One of them concerns the involvement of the polytheistic religion of voodoo, which is much loved by novelists but is so played down by the authorities here that you could run away with the idea that it died out with Papa Doc.

This is not so. Two nights ago — by candlelight on the seashore four miles from the football ground — I witnessed a ceremonial of such hideousness that if you are reading this over breakfast I would strongly recommend that you turn immediately to the *Mail's* Diary.

After an hour of orgasmic dancing, during which three girls writhed themselves into comas, a plump lady emerged holding a white pigeon by the tips of its wings. This she rubbed over our faces before presenting it to a 6ft. 6in. priest whose arms were on fire.

In a sudden frenzy the priest ripped out the feathers round the bird's neck, sank his teeth into its throat, sucked out the blood until it was running down his jaw and then passed round pieces of raw flesh to anyone who hadn't fainted.

The price to watch this aspect of Haitian culture was $4.

Mr Max Beauvoir, who invited me, is a Sorbonne-educated chemical engineer whose factory produces, among other things, cortisone. He has a white, French wife and has defended voodoo all his adult life.

'Hollywood sees us as black savages for doing this,' he said. 'But why should we stop? It is our religion. It is a religion which demands sacrifices. It is a religion still so widespread here that you will be erring on the side of caution if you write that at least half the Haiti football team practise it.'

Well, by way of a warm-up for the World Cup, Haiti play Northern Ireland on May 5 and I suppose you could argue that there's nothing more irrational about certain goings-on here than certain goings-on in Belfast.

Anyway here's a word of warning to the pigeons who make their home in the eaves of the Munich Hilton. Baby Doc's boys are coming and it could just be that the World Cup has never seen anything like them before.

The brief column that follows is an unashamed eulogy. There have been a handful of modern sportsmen as dominant in their own games — Nicklaus, Pele, Viren, Ali — but the art of Gary Sobers was cricket and at its many complex facets he was the master. Recklessly generous and not always a paragon off the field, he nonetheless played cricket throughout his career according to a code of honour now almost forgotten in the desperate determination to win.

'No man has ever earned his money with such honest toil and few have ever given such enormous pleasure to others in the process'

London. — It is hardly classified information that a dismayingly large whack of Gary Sobers's cricket earnings down the years has come to rest with the bookmakers.

We all have our peccadilloes and Gary's has been for playing the horses. He could make Ascot in 55 minutes flat any day rain washed out play at Lord's and a million trembling rabbits can testify to his anxiety to catch the last two races at some night meeting at Nottingham.

Literature for Gary Sobers was *The Sporting Life*; mathematics the art of calculating the yield from a ten-bob each-way yankee; philosophy a matter of keeping your woes to yourself when you're taking a beating.

I use the past tense because Gary slowed down his gambling the day he got married.

It was just as well. Gary's talent for picking fast horses never quite matched his genius for destroying fast bowlers. He caught a few costly colds.

There's no moral tutt-tutting about all this because no man has ever earned his money with such honest toil and few have ever given such enormous pleasure to others in the process.

When some sportsmen complain of fatigue you could almost laugh in their faces. When Gary Sobers talks of exhaustion your heart misses a beat. When he speaks of retirement, as he did for the first time yesterday, the sun goes in.

We must now actually contemplate the unthinkable prospect of a summer's cricket without Sobers and when we do that we can begin to think how fast and loose we have played with his incomparable talent. We have worn the man out with our insatiable demands.

As a matter of interest he had, as of midnight yesterday, played in 332 first class cricket matches, played 527 innings, made 78 centuries, taken 942 wickets and held 360 catches. Add to that Cup matches, knockout matches, exhibition matches, festival matches, the ferocious pressures of modern Test captaincy, the constant pursuit by the Press and the savage strain of unending travel, and you can understand why, at 35, he is talking like a man at the end of his tether.

What saddens me, apart from the selfish dismay at witnessing the beginning of the end of a man who has given me more hours of delight than any other single performer, is what Sobers has made out of it all.

These things are relative. He will not retire into penury. For a lad born in a three-roomed stilted house and reared by a widowed mother after his father was drowned off Bermuda, he has done uncommonly well. But he's not been paid the going-rates for a genius.

Gary Sobers's weakness was not really horses. It was being born to cricket instead of golf, baseball or, maybe, American football.

In the past few weeks I have met his equals in these sports — Jack Nicklaus, Joe Dimaggio and Joe Namath. They are, or were, the best of their age and it goes without saying that they are millionaires to a man.

You will hear it said in certain circles in cricket that Garfield St. Aubrun Sobers has been a fool with his money. It is no way to speak of a man who has still lost less on the racetracks of the world than Jack Nicklaus slips in tips to his caddie.

Another nation whose soccer team less than distinguished itself during the final stages of the 1974 World Cup in Germany was Zaire. It was some years since I had had to write 'running copy' at a night football game, a process involving dictating one's report to London during the match in a series of brief 'takes' which are immediately set in type, leaving the reporter with only the result and the opening paragraph to dictate at the final whistle. The report, therefore, is virtually written backwards so that it can be included in a first edition which it would have otherwise missed. Soccer correspondents and boxing writers are the masters of this technique which Paul Gallico, the greatest exponent of all in his days as a sportswriter, mockingly called 'literature under fire'. No literature follows and, in any case, Zaire at least had the grace to make the result a foregone conclusion as soon as they kicked off.

'Like Lord Cardigan, they charge straight at the guns regardless of casualties'

Zaire 0 Yugoslavia 9

Gelsenkirchen. — The Leopards of Zaire made a memorable last-but-one appearance in the World Cup in a pitifully populated stadium amid the chimneys of the Ruhr.

If they sound like an ice-hockey team that's fairly appropriate. They run like lightning, occasionally with the ball. Their attitude to defence is curiously like that of the late Lord Cardigan of Light Brigade fame. They charge straight at the guns regardless of casualties.

It just wasn't their night. They substituted goalkeeper Kazadi after three Yugoslav goals in 15 minutes. The poor chap was still dejectedly dragging his way along the touch-line when the fourth goal went screaming past his replacement. He brightened perceptibly.

This goal brought renewed anguish to a Zaire team who appeared to be experimenting with a 1-1-8 formation. Mulamba N'Daye, a household name in Kinshasa, was so overcome with emotion that he kicked the Colombian referee on the fleshy part of the right thigh.

Whatever sympathy Mr Omar Delgado may have felt for his assailant he had no option but to remove him from the contest.

In truth, the Leopards could not afford to lose one of their colleagues at this juncture despite the fact that Yugoslavia had reduced their game to training pace and were concentrating primarily on avoiding too many multiple fractures.

After six goals in half an hour the seventh didn't come for what seemed ages.

Then it was only by courtesy of Dimbi Tubilandu, the unhappy substitute goalkeeper, who completely lost his sense of direction and palmed the ball with curious deliberation into his own net.

He was still adjusting his gloves when Petkovic fired the eighth goal.

How was it, the intellectuals of the Press Box began to ask, that Scotland could only beat the Leopards 2-0 in the opening match?

It also raised the question of whether the presence of a team as clueless as this provides the World Cup with light relief it could well do without. As long as the zonal system of qualification is maintained it will continue, occasionally, to happen.

But when you remember that nations like Portugal and Hungary and Spain and — dare I say it — England aren't here it does lend some weight to the argument that the encouragement of emergent nations at soccer need not necessarily amount to inclusion in the World Cup final rounds.

The only question the match itself continued to raise was whether Yugoslavia could achieve double figures. They couldn't. They settled for nine goals, equalling the record for the final rounds.

The comedy was compounded afterwards when Zaire's manager, Mr Blagoje Vidinic, conceded that the referee was perfectly correct in sending off a Zaire player for kicking him. 'Unfortunately,' Mr Vidinic added, 'it was the wrong man. It should have been Ilunga Mwepu, not Mulamba N'Daye.'

When this article appeared in the Daily Mail *it was illustrated with a map, compiled with the assistance of a local police officer, detailing the exact locations where 101 competitive motor-cyclists had died on the Isle of Man circuit. Its publication was greeted with outrage on the island and in the motor-cycling trade press. This struck me then, as it does now after the deaths of several more riders, as an extremely foolish reaction.*

It was not the first shot in a campaign to stop TT racing in the Isle of Man or curtail the sale of fast motorbikes. It was a plea to avoid the unnecessary deaths of riders who should never be permitted to compete at the highest level.

Young men continue to go there with much courage, huge ambition and little else. They have neither a back-up team of mechanics nor enough money to rest in a good hotel bed or eat even adequate meals. Unrested, ill-fed, ill-equipped, inexperienced and nervous, they continue to kill themselves at very short intervals on a circuit which many of the great professionals will not ride because of its danger.

The day after this piece appeared I stayed up all night in a Douglas hotel arguing its validity with some of the most dogmatic amateurs I have ever met. They actually invoked the cause of bravery.

'I am not brave,' said Niki Lauda when he accepted an award for valour in sport in London, 'because I calculate the odds. When they are loaded against me I quit.'

There are the great professionals, always calculating the odds. Some of them die because they are hard-headedly gambling their lives against enormous wealth. That is their privilege. But then there are the others whose decision to race is unwise and there is no one there to dissuade them from doing it.

‘Violent death has become so commonplace that the show goes on regardless’

Douglas, Isle of Man. — As near as the experts can calculate, John Lawrence Clarke's career as a TT racer lasted 2 min. 15 sec.

He came very fast down the curve of Bray Hill from the starting line, braked to get round the acute right-hander at Quarter Bridge and was almost through the village of Union Mills with its toy town blue-and-white post office, when he made the mistake.

The straw-filled sacks roped to the stone wall outside the Railway Inn did not save him. Nor did his astronaut-sized helmet. His 250 c.c. Japanese machine left the road and Clarke catapulted into the stonework and died there and then of multiple chest injuries.

He had travelled less than three miles of the first lap of the opening race of this year's International TT Races in the Isle of Man.

Had he lived, and won, his prize would have been £100.

John Clarke, thank God, was unmarried. He was 25 years of age and a machine tool fitter from Towcester in Northamptonshire.

At his £1.50 a night boarding house digs in Douglas yesterday they were not too sure who was responsible for the expense of taking his body back to England.

‘We are trying to find that out now,’ said Mrs Daugherty, a small, nice lady who came to the door in a blue check dress but was too distressed to be asked more than a couple of questions.

Yes, she'd known John Clarke for some years. He'd stayed with her on all his Isle of Man visits, first as a mechanic, then as a rider in the September Manx Grand Prix races for amateurs.

Yes, he'd ridden the course before but never at this level of competition. This was his first year in the ranks that could lead to the fame and riches of men like Duke, Hailwood, Read and Agostini.

Neither Read nor Agostini, both world champions, are riding in the TT races this year. They are on record as saying that the course is too dangerous. No one in the Isle of Man will accept that. They smile knowingly and rub thumb and first finger together, implying that the prize money is too small.

I have no way of knowing the truth. All I do know is that Phil Read, who lives in Surrey, would have been riding for his 13th year in the Isle of Man, and was begged by his wife, Madeleine, not to compete this time. When Clarke was killed Read was on a yacht in the Mediterranean.

Personally I find the argument academic anyway. It is not for me to question the character or motives of the men who come here to ride at speeds of up to 160 m.p.h. round a 37¾-mile circuit with 200 bends, but there are certain facts to which even the leather-clad aficionados who come here in their thousands to watch must face up.

The most disagreeable is that according to the horrifying statistics of recent years at least two more men are due to die in motorcycle races in the Isle of Man this year.

John Clarke, who to many here is already a statistic, was the 101st rider to be killed on the Mountain Circuit since 1911. But the toll has been accelerating appallingly since 1951 when seven died in either the TT or Manx Grand Prix events. The total in those 23 years is now 72.

Violent death has become so commonplace that the show goes on regardless. Few in the start-finish line grandstand on Saturday evening knew of Clarke's death, for example, until they saw a few paragraphs in three of their Sunday newspapers.

They had sat through the completion of the International Production Race and the subsequent 750 c.c. sidecar event entertained by three hours of bubbling commentary, motor-sport commercials and pop music.

Yesterday the policemen who accompanied investigating Auto Cycle Union officials to the scene of the accident refused with immense politeness to answer any questions. 'It will all come out at the inquest,' they said.

What will come out at the inquest is almost certainly the evidence of a race marshal I spoke to who asked me not to reveal his name.

'What happened,' he said, 'was pretty obvious to me. The lad must have got away to a bad start. Anyway he was at the back of the field and trying to make up time. He just came into the bend far too fast. At that speed he never had a chance.'

It is hard for the average motorist, to whom an illegal 90 m.p.h. on a straight, dry uncluttered stretch of motorway is living dangerously, to begin to comprehend the fantastic speeds and skills of the men who *average* well over 100 miles an hour round this twisting course with its occasionally bucking surfaces and treacherous cambers.

'This point,' said Allan Robinson, a public relations man who rode three major races here and who guided me in a car round the course after the accident, 'is rather tricky.'

What was tricky apparently was that riders of the calibre of Agostini came off Bray Hill at speeds between 140 and 160 miles an hour and could only survive the bend by steering exactly eight inches from the right hand kerbstone to get round.

'You have to remember every deviation on this course like a tape recording,' said Robinson.

He is a charming, intelligent man, alert to the beauties of the mountain section where the gorse was almost bronze in the setting sun and you could look back over your shoulder to see the Scottish coastline as a blue silhouette on the horizon.

He spoke of it romantically. But there were terrible stories too, among them that of Les Graham's death on Bray Hill, of Gilberto Parlotti, who only last year had ricocheted off the wall of The Verandah, just above Creg-na-Baa, and pitched to his death among the sheep down the far side of the road.

John Clarke, on Saturday evening, never got that far. He was the fifth rider to be killed in the little village of Union Mills where for 50 weeks of the year the pace is so slow that life-expectancy is long.

They will hold his inquest in Douglas either tonight or tomorrow morning. The coroner, Henry Callow, is not exactly new to the procedure. In 1970 he conducted inquests on seven riders. He also used to be a marshal on the TT circuit.

'I have to force myself not to become emotionally involved,' he said. 'May I say that I have the greatest admiration for these riders.'

Mr Callow will sit in a building bearing the heraldic device of the Isle of Man.

This comprises three twisted, disembodied legs, a symbol which I do not find completely inappropriate.

From the start the coverage of the Muhammad Ali — George Foreman world heavyweight title fight in the African republic of Zaire was a series of hilarious disasters. The British Press contingent were still checking in at London Airport when news came through that Foreman had severely cut an eye in training. A long postponement seemed inevitable. Did we go home or go ahead?

My own view was that Muhammed Ali, frustrated and fretting in the Congo, was a suitable subject to write about. So did my editor. We hopped aboard the plane. So, at an enormous corporate cost to Fleet Street, did everyone else.

At Nselle, Ali's training camp, they had installed a battery of telex machines to communicate with London. Unfortunately there were no holes in the wall to plug them into. Nightly we made the 120-mile round journey into Kinshasa. There, in the unforgettable Memling Hotel, there were more telex machines. Some worked sometimes. Unfortunately the gentlemen nominated to operate them didn't. At least not without large inducements known as bribes.

Taking unilateral action one evening I decided to operate the telex myself, undeniably giving vent to certain personal feelings. This was an error. Apparently calling President Mobutu Sese Seko Kuku Ngbendu Wa Za Banga by any other name, particularly his former one of Joseph, was jolly bad form. While the words were safely coming out in London they were also being read over my shoulder by one of the President's lieutenants who saw fit to tear them from the machine and have me escorted by two soldiers into the presence of a Mr N'Godu whose room, several floors up in the hotel, bore an uneasy resemblance to a Gestapo interrogation cell.

I remain eternally obliged to men like Neil Allen of the Evening Standard, *Frank Butler of the* News of the World *and Alan Hoby of the* Sunday Express *for planting themselves outside the door and refusing to budge until they knew what the hell was going on. What was going on was that Mr N'Godu and I were failing by some light years to see eye to eye.*

We all returned to London the following day and flew out again a month later to report the rescheduled fight. It took place at a hour in the morning when it was possible to dictate an off-the-cuff story to lead the front page of a special edition that could be sold to crack-of-dawn commuters at the major London railway stations.

By a miracle the ringside telephone worked. Cheerfully we began dictating to a typist in London whose voice, of course, one cannot hear above stadium din. All, I thought, was going rather fluently particularly the description of Ali's knock-out blow. When the noise subsided I asked London to confirm that all was well. There was only an appalling silence. The line had been cut in the third of the eight rounds and the remaining two-thirds of the story that appeared were written by my colleague Peter Moss, equipped with a telephone in front of a closed-circuit television screen one-third of the way up the London Post Office Tower. The resumè report which is reproduced here was written later that morning for the following day's newspaper.

It was a marvellous fight even if we did have to travel a total of 16,896 miles to watch it.

'Up the Congo without communications is no place for 600 journalists to be'

The Zaire Government cut off Ian Wooldridge in mid-sentence last night as he was cabling his column to London by telex.

Wooldridge was well into his satirical stride about the poor communications from Kinshasa when the copy was torn from his telex machine for 'undesirable writing'. President Mobutu's men refused to allow him to send any more copy.

This is the story Wooldridge was sending when he was cut off.

Kinshasa, Zaire.— When a reporter called Stanley passed this way in search of a doctor called Livingstone he was wise enough to be carrying smoke signals, cleft sticks and towing along a relay of foot-runners. We should have learned.

Up the Congo without any visible means of communications is no place for 600 journalists to be. This, of course, is why the Ali-Foreman fight has been receiving such filthy publicity from Sacramento to Surbiton.

It must be galling to a Zaire Government whose president, Joseph Mobutu, moved heaven and about ten million tons of earthworks to get the fi . . .

‘He was wearing a Big Fight accreditation badge bearing the emotive numbers 007’

London.— As I was saying when a furious Zaire Government censor ripped last Friday’s dispatch from my telex machine in Kinshasa:

‘. . . ght here and thus put his country on the map. For all our personal aggravations as journalists we should not be too critical. Now for the good news.

‘There are few modern cities where you can walk about the streets in greater safety than Kinshasa. You could not meet people with greater warmth or anxiety to please. You could hardly stay in quarters more comfortable than those in which we have been encamped near the fighters.’

Unlike my earlier words, which were intentionally highly critical of Zaire’s woefully inadequate communications system, this near eulogy of President Mobutu’s capital and people never saw the light of publication.

Instead they were borne away ahead of me to a darkened fifth-floor office where a Mr N’Godu, government official, gave me 25 minutes of his mind.

This appeared to be his prerogative. It was equally mine to notice he was wearing a Big Fight accreditation badge bearing the emotive numbers 007.

Next morning Mr Tshimpumpu wa Tshimpumpu, Zaire’s Chief of Press for the Ali-Foreman fight, summoned American, European and British reporters and assured us: ‘There will be no more censorship.’

Before the sun had set Mr Reg Gutteridge, boxing correspondent of the London *Evening News*, had been prevented from informing his editor that a delayed dispatch was due to an overnight storm putting the only remaining telex line out of action.

Mr Hugh McIlvanney, the highly literate columnist of *The Observer*, suffered even greater irritation. His 1,800-word column was returned to him before transmission with the words: ‘You must understand we cannot send any of this.’ He hopped on a plane, travelled 3,193 miles north and dictated his report from Rome.

Several American writers were similarly censored out of existence. Invoking Bills of Human Rights was pointless. Explaining that censoring material mostly concerning a boxing match was to invite ridicule was useless.

Fight promoters see publicity as blood-plasma. They are unlikely to receive it from a country whose communications broke down completely under the mild demands of 70 reporters when 600 are accredited for the night of the fight.

In one centre a bank of 14 telex machines gleamed as though it were a Harrods' showroom. Not one worked. Room telephones were ornaments with numbers inscribed on the front. They never rang.

Newspaper communications, I am the first to appreciate, are not the be-all of our existence. Meeting the mortgage, paying the rates, schooling the kids and even a General Election, may be of greater importance. But one principle, even beyond the question of censorship, is involved.

It is whether a country which applies to stage a major spectacle, be it a heavyweight championship fight or the Olympic Games, is immune to criticism because it is young, emergent and black.

This is dangerous ground. There are those who will read into it attitudes of Colonialism and Kiplingism and racism or, at the very best, insufferable paternalism.

I can only hope that regular readers of this space will recall that a succession of white South African Ministers of Sport have rarely received the time of day here and that George Best, Brian Clough, David Bedford et al may well think they have as much cause for bitter recrimination as President Mobutu Seso Seko of Zaire.

It is all a question of whether we are prepared to apply double standards. I, for one, am not.

Zaire may well be capable of getting Messrs Foreman and Ali into the same ring for what may well be the genuine Fight of the Century. But whether Zaire is yet geared to informing the world swiftly, accurately and without hitch about what happens must be very much open to doubt.

There is more to the Ali-Foreman fight, as you will have guessed by now, than meets the eye or gets into the newspapers.

It involves highly-complex financial deals. It involves taxation and currency exchange. And it involves President Mobutu's personal standing with his own people.

The investigator is not yet born who can get to the bottom of these things and print his findings with total assurance or without running close to the wind of the libel laws. For now a mild scepticism must suffice.

So far, Zaire's handling of the Big Fight has, on the personal level, been friendly and charming. On the professional level it has been an unqualified disaster.

To say otherwise, or to avoid saying anything at all, is to avoid criticising a circus that would be run out of town on the more beaten paths of sports promotions.

In due course, if the contest is still on, I intend to return to President Mobutu Seso Seko's ringside and report the action.

The decision is his. It's his country. We shall come in peace and be delighted to have a drink or two with his unemployed censors.

'He sprawled there, blinking and subconsciously mouthing the count. He had not one chance in 50 of getting up again'

Kinshasa, Zaire.— The sun had the audacity to rise over Central Africa yesterday while Mr Muhammad Ali was still speaking.

His message was really quite trivial. He will require 10 million dollars, he informed the universe, to perform his next miracle in the boxing ring.

This works out at something slightly over £4 million an hour or, alternatively, precisely twice as much as he received for exposing George Foreman as not quite the immovable object we thought.

Naturally, we shall pay it. We shall rob banks, surrender life policies, short-change widows and sell the new dishwasher to raise it. His recapture of the world heavyweight title here, on a morning the memory of which I shall take to the grave, entitles him to name his own price.

By the eighth and providently last round he had, according to a communal round-up of statistics, hit Foreman 65 times flush on the face.

It was then, from an entrenched and contemplative position, that he saw an opening which lasted as long as it takes to fire a hair-trigger pistol.

Foreman is a man of ingenuous honesty. 'A boxer,' he said when his mind was functioning again, 'never sees the big one that hits him.'

What hit him, in fact, was a Bren-gun burst of quick blows, a left-hook that spun him round into the real line of fire and a right that put him on the floor for the first time in his professional career.

He sprawled there, blinking and subconsciously mouthing the count to himself. He had not one chance in 50 of getting up again. It was like watching a tank going over the edge of a bridge in slow motion.

The allusion is not all that absurd for Foreman fought the most important fight of his life with all the intelligence of a piece of armour-plated machinery.

He became so confused by Ali's tactics that he finished the fourth round hurling wild swings into the air and later missed so badly with the punch that was meant to finish it all that he almost went through the ropes.

Ali slapped him on the bottom. Throughout the fight he talked to Foreman in all the clinches and carried on a running conversation with a black American reporter in between rounds.

In the fifth round he indulged in a piece of exhibitionism so dangerous that it would not be tried by the resident professional fighting farm-hands in a fairground boxing booth.

He sagged back so far on the ropes that he was almost in the laps of the TV commentators. And there he stayed for well over a minute, defending himself from Foreman's frantic hitting only with his forearms and cupped gloves.

Ali took the wildest liberties and still rode back to the world title he regards as personal property with a performance of total genius allied to immense physical courage.

The fight that was reckoned to be his five million dollar retirement pay-off went precisely as he raved and bragged it would. 'I shall be the matador and Foreman the bull,' he told his Zairois brothers last week. The metaphor was exact.

Regrettably, another of his graphic forecasts came true as well. 'Foreman's face will be a disaster area,' he said. And so it was, with a ghastly purple bruise dead between the eyes, a right eye still swelling as we commiserated in his dressing room, and a cheekbone long disappeared beneath a mound of flesh.

Foreman's style throughout these many weeks in Zaire was quiet dignity and it did not desert him in defeat. Of the man who but 30 minutes previously had been abusing and taunting him in the ring he said: 'The man who is champion should now be respected. He is a great gentleman.'

He repeated three times in a minute: 'I followed my directions to the best of my ability.' He did not have reproachful looks for his manager, Dick Sadler, but one wonders whether their partnership will now survive.

Ali went down, too. Ten seconds after Foreman was counted out, he was knocked down as his faithful leaped into the ring. From then, long into the dawn, he was besieged.

He kissed his wife, embraced his mother, teased those of us who had doubted his durability and then put a pistol to boxing's head.

'I'm going to haunt boxing for the next six months,' he shouted. 'I'll talk to the man who first offers me ten million dollars.'

You may say a man requires supernatural powers to command such a sum. But maybe Ali has.

At breakfast the sun went in and the rainy season started.

ITEM: The unusual circumstances surrounding the departure of Mr Yukio Mishima were, as I recall, widely reported at the time. The matter did not quite end there.

'By prearrangement one of Mr Mishima's colleagues then severed his head'

For the first time in just over 24 years Mr John Arlott, the most literate sports commentator in the English language, is totally speechless.

It is a long and sad story concerning a massive reference book which is due to appear some two years from now called *The Oxford Companion to Sports and Games.*

Mr Arlott is the editor.

Such is the compass of the book's ambition, however, that he spent two long years searching for an expert capable of writing authoritatively on the sword-play section of the Japanese martial arts.

Eventually he was put in touch with his man: an author, playwright, actor and stage director by the name of Yukio Mishima. The article was commissioned and Mr Mishima accepted. To celebrate Mr Arlott opened one of his several thousand bottles of claret. The celebration was somewhat premature.

At almost the same moment Mr Mishima — wearing a Rising Sun badge, shouting 'Long live the Emperor,' and bearing very definite ideas about the degeneracy of Japan since the arrival of the Americans in 1945 — was storming into an Army barracks in Tokio, tying up its commandant, and lecturing its startled troops about the glories of Nippon imperialism.

As an appropriate pay-off to the performance, Mr Mishima, encouraged by the presence of a TV camera crew, produced a two-and-a-half-foot-long Samurai sword of ancient origin and plunged it into his own stomach.

By prearrangement one of his colleagues then completed the classic ritual of hara-kiri by severing Mr Mishima's head.

Mr Arlott missed the TV performance but read all about it, without wild enthusiasm, in *The Times* the following morning.

On the one hand, as a liberal, he could hardly have mourned the passing of a dangerous militaristic fanatic.

On the other, if anyone knows anyone capable of writing an authoritative article on Japanese sword-play, will they please contact Mr Arlott immediately. Sooner if possible.

There are two facts that amaze me about Las Vegas. The first is that people go there on holiday. The second that people who have been there on holiday go again. This column was strictly business. It is about a tennis match, the second set of which contained the highest quality play I have ever seen. In the end Rod Laver lost.

'They want XXXVI-year-old Rod Laver to come out dressed like some gladiator emeritus'

Las Vegas.— When the organisers of tomorrow's big tennis match here in Las Vegas asked Rodney Laver to arrive on court wearing toga, sandals and laurel crown as last modelled by Mark Antony, Mr Laver's reply was duosyllabic, very Australian and much to be admired.

I would not attempt to quote it since my mother buys this paper, but at least I can confirm it was so effective that in the region of 40 million American tele-viewers will see Laver come out to take on their darling Jimmy Connors in the simple traditional attire appropriate to the greatest tennis player who ever lived.

What Connors will come up with is anybody's guess. At 22, with an ego unsuited to his youth, he could well play the first rally with a violin purporting to be Nero's. It probably depends on what sum the promoters have whispered in his ear.

Why in Imperial Caesar's name, you will ask, all these references to bygone Rome? Very simple.

The owners of a Las Vegas hotel, where Paul Anka is singing this week and Sammy Davis is shortly due and Frank Sinatra promises to make his last-but-250th final farewell appearance in March, are staging on their own premises the most lucrative tennis match in all history.

The great Laver (Australia) plays the brash Connors (America) over five sets for a purse of $100,000 which, according to last night's Wall Street conversation, is exactly £45,454.

Why such a daft, inflationary and quite unnecessary sum? Because it is publicity from super-colossal events like these which has made Caesar's Palace, Las Vegas, probably the best known hostelry on earth.

Tomorrow's match serves off at the anti-Godly hour of 10 a.m. precisely to catch live coast-to-coast American TV. Reporters from all over the world are here.

Caesar's Palace, an ancient Roman allegory set in Nevada badman country, and architecturally accurate down to the last plywood arch and plastic blade of grass, knows full well it will recoup the money. Mostly its clientele are rich, compulsive gamblers.

In fact, the owners are spending much more. They've paid out a further £230,000 to erect an indoor tennis pavilion to stage the contest, though, admittedly, this may be regarded as capital investment.

According to an incredible handout I was given, this pavilion is, and I quote exactly, 'surrounded by lush foliage and sprinkled with colourful flowers; an oasis that would impress even Sir Lawrence of Arabia'.

Sir Lawrence must be spinning in his benighted grave.

Set in a sea of sawdust and carpenters' chippings, his oasis, looking as Roman as any other aircraft hangar, was yesterday still being sawn and hammered into shape by a legion of slaves who'd parked their Cadillacs outside.

I do hope the paint dries by tomorrow, because the cheapest seats cost £11 and the dearest £48.

Anyway, those are the strictly business reasons why they want XXXVI-year-old Rod Laver to come out against Connors, XXII, dressed up like some gladiator emeritus.

Outside Caesar's Palace, on an illuminated signboard twice the size of Harrods, they billed the match as the heavyweight tennis championship of the world.

They have also appended the half-truth that the winner takes all which, in my naivety I inferred and then reported to you yesterday as meaning that the loser gets sweet nothing at all.

Not, I now discover, so. Vicariously appealing though this may be to the likes of you and me, Mr Laver was swift to point out that tennis players are not idiots.

'It's true the winner takes the $100,000,' he said, 'but you don't think either of us would play, do

ONE HERO: *Franz Klammer, son of an Austrian farmer,
brought a new dimension to downhill skiing.
Pictured here in the World Championships, his greatest
descent was in the 1976 Winter Olympics.
"What do I need to do?" he asked his coach,
before coming down 15th. "Kill yourself," was the reply.
Klammer flung himself down the mountain,
lived and won.*

INTERVIEW MOUNT FUJI: *Minutes earlier James Hunt had won the world Grand Prix drivers' championship in the foothills of Japan's holy mountain. In blinding spray he drove at 190 mph with manic determination. "Now," he said, "I'm going to get drunk." In fact, one cold beer proved more than a match for his overheated digestive system.*

INTERVIEW MADRID: *The Duke of Alburquerque, recovering from his near-fatal Grand National crash. "I do not regard age as something which automatically eliminates a man from doing anything," he said. But they banned him from Aintree a year later. Tragically the photograph does not do justice to his duchess. She is one of the world's most stunningly beautiful women.*

INTERVIEW BRUSSELS: *Eddy Merckx, four times Tour de France winner, grants a rare interview in his Belgian home. Visitors are not encouraged because of the kidnapping risk to the Merckx children. The resident 'mechanic' turned out to be a security guard. Despite the regiment of bottles Merckx, the world's wealthiest cyclist, rarely drinks.*

INTERVIEW KAMPALA: *John Akii-Bua, Olympic gold medal hurdler, back home on the campus of Uganda's Makerere University. Some day we shall learn how many students were murdered here at the height of Amin's reign of terror. One morning Amin stopped his car to talk to Akii-Bua. Akii-Bua gasped: "Can't stop. I'm training." He ran on. And lived.*

TWO BRAVE FRIENDS: *Ex-Cpl Raymond Peart, blinded when a terrorist bomb exploded in the Divis Flats in Belfast, now a swimmer, athlete and horse-rider. Sir Matt Busby, survivor of the Munich air crash, who re-built a brilliant team.*

THOUGHT TRANSFERANCE: *From South America I wrote a column describing the long dreadful wait for a Grand Prix to begin. In London, Daily Mail artist Michael Frith drew an illustration. The positions, expressions and even attitudes of the drivers were so exact it could almost have been a photograph.*

you, if we weren't covered by an appearance fee in case we lose?'

He wouldn't tell me for publication how much it is but it sure would keep you and me in petrol for a year or two.

However, we should not be blinded by the absurdities of a Kelloggs conflakes packet Rome into losing sight of the fact that quite a remarkable tennis match is about to be played.

The genuine billing would be: Laver, best ever but growing old with visible regret, versus Connors, best find of the past five years and getting nastier by the minute.

Few duels in modern sport have thrown up adversaries of greater contrast.

Rodney George 'Rocket' Laver, child of the Australian outback, now has a Californian home with seven bathrooms and enough money never to have to think again.

But sophistication continues to evade him. Charming in private, morose in public, he still sniffs continually on court, thus giving the impression that he's been dragged away from his favourite television programme to play some upstart.

Incapable of trendiness he will remain a bushwhacker forever.

James Scott 'Jimbo' Connors, son of a masterful mother, now has the world at his feet and is using both to kick the opposition off it.

He doesn't lodge, eat or travel with other colleagues, spurns doubles matches, and had second thoughts about founding a tennis dynasty when he cancelled his match with Miss Christine Evert.

Loud, aggressive and with the face and hairstyle of a medieval varlet, he personifies a generation which tips its hat to no man.

What they have in common is confined to sporting fundamentals: they are both lefthanders of undisputed brilliance, tremendous power, no visible generosity on court and a grinding determination to win.

Amazingly, in the incestuous world which commerical tennis has become, they have not played each other before.

In short it could just be this year's match of the century.

The pressure, inevitably, is on Laver. He's just beaten Arthur Ashe, 6-3, 7-5, in the final of the American CBS classic but that doesn't quite add up to a second coming.

He has been practising here for a week, against Roy Emerson and our own Mark Cox, a minimum of four hours a day. Connors has merely breezed in for a warm-up.

I asked Cox how Laver was playing. 'He's getting it back all the time,' he said, and the innocent innuendo of the phrase was interesting.

I asked Laver how the tension differed before a blatantly commercial match like this, and, say, a Wimbledon final. 'There's no comparision,' he said. 'Here you're only playing for money but a hell of a lot of it.'

He isn't of course. He needs a last big pay-day like I need a tuppenny stamp. He is playing because it would gratify him no end to put down just one more young messiah before the cause becomes quite hopeless.

The best high-jumper in the world did not win the gold medal at the Montreal Olympics. He had spent his energy informing the Canadians they were 'rude and ignorant' and breaking camp to join his girl friend. This was quite predictable since his name was Dwight Stones.

'Do you know what government is -it's another word for organised crime'

London.— Gravity is the first and last enemy in the young life of Dwight Stones but, as he points out ad infinitum, there's shoreashell plenny of other things that give him a pain in the groin.

Volubly he detests all politicians, cheating French blackjack dealers, dilatory waiters, girls whose cigarette smoke makes his eyes water, undersized British fillet steaks and his Dad. Particularly his Dad.

'I'm going home from here to try and bury the hatchet with him,' he said, 'but for the past ten years all I've wanted to do is bury the hatchet in his head. I'm going to demand to know from him why he absolutely dedicated so much of his life to making me miserable.'

Dwight's father left Dwight's mother for another woman when Dwight was five. Dwight is now 20 and concedes, with perverse generosity, that he owes all his current enormous fame to his father's insouciance.

'Can you imagine, can you just *imagine*,' he cries, 'how a bum trick like that just *crushes* a sensitive child? I was so crushed I crawled round like a tortoise which pops his head out every now and then to see what new disasters are happening.

'Well I woke up one morning and I told myself: "Dwight Stones you gotta fight. You gotta fight or go under." So I decided to take up athletics and fight my way out as a high-jumper. Now nothing scares me except the thought of an injury or maybe getting appendicitis a week before the next Olympics.'

Stones Bren-guns the words, the

colour-imagery and the scathing positiveness of irreverent youth, for hours on end. You listen not only because he's ravingly entertaining but because he's also the greatest high jumper the world has ever seen.

Last year he sprang to a world record of 7ft. 6½in. and lay there, transfixed, watching the bar wobble for fully ten seconds before it fell off. 'It didn't count' he said. 'Absolute ecstasy, absolute dejection in the space of ten seconds. Just like life itself.'

He philosophises, self-analyses and criticises at a usual speed of around 160 words a minute. He will remain silent, briefly, this evening to complete before the biggest British athletics crowd of the year at the Coca-Cola meeting at Crystal Palace.

Stones is certain to produce a prodigious leap. But his proposed attempt on his own world record is now likely to be unsuccessful. He has a tendon injury which, though minor, is playing on his mind so much that he even breaks off from a verbal blitzkrieg on the morality of the world's statesmen to refer to it every five minutes.

'All politicians,' he states, in the manner of a man dictating the opening paragraph of his Life and Thoughts, 'are a bunch of pompous old bastards. I don't think there's such a thing as an honest politician. By definition you have to do shady things to get yourself in a position of power. Politics make me tired.'

High-jumping doesn't make him tired.

Since June 25 he has jumped in 21 meetings all over Europe, from Athens to Finland. In the nine days between June 21 and June 30 he leaped 7ft. 5in. in Siena, 7ft. 4⅝in. in Turin, 7ft. 4⅝in. in Nice and 7ft. 5¾in. in Oslo. It was the most staggering sustained spell of high-jumping in history.

'Yes, I agree with that,' said Stones, who stands 6ft. 5in. tall, weighs 175lb. and eats things like spaghetti, suet pudding and chocolate without introspection. 'But it's not so much that I'm outstandingly good, though I am, but that most of the others jump so badly. I just can't understand why I'm the only one who is jumping so well.'

After three more meetings he is going home for a five-week rest.

Home is Hollywood, California, where he lives with his 40-year-old mother and you can't help thinking that that brash, neurotic, tough, plastic and fearsome city has also played its part in moulding Dwight Stones into the spectacularly unboring young man that he is.

Everything is premeditated. Like girls. 'I've got girls all over Europe,' he said, 'and do you know something, they're all short, short girls. I've got to dominate, you see. I used to have a terrible inferiority complex about girls. I don't just *pick up* girls, I *choose* girls with whom I can have a meaningful, sensitive relationship.'

Dwight Stones has also discovered gambling. He started with a 145-dollar win first time out in Las Vegas and found blackjack the perfect relaxation until he was cheated of £100 by a bent dealer in St Tropez the other day. He's still gambling, though, but I didn't have the heart to ask him where he gets the money from.

He had no idea about a future career. 'Whatever it is when I get there,' he said, 'I shall be good at it. For now I just want to keep jumping until my legs fall off. That means two more Olympic Games at least.'

He will not accept the theory that there must be a ceiling of achievement.

'It's illogical,' he cried. 'That's suggesting you can measure evolution. I shall break the Olympic record by a huge margin in Montreal. Then, between there and the 1980 Olympics, I shall take the record up to either 7 ft. 10¾, or possibly 7 ft 11in.'

There was not a waver of doubt in his voice. Nor was there when he said that by the time he's 70, with lots of meaningful sensitive grandchildren the world high-jump record will be 8ft. 6in. which is roughly the athletics equivalent of a three-minute mile.

Come to think of it, Dwight Stones had doubts about nothing at all except ever completely forgiving his father who is 42 and builds bridges in and around Los Angeles.

'I'll try goddamit I'll try,' he said, 'but it's just that he's such an immature man.'

It was at this point that a uniformed guardian asked us to leave the royal park of St James's for photographing Mr Stones without a permit.

Mr Stones clutched his stomach and fell over laughing. 'Hell,' he gasped finally, 'waddiditellya? We have just been approached by an arm of the Government. Do you know what Government is — it's another word for organised crime.'

It's just as well Mr Dwight Stones is extremely good at athletics. He might need them some day.

The words that follow were slotted together while sitting on the edge of a bed in the Ukraine. They were the product of a near terminal hangover, an integral affliction on all semi-official tours to the Soviet Union. Two days later in Moscow I was telephoned by the Daily Mail *and asked to go to Leningrad and fly from there to Vienna with the Panovs, the ballet dancers whose request to leave Russia and live in the West had surprisingly been granted. Permission was refused. I subsequently complained about this to Mr Sergei Pavlov at a Press conference at which he had just been pledging freedom of movement throughout the Soviet Union to both journalists and tourists if Moscow were successful in their bid for the 1980 Olympics. Mr Pavlov smiled and said: "We have no trains to Leningrad but an excellent air service to Siberia." From time to time I still puzzle about that remark. Moscow was later awarded the Games.*

'The idea, you understand, is that we should write favourable if not flattering comment about Soviet facilities'

Kiev.— The whole world was an infinitely wonderful place by the time we rose here last night to dedicate the 183rd and final toast of the evening to the health, prosperity and continued gastronomic genius of the deputy under-chef of the Dnieper Restaurant.

For reasons not immediately apparent this morning we coupled his name with that of Mrs Mary Whitehouse, placed our glasses upside down on the table in accordance with ancient Ukrainian custom and walked as nonchantly as possible into the awakening dawn.

Our hosts beamed. So did we. We are all old hands at this game.

In the past 72 hours we have lived the life of Tovarich Riley.

This means caviare, champagne, vodka, VIP lounges, watching real tigers leap through hoops at the Moscow State Circus, shaking hands with Hero of the Republic Valery Borzov and standing, truly respectfully, in front of the remarkable monument to the ten of the 11 men of the Kiev Dynamo football team who were taken out and shot dead after beating the German Luftwaffe team 4—3 in 1942.

Well may you ask what this is all about.

It is about the intricate politics of sport. The Soviet Union is determined to stage the 1980 Olympic Games in Moscow and to win that dubious distinction they have to convince the International Olympic Committee at a meeting in Vienna that their claims are superior to those of Los Angeles.

To this end and at an expense which would make a British Chancellor blanch, they have invited to Russia 23 sports writers from such far-flung parishes as Nairobi, Montreal, Atlanta, USA, Israel, Tunisia, Dublin, Austria and London.

The idea, you understand, is that we should write favourable if not flattering comment about Soviet sports facilities and thus influence the IOC in their decision.

They are paying our air fares, our hotel bills, giving us three-hour lunches, four-hour dinners, bouquets of carnations, notebooks and free telephone calls.

They even went so far two evenings ago to slip into our hands, under plain cover, an envelope containing 20 roubles, which is roughly £8, for pocket-money.

This, in plain English, is known as a bribe and I had no hesitation whatsoever in accepting it and spending it on drinks for our party.

Last year's sports budget for the Ukraine, which is only one of the 15 Socialist republics which form the Soviet Union, was £400 million.

The figure is so phenomenal, unrealistic and unbelievable, that we checked it five times. It proved to be right.

It is justified locally by the fact that at the Munich Olympics of 1972 the Ukraine provided 72 athletes who between them won 20 gold medals plus 43 silver or bronze. As you will recall, Great Britain won one gold medal on the track.

At the moment the Ukraine alone has 500 athletes in full training for the Montreal Olympics, which are still two years and two months away. The number includes the aforesaid Mr Borzov, the double sprint champion at Munich, who is but one of 45,118,918 officially registered Soviet sportsmen belonging to 211,849 officially registered clubs.

It was in view of these overwhelming statistics that we decided that 20 more roubles would make little difference one way or the other.

What of course is blatantly obvious is that any nation with resources like these, which has fired men into orbit round the Moon, which can split hydrogen atoms and transplant human hearts, can stage an Olympic Games standing on its head.

It is not as simple as that. Winning the Games now is a matter of influencing 80 mainly capitalist votes in Vienna, and that is why we are here, dining lavishly beneath pine trees in a city older than Christendom and freeloading it on a junket so congenial that no one raised an eyebrow the other evening when one of the American delegates cried: 'Jeez, there's red pepper in this vodka' and slumped across the table at a solemn moment in the speech-making.

What has yet to be determined — and we await the arrival of Mr Sergei Pavlov, the Soviet Minister of Sport to assure us — is that the athletes of all nations, including Israel, would receive a similar welcome in 1980.

The Israeli problem, and the bad publicity the Soviet Union received during the World Student Games in Moscow, is Russia's biggest problem.

It is also the reason why Mr Moyshe Lehrer, the Tel Aviv delegate, is receiving VIP treatment which includes an invitation to stay on for an extra fortnight at the Soviet Government's expense.

It may astonish you that such wheeling and dealing is necessary to assume the horrendous burden of becoming host nation to the Olympics, but, to date, they have never been held behind the Iron Curtain.

The Russians were so convinced that they had won the 1976 Games that they actually released a Press statement saying so some hours before they were awarded to Montreal. This time no expense, no effort, is to be spared.

There can be no question that if they are awarded to Moscow we will witness in August 1980 the most gigantic sports spectacle in the history of the human race. They will out-charm those of Tokio, out-automate those of Munich.

Russia's athletes and Russia's facilities are ready. They have even turned a swamp on the outskirts of Moscow into a rowing course which has a mobile stand for spectators which moves abreast of the rowers.

Nothing it seems is beyond them. Except complying with one request made here yesterday.

'Where', asked the Irish delegate, 'can I go to Mass?'

Our hosts looked suitably blank.

If the sudden acknowledgement of a teenage son amounts to a scoop, the following piece was a scoop. It is a curious story with a happy ending. In South America to cover motor-racing I called on Garrincha, whom I had last seen playing in the 1958 World Cup soccer finals in Sweden. Garrincha speaks no more English than I do Portuguese. After two hours he and Paulo Paladino, my interpreter, had an earnest private discussion for several minutes before Paladino said "There's something he wants to tell you." What he wanted to tell me follows here.

Within 48 hours, through Tom Clarke, my sports editor in London, and Margareta Rost, news editor of Stockholm's Expressen, Garrincha's first son had been located on the west coast of Sweden. Adopted, happy, an outstanding junior footballer and well aware of the real father he had never met, the young man was as well pleased as Garrincha that the secret was out. It was a risk, I suppose, but mercifully no damage was done.

'If Denis Compton and Miss Vera Lynn had come to the same arrangement the impact might have been somewhat similar'

Rio de Janeiro.— The birth here last year of Master Manoel dos Santos II — accomplished without even the benefit of wedlock — was greeted by nothing short of a nationwide ovation.

Well, the odd priest may have coughed discreetly. And doubtless a few nervous mums suggested to their daughters that there are other ways of proving nature wonderful. By and large, however, Brazil roared its approval out of relief, romance and sheer idolatry for the two parents who'd pulled it off.

The father, Manoel Francisco dos Santos, is better known here and to the world as Garrincha, the winger who helped win two World Cups for Brazil and is rated one of the two greatest footballers ever produced by this prolific soccer nation.

The mother, Elza Soares, is a gorgeous slant-eyed tigress of a singer whose voice throbs out all day every day on what seems like every Brazilian radio channel.

There is no immediate British comparison to their respective statuses, but if the Denis Compton of the 50s had come to the same arrangement with Miss Vera Lynn — and a thousand pardons for even suggesting it — the impact might have been somewhat similar.

It is a strange story which becomes even more curious as it goes along.

Garrincha, now 40, married young in his tiny up-country home town of Pau Grande and with his wife, Nair, began assembling a formidable collection of children.

First came Tereza, now 22. Then, almost at yearly intervals and sometimes less, came Edenir, Marinete, Juraciara, Denizia, Maria Cecilia, Terezinha, Cintia and finally little Iraciara, who is now 11.

The joy of such a large and healthy family, however, was tempered by one fact. To Manoel's regret, Nair's despair and the nation's stupefaction all nine children of their great hero were daughters.

There was no son to inherit Garrincha's incomparable talents and thus bring more glory and World Cups to Brazil.

However, as the years went by, Garrincha was to be seen more and more frequently in the company of the exotic Miss Soares who, between nightclub and recording contracts, was making her own not inconsiderable contribution to a Brazilian population now rising beyond the 110 million mark.

She had already given birth to Joao Carlos now 22; Gerson, 21; Dilma, 20; Gilson, 18; and Sarinha, 11. 'Two more were born dead,' Miss Soares said, 'but I have three grandchildren and they have brought much happiness to our house.'

By 'our house' Miss Soares was referring to the elegant ten-bedroomed villa in the wealthy Rio dormitory town of Jacarepagua where she and Garrincha set up home some while ago without abashment or apologies to those bureaucrats who enforce the Brazilian law forbidding divorce.

It was here that their mutual son, Manoel dos Santos II, was born on July 9 last year to such national rejoicing.

His arrival raised to 22 — if you count the grandchildren, a son-in-law and Antonia, the indefatigable housekeeper — the number of permanent residents at No. 60 Rua Tomas G. Masariky, with its private swimming pool and three family cars parked in the driveway.

Brazil's newspapers led the celebrations. 'At last a son for Garrincha' . . . 'Finally an heir,' trumpeted the headlines.

They were wrong. Garrincha had already had a son for 17 years.

What induced Garrincha to divulge to a foreign reporter a piece of information that he had kept from the Brazilian public throughout his career, the national testimonial match which brought him £230,000 and had taken safely into retirement, I have no way of knowing.

But we had been talking of this and that, mostly football, for almost two hours when he suddenly said: 'I have a son I have never seen. He must be 17 now and I only know him by the name of "Johnny". He lives in Sweden and I have only ever seen pictures of him taken when he was a baby. I don't know how to get in touch with him now but I would very much like to meet him.'

The explanation is very simple and not unconnected with Brazil's glittering victory in the World Cup Final in Stockholm in the summer of 1958.

'On the evening of our victory there was a very big party,' said Garrincha. 'I met a Swedish girl there and you will understand the rest. Johnny was born the following year.

'I was back in Sweden with the Brazilian team the following year and I was asked to take a blood test to discover whether I was the father. I accepted that I was and I paid some money. Then the child was taken into a home run by the government. Apart from the photographs many years ago I have seen or heard nothing of him.'

Garrincha is now a rich man, but football remains his life. Spectacularly fit he still plays some 30 matches a year for The Millionaires, a Brazilian team of ex-international stars who raise enormous sums for the nation's less fortunate citizens.

He is not impressed by the present Brazilian side and regrets the global sickness which has transformed football from a sport of spectacular improvisation into an overtactical and largely defensive exercise.

He has never been invited to coach in Brazil but, despite his wealth, would relish the chance to be able to halt soccer's sickness somewhere. 'I would enjoy coaching in Europe,' he said, 'and tell them in England that I would particularly like to coach there.'

It was time for Miss Soares to leave for the first of her evening's public appearances and Garrincha escorted her tenderly to the car.

Actually, she is Mrs dos Santos now.

Nair, the mother of nine daughters, died last year and now the footballer and the nightclub star are married.

Three weeks after returning from the Soviet Union a product of its tennis conveyor belt played in one of the outstanding matches at Wimbledon. Like the Panovs, Mrs Morozova soon developed more than a passing interest in life as lived in the West.

'Some had queued and stood for 26 hours to witness it, and some had paid £30 for a black-market ticket'

Wimbledon.— Heroine of the Soviet Union Olga Morozova wore pale pink on the Centre Court last evening as a concession to the Tory voters of Wimbledon. But that was as far as it went.

By this point in the championships the Russians are usually out and on their way to Moscow or any anywhere, but what we saw this time was not only one of the most remarkable tennis matches in history, but yet another example of Russian character and attitudes to sport.

After the first set, when Miss Wade brushed Mrs Morozova aside as brutally as the Panzers scorching their way through the Ukraine, I felt like sending a telegram to General Nikolai Kosolev pleading clemency.

It was in Moscow only three weeks ago that General Kosolev, head of his nation's tennis programme, was informing me with a frown that his country's progress in the game had been gravely disappointing.

That tennis means about as much to the average Russian tovarich as volleyball does to the average British stockbroker did not concern him.

'We have 27,000 players under training, we have employed some of the world's finest coaches, we have all the facilities,' he said. 'But we have still not achieved anything of note.'

General Kosolev, who was a pretty tough tank commander around places like Stalingrad and Minsk in the war, should have been in SW19 last night.

For a start it was an almost classic confrontation of character with only the weather on Mrs Morozova's side. It was as cold as Siberia and half a day's rain made the whole place smell of damp army blankets and sodden strawberries.

It was always, of course, a contest beyond the normal limitations of sporting interest.

It was West versus East. It was bishop's daughter versus electrician's wife. It was ideology versus ideology.

Miss Wade has one of the most acceptable faces capitalism has ever fashioned. Mrs Morozova only needed a scarlet head scarf to have stepped straight out of one of those communist posters calling on factory workers to double their productivity norm to the glory of Lenin.

Instead, she wore pink and a pair of frilly pants that didn't come from a Soviet GUM store and fooled us all into believing that she couldn't pull out a miracle two days in a row. She did.

Some had queued and stood for 26 hours to witness it, and some had paid £30 for a black-market ticket. Both time and money were justified.

It was a stupendous achievement, bereft of temperament of feminine squeals, and the implications are likely to be as big. By reaching a Wimbledon final Mrs Morozova, seeded eight and rated nowhere by the bookmakers, has achieved the breakthrough for which Moscow has waited 25 years.

To have seen the Soviet sports machine at work is to know something of what will happen next. She will be feted and paraded to inspire a generation of tennis players who must have been beginning to feel that genetically tennis just wasn't their game.

With its 70 stadiums and six Palaces of Sport, with its 36 tennis courts in the Luzhniki complex alone, the Soviet Union will employ them all to pile through the breach achieved by one woman at Wimbledon.

They will even claim back 90 per cent of her prize money — £1,200 if she loses the final, £2,000 if she wins — to foot one tiny item on the bill.

How much of this occurred to the spectators in the Tia Maria belt of South London last night is open to doubt but they were certainly watching a political match.

Olga, with her humour and charm and a brand of sportswomanship that Mrs King could do well to emulate, concealed it well. But here is one lady who won't be defecting yet awhile.

That apart, it was one of those matches you would have marched from Moscow to see. Character and nerve and resilience won it and it was an historic moment in championships which were already well established when the last of the Czars was gunned down.

Unlike America, where major sports teams employ publicity men to disseminate information to newspapers, radio and television, many British professional sports clubs regard inquiries from journalists as intrusion. This is particularly true of soccer clubs. Those fortunate enough to reach a Wembley Cup Final are misguided enough either to turn a blind eye, or actively encourage their players, to create a 'perks pool', which is a fund to which newspapers are asked to contribute for 'co-operation'. If a newspaper does not 'co-operate' its photographers are liable to find themselves barred from taking pictures at practice sessions. 'Perks' have become a major industry in sport and have thus proliferated the growth of the agent.
Mr Justin Vilegrab, of Rapacity Enterprises, isn't actually one of them.

'Congratulations on getting to Wembley. Of course you'll have to give up training completely'

London.— Well lads, we don't get in the Cup Final every day which is why I've asked Mr Vilegrab of Rapacity Enterprises to come and advise us how to screw . . . sorry consolidate . . . the situation financiallywise. All yours Mr Vilegrab.

Thank you, Mr Manager. By the way, just call me Justin. We're very informal at Rapacity Enterprises, so informal, in fact, that we're not even registered in the *Companies Register.*

Anyway, congratulations on getting to Wembley lads which means that your work's all over and mine's just beginning. Of course, you'll have to give up training completely. No time for any of that if we're going to screw . . . sorry, exploit . . . the great honour you have brought to this fine club and its loyal supporters.

You will, of course, already have made your own arrangements to distribute your fistfuls . . . sorry, personal allocations . . . of Cup Final tickets through the usual channels, thus maintaining the tradition that lifelong fans have no hope of getting one.

However, that's only skimmed milk compared with what Rapacity Enterprises have in mind. TV shows, radio phone-ins, signed newspaper articles, photographic sessions, personal appearances, commercial endorsements, souvenir handbooks, nightclub ball-juggling acts.

You name it and I'll con . . . sorry, negotiate . . . terms. With luck you'll be too clapped out to come to attention for the national anthem on the big day.

It's the law of supply and demand, lads. You supply, I demand, somebody pays and we split it up 50-50. That's 50 for you 15 lads and 50 for Rapacity Enterprises, not including VAT, of course.

As usual we'll start with the newspapers. The *Daily Smirk* have offered £25,000 for an in-depth dialogue between two players' wives about the hats and dresses they'll wear to the game. Naturally I've made a few inquiries and I've fixed them up with two who can neither read nor write so that they won't be able to give too much away.

Of course we can kid . . . sorry, suggest . . . that one of the Sunday colour supplements carries the same sort of piece. And I have great hopes that one of the Sunday naughties will go for my Cup Final Star Found in Mayfair Love Nest idea, so I want one of you to volunteer for that. Obviously a bachelor's no good because we want Heartbroken-Wife-Blinks-Back-Tears-and-Pledges-I'll-Still-go-to-Wembley for follow-ups during the week.

The real loot . . . sorry, professsional fees . . . are from photographs. The *Daily Grope* have already offered £10,000 for your leading goalscorer to dress up as Albert Pierrepoint and stand over a trap door with the name of your opponents painted on it.

But I have a better idea than that. I want the back four to get down to Hickstead and ride around on show-jumping horses made up as War, Death, Famine and Pestilence. If we can get all of Fleet Street bidding for the Four Footballers of the Apocalypse we ought to clean up . . . sorry, receive reimbursement . . . that will settle all our gas bills for years to come.

I've already booked the *Jimmy Young Show* all the week before the match so that some of you can go and give recipes, but that's only £25 a time, I'm afraid.

Still, we should do better from Michael Barratt if only one of you concentrates long enough to answer questions for 30 minutes but I must warn you that he asks really smart things like 'In view of the Cambodian conflict do you feel a professional footballer's contribution to society borders on the insignificant?' So for God's sake don't ask what League Cambodia play in.

I've succeeded in getting the Duke of Edinburgh thrown off *Desert Island Discs* so I'm equally anxious that whoever fills in there won't let us down. Choose lots of Bach and say that Bertrand Russell is your favourite writer and before you know it we'll be getting offers from really influential publications like *The Economist* and *Sports World.*

I understand that there is a certain player among you sufficiently well endowed to do a full-frontal for one of the bedsitter-lady mags and that really is worth a lot of bread . . . sorry, artistic fees . . . and I don't want to be let down on that one.

Obviously we'll be opening new branches of Tesco's and W.H. Smiths and things like that but I don't want you to forget to go to the Football Writers' Dinner. They don't, unfortunately, give you a fee for turning up there but it's very useful if you happen to have an absolute stinker in the game itself. Some of these reporters are nearly human and they'll criticise you less if you were a guest at their table a couple of nights earlier.

When you walk out at Wembley you will, of course, be wearing track suits bearing the trade name 'Anglican'. The Church of England have paid us a really substantial fee for this in the hope of increasing Sunday congregations, so I don't want any of you making V-signs or anything vulgar like that while you-'re wearing them.

Your boots will have a distinguishing white star on the side, which is the trade mark of Cornish Cobblers who have been daft . . . sorry, enterprising . . . enough to pay us £500,000 for using them on television.

Unfortunately the boots can be delivered only on the morning of the match. They probably won't fit properly but just console yourself that this is Your Day of a Lifetime and you might as well make a bob or two while you can.

After the match make sure there are plenty of Press photographers around when you step up to get your loser's . . . sorry, finalist's . . . medal from Her Majesty. We will get lots of copies made so that you can sell them to your children and friends.

In the unlikely event that you have a good game, David Coleman will probably want to interview you. In recent years players have always gone into the interview room drinking milk from a bottle because they were paid to do so by the Milk Marketing Board who know as well as you and I do that footballers only ever drink beer or champagne after a match.

To be more in keeping with the dignity of the occasion I have this year arranged that you undertake these interviews while eating an artichoke. For this the Britanny Artichoke Growers' Association are paying us more money than Edward Heath is paying for his new yacht, so I implore you to tackle them as though you've actually seen an artichoke before.

Well, lads, that's about it. You'll probably have a few ideas of your own that you'd like me to kick around for you.

But while I'm still on my feet it remains only for me to wish you everything that Rapacity Enterprises wish for you, namely, about £10,000 in perks per man less, of course the usual agent's fee and expenses.

Ex-Corporal Ray Peart competed in the Paraplegic Games that followed the Olympic Games in Canada in 1976. He won no medals at anything. He is the bravest man I have ever met.

'I would like this to be read by a man in possession of all his faculties in one of H.M.'s prisons'

Gloucester.— The last thing Ray Peart saw on God's Earth was a candy-striped mattress.

It was protruding from a fuse cupboard on a third-floor landing. He leaned forward, cautiously, to examine it. It exploded.

In that instant in the booby-trapped Divis Flats, Corporal Peart became another Belfast statistic worth five words on the night's news: 'Another soldier was seriously injured.'

The two men flanking him that July afternoon in 1973 were killed instantly.

It was another ten weeks before they asked Peart's wife, a girl he'd fallen in love with in Londonderry, to break the news to him that he was totally blind.

He missed seeing his new-born second son, Jonathan, by three days. 'That' said Ray Peart 'was upsetting.' It was the closest he came to self-pity all day.

It isn't often that a sports-writer passionately hopes his words are read by a particular person, but I would like these to be read by one man who is alive and well and in possession of all his faculties in one of HM's prisons in Ulster as a result of having detonated the bomb which killed two and blinded Ray Peart.

He may discern something about the true nature of courage.

In July next year, almost on the third anniversary of being blown up, Peart will fly to Canada to represent Britain in the Paraplegic Games which immediately follow the Olympics.

He will swim, sprint, long jump, putt the shot and throw the discus, and being Britain's sole blind entry in the pentathlon and a man of certain old-fashioned values, he has every intention of winning.

To this end, having already disposed of the tiresome but necessary business of learning how to read and type Braille, he is training as assiduously as Mohammad Ali preparing for his next title defence.

As we left his neat home on a new white-collar estate on the outskirts of his native Gloucester, it was wet and freezing.

Dorothy, his 24-year-old wife, drove us to the Gloucester Leisure Centre, where he swam 24 lengths, breast-stroke and front crawl.

About once each length he grazed his cheeks or got an arm tangled in the lane-ropes and immediately corrected his direction. Just before his head was due to crash into the end of the bath his coach, Chris Maloney, tapped him on the back with a stick. His speed was terrific.

In the centre's big pool, they asked the kids to swim out of range while Peart walked unerringly out on a springboard and produced three piked dives. Two were nearly perfect.

Most days he also just jumps off the top board for the fun of it, but with so many children about it was too dangerous the day we were there.

'He's fantastic,' said Maloney, who is one of Britain's leading swimming instructors. 'The other day I tried swimming fast with my eyes closed and finished up going round in a circle.'

Maloney is a benevolent bully. For the next hour, in the centre's gymnasium, he shouted, stop-watched, cajoled, exhorted, coaxed and drove Ray Peart through a session of circuit training that would have rewarded any man less than supremely fit with nothing more valuable than a heart attack.

It was belting with rain by the time we arrived at the athletics ground but Peart said it was better than being dead, surely.

By Olympic standards the results were necessarily unsensational. The long jump is performed from a standing start and the shot and discus are hurled without the benefit of a full body-turn. The left foot is jammed against the stop-board and the rest is sheer strength.

With his third shot-putt Peart broke his personal record. But he couldn't get the discus to come out flat and cursed a bit about that.

Then he sprinted. The technique for blind sprinting is that another athlete runs behind yelling 'Left, left,' or 'Right, right' to adjust direction. Ray Peart, at full speed on a greasy surface over 80 yards of engulfing blackness, didn't need the commands. He deviated precisely one yard to the left.

Training over, ex-Corporal Peart of the Gloucestershire Regiment, then retired to the dressing rooms where, declining assistance, he changed into riding kit and was driven to the riding school of Charlie and Ann Francis.

Arrondell, a 17.2 hands chestnut hunter, and Miss Fiona Ashley, a jolly girl with an expensive accent, were both pleased to see him.

Fiona fixed a 40ft. lead rein on Arrondell's bridle, and Ray Peart just cantered around a bit before going over a few jumps.

Earlier this year, by way of a

change, Ray Peart got himself roped up to some expert climbers and clambered and bruised his way up a 2,900 ft. mountain in Wales. For his next trick he skied down part of a slope at Aviemore and then fell the rest.

His proudest achievement, and the only one about which he is boistrously immodest, was witnessed by England footballer Colin Bell. On holiday in Ibiza, Peart spent ten days on the beach listening to the noises people make when they try to water ski.

'I couldn't stand it any longer. I whacked down a few brandies and had a go. I got up on the skis first time and I stayed up on them right round the bay. That was a hell of a feeling, so I had a few more brandies to celebrate.'

At 30, supremely fit physically, apart from his eyes and part deafness and a terror of answering the doorbell when he's alone in the house, Ray Peart has no doubts that the best years of his life are ahead of him.

These include next year's Paraplegic Games, a career, he hopes, as a telephone switchboard operator, some drinking, much dancing, quite a number of nights out with the boys so that he can keep up his darts and any new sports that might occur to him.

For the moment his income comes from an Army and a disability pension. At a guess they probably gross him what a London businessman might spend on dinner for four in a West End restaurant.

So far he hasn't received any Government compensation. But that could be because all those bureaucrats with two eyes haven't had time to get round to it.

Paul Gallico died in the south of France about 18 months after this piece was written. During that time he wrote me several notes of criticism and encouragement. I was astonished and grateful that a man who apportioned his time so ruthlessly should take the trouble. He was quite amused, I think, to know that a book he had written nearly 40 years earlier had actually fired another human being with the ambition to try sportswriting for a living.

'Above all, sport has a perpetual drama which even the theatre can't rival'

London.— Mr Paul Gallico first came into my life when I was maybe 15 and bought a book of his in one of those oblong American Forces editions which had two columns of type on each page.

It was so grubby and dog-eared that it would have been dear at a shilling had the contents not amounted to the most magical prose ever written about sport in the rich English language.

Dempsey and Walter Hagen and Babe Ruth and Sarazen and Helen Wills Moody came tumbling out of its pages, reeking of liniment and after-shave or whisky or Worth, so that you were simply sitting there drowned in the golden age of American sport.

Gallico wrote them, warts, tantrums, grunts, vanities and all, chronicling their shortcomings, acclaiming their ability but, above all, stripping them of the glossy images that had been built up by years and columns of mindless obsequities.

He called the book *Farewell to Sport* and then, after 14 years of reporting boxing, baseball and tennis, went away to write about snow-geese and cats.

He is now, of course, a distinguished novelist with a house in Antibes and a pied-a-terre mews cottage behind Eaton Square where two nights ago he poured himself a cut-glass of Irish whiskey and said: 'Paul Gallico and Mr Bushmills are now entirely at your disposal.'

Gossip came first, because for 25 years I had been curious why, in *Farewell to Sport*, he had concentrated his enormous powers of invective to knife Helen Wills Moody, the imperious Wimbledon queen of her day, out of the public's affection.

Gallico smiled: 'I was in love with her. I just liked to sit and look at her because she had that lovely Grecian nose. I remember taking her to the El Morocco where they had two bands, playing in relay, and when we'd been on the floor for what seemed about 35 hours she looked into my eyes and said: "You know, Paul, your dancing is very good for my footwork." '

It was not the oblique criticism of Gallico's fox-trotting that sealed the lady's fate. They later fell out over a business deal. 'That and the way she walked off the court against Helen Jacobs, pleading sick, were the reasons I beat up on her,' said Gallico. 'I never forgave her for either.'

But scurrilous locker-room secrets aside, what I really wanted to hear from Gallico was whether he believed any reasonably intelligent person could justify spending a lifetime getting passionate about anything so basically unimportant as two football teams or two boxers trying to win the same thing.

Reassuringly, coming from a man who has acquired much wisdom on his graceful passage to 75, his answer was yes.

'My disenchantment was not with sport,' he said. 'My disenchantment was with me. After 14 years of writing about sport seven days a week I had nothing left to say. I was beginning to repeat myself.

'But sport hadn't changed then and it hasn't changed now. It preserves adolescence, which is not a bad thing. It is a meeting ground for minds which might otherwise be completely empty of anything. Above all, it has a perpetual drama which even the theatre can't rival.

'Sport is all about some poor bastard of a golf pro who suddenly gets hot and comes away with $25,000. One day he's poor and the next day he's rich and nobody's written the plot.

'You talk of the golden age I was writing about. It's a golden age now. Cassius Clay is every bit as colourful as Dempsey, Lee Trevino could up-stage Walter Hagen. It's one of the tragedies that the golden age we so rarely recognise is the one that we're actually living through.'

Gallico still fences and in London this summer has sat mesmerised in front of the television watching cricket which he rates an immeasurably superior game to baseball because of the additional dimension of the ball's movement off the pitch.

Tragically, for a generation who have never read the arena-side dispatches which he pounded out with speed and perception and glorious style, Paul Gallico will never write about sport again.

He is constantly under pressure to do so, to the point where he could make more money for one article in *Readers' Digest* than Dostoyevsky coined out of *Crime and Punishment*. He resolutely resists.

'My family will perhaps not enjoy me saying this,' he said, 'but my time is so short and my ambition remains so great to write something that will really satisfy me.'

It was Paul Gallico speaking. Not Mr Bushmills.

The kindest people you ever meet in sport live in what is irreverently known as 'the sticks'. Lost in Ebbw Vale, which is not so difficult as it sounds, I asked a man the way to Blaina's rugby ground. 'You could well get lost,' he said, 'I'll lead you in my car.' This he did, round the head of the valley, accelerating occasionally to as much as 20 mph. In a Darlington pub on the eve of the match another man said 'Don't waste your money on that hotel, come and stay with the wife and me.' I didn't, but he meant it. Things like that don't happen in London or Las Vegas. The next two columns are about Saturdays in 'the sticks'.

'I smashed one of their fellers straight in the face and all he did was shake his head and waggle a finger at me'

Blaina, South Wales.— A cold white mist was already rolling up the valley like the wrath of God when Vasili Korotaev shook off four Welshmen as though they'd never been born and torpedoed over the line just inside the left corner flag.

Korotaev, a 6ft. 7in. atheist from Moscow, is claimed by his coach to be a watchmaker, which strikes you as odd since he is only 22 and has fingers like frankfurters. Anyway, his try made the score 10—0 and my Welsh neighbour, in the vibrant tones of a lay-preacher interpreting the *Book of Revelations*, announced: 'It's all over.'

It wasn't actually. Later the Russians went over for another try wide out on the right to make the final score Slava Moscow 14, Blaina 0, thus undermining both Welsh religions in a single afternoon. It was the Soviet Union's first rugby victory on British soil.

'They reckon,' said a Blaina forward, alternating spoonfuls of brown windsor soup with whole pints of beer at the after-match banquet and dance, 'that they've only been playing rugger two years. Crafty bastards, they are. Do you know they were in bed at six o'clock on Friday night instead of coming out for a drink? I'm going to get as drunk as a rat.'

Mission accomplished, the 15 players, five reserves and four officials of Slava Moscow RFC marched solemnly through the soup, lamb and two veg., and crackers and cheese.

They sipped lemonade. 'They do not drink,' said Edward Tatourjan, 38-year-old rugby coach to the 11, 000-employee Slava Watch and

Clock Factory in Moscow, because they are Soviet sportsmen and do not wish to drink.

I asked Mr Tatourjan whether, in the Soviet Union, it was the better class of person who took up rugby?

He looked blankly back at our interpreter. 'Explain please,' he said. I explained that, outside the Principality, rugger was largely a game for smoothies, mostly bank clerks who wear suede Hush Puppies and brown trilbies as affected by off-duty subalterns from the Queen's Hussars.

In bewilderment, Mr Tatourjan glanced briefly round at a Blaina team by now deeply anaesthetised against the afternoon's shock-horror result. Unwilling to be snared into some dialectical argument about Western class structures, he announced: 'In the Soviet Union rugby is a game for all the people. We have eight centres across the country where boys of between 11 and 13 are learning to play. They are tested for their psychological ability.'

If the Soviet Union are going to all that trouble, it was probably less than coincidence that they chose not the trendy Home Counties but the valleys of Nye Bevan Socialism in which to initiate their first generation of players into international rugby mystique.

'It was only to be expected, I suppose,' said Ron Adams, vice-chairman of Blaina. 'But they've dropped a few clangers. Won't turn up at receptions, see. We've laid on parties and dinners for them but they keep saying they've got to go to bed. Well, I mean, I had to take 'em aside and say. "Now, look 'ere, lads, playing rugby is only the half of it. There's a social side, see." '

So there was still mutual misunderstanding in the air when the Russians, with unintelligible Cyrillic lettering on their track suits, came out from the green corrugated iron dressing-rooms to play under the shadow of the almost vowelless Mountain of Mynydd Carn-y-cefn, which separates Blaina from Ebbw Vale.

Blaina's pitch, a rectangle of grass perched on the side of a coal tip; was hemmed in four-deep by the kind of people who made Dylan Thomas the richest man in the graveyard.

They've had a rugby club for 101 years, regard their present 12 per cent. unemployment as prosperity compared with the '30s, recall visits by Cliff Morgan and Gareth Edwards as the highlights of their whole lives and, by nature, are the most resilient, generous and kindly people you've ever met.

Before the kick-off the Blaina team could be heard going through the traditional Welsh 'We will smash them' chant in the privacy of their un-soundproofed changing room.

Nothing of the sort, however, transpired. In a hard and entertaining game, end-to-end play only ensued when it was far too late for Blaina to recover. 'I'll tell you what,' said a Blaina forward afterwards, 'I smashed one of their fellers straight in the face and all he did was shake his head and waggle a finger at me. They're real 'ard.'

The disaster was probably best summed up by a Welsh Rugby Union observer. 'It strikes me as extremely unlikely,' he said, 'that this Soviet team have been playing rugby for only two years. God 'elp us if that's true. They'll be beating the world in five years time.'

That, of course, is precisely the Soviet Union's intention. Slava— the word happens to mean 'glory', for what that's worth — are merely a factory club with 300 players, six regular teams, a full-time coach, and more training facilities at their command than the British Ministry of Sport could afford to grant our rugby, soccer and athletics teams put together.

Their coach, the extremely guarded Mr Tatourjan, mysteriously informed me that his own interest in rugby stretches back to 1958, since which time the Soviet Union have been establishing an information bank comprising every book, film and TV tape about rugby they can lay their hands on from the West.

That all this led to a club in a Welsh valley where, to save money, dinner was served by a committee of nine ladies should be a matter of great pride to the community of Blaina. They gave the Russians a brass pit lamp, worth £35, and a tie apiece, and John Powell, the Blaina chairman, less made a speech than an impassioned appeal.

'For Christ's sake, lads,' he said, looking down the two lines of uniformly-suited Russian players, 'enjoy yourselves, will you?'

Two hours later, as Mr Tatourjan tapped his foot on the pavement awaiting the team coach, the message was getting through.

Experimentally at first, then with accelerating concentration, the Russian players were getting into the pints of beer being lined up before them.

Shyly at first, then emboldened later, they began to size up the daughters and sisters and distant cousins arriving for the dance.

The day's detente was completed by a small Welshman educating a large Soviet citizen into the finer points of the game. 'Listen Charlie,' he was saying, 'it's all about aggression. When he whacks you in the face, you have to whack him back. That's what it's all about.'

'Da,' said the Russian, wondering what the hell you've got to do to win a rugger match in Wales.

‘He had a drill-sergeant’s vocabulary and about as much compassion as a Gestapo thumb-screw exponent’

Darlington.— There was only a very small riot when Darlington were obliterated 7—0 for the second match running last Saturday. Maybe 20 men, some of them gnarled enough to have voted for Ramsey MacDonald, rose up in the stand and shouted ‘Tait must go.’

Tait is George A. Tait, who bought the chairmanship of Darlington Football Club 21 years ago by promising to underwrite their expenses up to £75,000 over three years. He is widely disliked in Darlington because he is a foreigner. He comes from Newcastle, 33 miles to the north.

George Tait is an archetypal English football club chairman: self-made, thickskinned, friendly, very rich, deferred to by his employees, envied by his contemporaries. In 1930 he launched out in the carpet business with £10 capital. He is now a millionaire.

He brought the only splash of colour to Saturday’s freezing, fog-shrouded match: powder-blue 4.2 Jag, brown suit in bookmaker-check, ochre nylon shirt and one of those narrow ready-made bow-ties much favoured by 1959 band-leaders.

What the demonstrators failed to realise, or blindly ignored, was that without George Tait there would have been no match to abuse. The economics of Darlington Football Club are so absurb that only philanthropy keeps them alive.

Take Saturday, when 1,088 of Darlington’s population of 84,830 paid £232.55 at the turnstiles.

They had to give Southport, the visiting team, the statutory minimum of £250. Their wage bill for the week was £650. Printing 1,000 programmes cost them £28.75. They had to pay 15 gatemen and the nominal bill for police protection is still to come in.

But the financial strain is nothing compared to the nervous stress of being manager of the 92nd of the 92 League clubs with only three wins in 24 games. At Darlington they share it about a bit. They’re now on their fifth manager in 15 months.

This may explain why Ralph Brand, who took over three matches and 17-goals-against ago, was stopped at the entrance and asked to pay 40p for the privilege of doing his job on Saturday.

Brand, at 35, is a one-time Scottish international who became so bored after two years as an Edinburgh newsagent that he took up the Darlington challenge in the one-to-50 gamble that it would launch him as the next Clough or Shankly in soccer management.

His style owes much to both of them. Short, with fanatical blue eyes, a busted nose, fearful articulacy, a drill-sergeant's vocabulary and about as much compassion as a Gestapo thumb-screw exponent, he last week flayed and cursed Darlington's 16-man staff through a practice match until they trembled in their boots.

'Get up, get up,' he screamed as a man fell from exhaustion. 'You'll die three times before I bring you off.' Then, back in the dressing room: 'Just get it into your heads that this time next season you'll be on the dole or driving a bus if you don't start fighting.'

On Friday afternoon a forward phoned Brand complaining of back pains. 'It must've been something I've eaten,' he said. 'Eaten?' scorned Brand, 'Jesus Christ, you must have swallowed a whale bone to get pains in the back. Listen son, get to bed and send your wife off to another bedroom. I don't want you waking up and finding your wife all nice and warm there beside you. Remember that you belong to me till five o'clock tomorrow. After that you can make up for lost time.'

Saturday dawned auspiciously for Darlington. They had their first full-strength side of the season. Then, at midday, goalkeeper Ernie Adams arrived. He was shuddering with flu.

Adams was sent home and Phil Owers, a quiet, shy lad who'd been cleaning the players' boots the previous afternoon, was sent for. Owers is a 17-year-old amateur who is still studying for his geography A-levels at Tech. It was to be his first League match. Ever.

After two minutes Owers went flat for a marvellous save. Of the seven goals that went past him one may just have been his fault. The other six left him helpless behind a defence that looked like a Toc H team appealing to Rommel's better nature.

As the seventh goal went in someone started singing *We Shall Not be Moved.* A lot of people laughed. The alternative was to weep for Darlington's joyless fate and seemingly hopeless future after 99 years existence and 52 years in the Football League.

There is no moral to the story. Only, just a week before the League chairmen meet to debate whether the Darlingtons have anything to contribute to the future structure of English professional football, observation.

The local arguments — that 40p is downright robbery to get in, that George Tait has failed them by spending none of his £75,000 on new players — are petty, pointless and parochial.

All Tait wants to do now is see the club steer clear of re-election and hand it back to the town.

All Ralph Brand hopes to do is to achieve that miracle, for it will be no less, and move on and upwards in the cut-throat business of football management.

In the end it comes down to a town visibly caring whether or not it has a football team and on that score, last Saturday, Darlington's apathy was even denser than its fog.

There was a period during the quite recent history of Australian culture when it was possible to buy the most explicit pornography in King's Cross, Sydney, but quite impossible to lay your hands on a copy of Portnoy's Complaint. *It had been banned, presumably on the assumption that any tacit acknowledgement of onanism could encourage the criminal waste of the gross national product. This ambivalent attitude should have warned me that The Tomkins Papers were likely to test Australian tolerance to the extreme.*

They did precisely that. While completely fictional and written for fun, they provoked much acrid correspondence from Australia, where a couple of them were reprinted, and even inspired the management of a visiting Australian cricket team to contemplate legal redress. This they wisely decided against before it involved them in quite unnecessary expense.

In fact you could only parody Australia and Australians if you love the place to distraction, which I do. Brash, vigorous, generous, proud, chauvinistic and incurably insular, its sheer capacity for living far outweighs its more hilarious foibles.

The only way to survive there, a fact not always assimilated by English immigrants until they are on the disillusioned trip home again, is to give as good as you get. If you can't beat them, join them. If you can't join them, beat them.

Hence the Tomkins Papers, the mildest of retributions for the calumny which the Australian sporting Press has cheerfully poured over successive generations of visiting Pom cricket teams. Long may this institutional harangue survive since there is nothing in sport to compare with an England—Australia Test match when the gates are closed and the heat is on.

‘Our biggest problem is that we won’t have 11 men strong enough to take the field for any match’

London. — To the rich treasury of sporting *belles lettres* Sportsmail today adds a document of compelling socio-cultural interest. After four days in England Terror Tomkins, Australia’s Pin-a-Pom fast bowler, has compiled his initial impressions of England in a letter to his mother, Ada. We thank Mr Tomkins for allowing us to reproduce it unabridged, and at his specific request, are forwarding his usual fee of £3,000 to the Freddie Trueman Homes of Rest for Paralytic Opening Batsmen.

Dear Mum,

Well it’s just wot Dad said it would be like, freezing bloody cold and all the Poms which aren’t on strike are saying the old country’s knackered which is why they’re going to vote for a German prime minister or something on Thursday. Incidentally is there any news about Dad’s parole?

We nearly never got here, I can tell you. At London Airport they waved all the abbo’s straight through immigration and made us get on the end of a queue about ten miles long. ‘Come on, let’s pizzoff,’ said my oppo, Dennis, but I said ‘No, let’s stay and kill an extra couple of their batsmen.’

The bloke at the passport desk said: ‘What is the purpose of your visit, Mr Tomkins?’ I said: ‘To kill an extra couple of batsmen.’ And he said ‘That is not the spirit at all, sir,’ and it just shows how the Establishment works in England because by the time we got to Lord’s they’d changed all the laws of cricket so that you couldn’t bowl bouncers in the World Cup.

You’ve got to give it to the Poms, they cheat with style. They used to rough up the wickets to suit their spinners, like they did at Leeds on that famous occasion. Now they change the rules to make all bouncers into wides.

They also tried to con us into playing two warm-up matches against some place called Gloucestershire. Well, we jumped at that because we thought that was right next door to Chelsea where all the birds are. Not at all. We were thinking about Gloucester *Road*. Gloucester*shire* is bloody nearly in Chicago. It’s wild west country so we told them to stuff it and sorted out the local talent.

You can't move for birds here. They've got this thing called the Permissible Society. You don't have to join or anything. You just write a couple of pieces for the newspapers saying you're highly-sexed and all that and they're queueing up for a meaningful experience every time you come down in the lift.

Our biggest problem is that we won't have 11 men strong enough to take the field for any match.

I've already been photographed with models, hotel receptionists and some Swedish au pair girls. Apparently you can't sell newspapers in England unless you have a couple of beauts on every page.

I'm real sorry that you and Dad won't be able to watch the Test matches on TV. The reason is that the BBC are broke, cricket is broke and they won't do anything to help one another. They don't give a damn about the public so everybody suffers.

By now you will have read that Snowy is back in the England team which is bloody bad news for us. They can't stand him at Lord's because he's a sort of anerkist who writes poetry and that but they're so short of fast bowlers that they've had to bring him back at the age of 60.

Anyway, Geoff Boycott's lady friend won't let him play so that's something. Funny thing about Boycott. He's one of the world's four best batsmen and yet no overseas bowler can remember what he looks like. They say he's going to emigrate to South Africa because he's fed up with the English Press being so nasty to him.

Mostly all we've done so far is drink gin at cocktail parties but that's all anybody seems to do here. They keep on ordering up another round of doubles and complaining about the way the cost of living's going up. There's also some bloke called Benn who's even more unpopular than Boycott.

Give my love to Gloreen and tell her not to believe anything she reads about me and other birds in the papers. I'll definitely be fit in time for the Tests. Also that we're going to a party at Buckingham Palace at the weekend, only by then we'll be foreigners because England will be joined up with Germany which seems a bit daft after what happened to Uncle Bruce at Tobruk.

Did Sis get away with probation? They're much more lenient about things like that here. Some English blokes smashed up a football ground last week in Paris and then broke a lot of windows, and they've got the bloody cheek to call us wild colonial boyos.

Well, new rules or not, we're going to give them plenty of bouncers because, as you know as well as I do, I can't bowl straight enough to bowl the bastards out. Not after a heavy night, anyway, and the way things are going the only thing we're going to have a shortage of is sleep.

Anyway, a couple of papers here are paying me plenty to become a sort of sex symbol now that Fred Sinatra's too old to cope. The phone never stops ringing with offers of every kind and I shall do my level best to keep my end up.

Got to go now because we're all off to one of those posh clubs called Raymond's. That's one of the reasons we didn't go to Gloucestershire but don't tell anybody that because it could get in the papers. By the way, please let me know whether it was only a rumour or not about Sharon. I know she's my sister but 14 is definitely too young to become a mum and I can do without that sort of thing damaging my image.

Yours in sport,
Your loving son,
T. Tomkins.

'Thanks for the Oxo cubes and woolly underwear. It was 92f here last week'

London. — Once again Sportsmail enriches the tapestry of sporting literature with the complete, unabridged reproduction of a letter home from Australian fast bowler Terror Tomkins to his mother, Ada. As before, his fee for permitting us to read this fascinating document will be forwarded to the Freddie Trueman Homes of Rest for Paralytic Opening Batsmen . . .

Dear Mum,

Sorry I haven't wrote for so long, but what with the other for one thing I've hardly had time to put pencil to paper. Thank you for the Koala bear colouring book. Also the Oxo cubes and woolly underwear. It was 92f here last week.

We are now in a town called Yorkshire where Captain Cook came to Botany Bay from. It's full of white abbo's who say things like 'Ey oop, laad, th's abaht t'get stoofed.' Mostly we give them the elbow.

They're very sneaky with it. Bradman always used to get 300 on this ground, so they started planting fungus and things in the pitch, which is why Australia have lost three Test matches here since the war.

What I'm trying to say is, by the time you get this, we might have lost another one.

Don't tell dad if we do. Coming on top of learning that the sentences aren't to run concurrently, he'd do his block. I know the Aussie papers won't print it if we do go down, but you know how rumour spreads.

Incidentally, if Gloreen's heard any rumours about *me* tell her it's all lies made up by the British Press. The whole country's so bored with the economic concussion and soccer fans stabbing one another that all they print is scandal and pictures of birds with big knockers.

Funny lot, the Poms. When we smashed them at Birmingham, they smiled and said things like 'Well, it's only a game, dear boy.' But it didn't stop them hiring a South African captain, a Belgian spin bowler, and some old bloke called Steele who looks as though he invented nuclear fishing.

Thank Sis for the picture postcard from Alice Springs. I know it's a long way from Sydney, but it's only right she disappeared in the circumstances. There are still some people who are very sensitive about that sort of thing and it might have affected the sales of my autobiography.

I still haven't met the bloke whose writing it, but he's calling it *Rain of Terror*. I don't know what that means but the publishers say it's brilliant.

Tell Sis I still haven't got Geoff Boycott's autograph, but we haven't seen much of him because the England selectors just won't pick him. He did try to attract their attention by running down the pitch during the Lord's Test, but it didn't do any good. At least, I think it was Boycott, but you couldn't be sure because he didn't have any clothes on.

Everybody laughed and said 'What jolly fun,' but if it had been an Aussie they'd have said he was adrianed.

The Poms are like that, e.g. the whole crowd went real quiet while I was writing part of this because it looked, ey oop, as if we was going to plaster the Belgian all over Yorkshire and win. I bet Dad would give up a year's parole for that.

Anyway, there's only one more Test to go so don't bother to send on any more food parcels.

If we lose this one and you do get to hear about it, bear in mind that all we were doing was upping the betting odds for the Oval match.

We were 1—5 with Ladbrokes for the Lord's Test and there doesn't seem much point winning if that's all you can make out of it. Obviously, we'd never bet on the Poms in case it got into the papers.

Well that's about all I can think of for now. Anyway, it's hard to concentrate here in the dressing room because everybody's banging their bats about over an lbw decision.

I didn't see it myself because I was looking up how to spell parole in the dictionary. This Test series has been a real education.

Your loving son,
Sgd. Terror Tomkins

‘It was a real shock to see that Englishmen are black’

London. — In response to incessant public demand *The Collected Letters of Terror Tomkins, Australian Fast Bowler*, are shortly to be published by Claptrap & McGhee (leatherbound 21 guineas, limp 35p). While awaiting this profound literary landmark we are privileged to reprint a document of equal significance: a reply to the great antipodean athlete, raconteur and essayist from his mother, Mrs Ada Tomkins. Reproduction is strictly forbidden.

87b, Whitlam's View,
Cronulla, N.S.W.

Dear Son,

I am writing this in Mr Robinson's because they came and took our telly away after Dad failed the identification parade. The Robinsons are real dinkum neighbours and they're only 73 miles up the road.

Also they've got a colour telly so we was able to sit up all night watching you stuffing the Poms at The Oval by saterlight. Mr Robinson got very wobbly and kept on shouting ‘Goodonyer, Terror’ and ‘That'll teach the bastards to dissolute the Empire.’

When those Poms had to follow-up, Mr Robinson got out the champagne but this time I was sensible and stuck to wine. Gloreen had to go outside a few times and I've told her she'll have to mend her ways if she's going to marry you and meet all them Indian Rajers and the Queen and things.

As you know colour telly is new here so it was a real shock, when the cameras went round the crowd, to see that Englishmen are black. ‘Why isn't the Queen black then?’ I said to Mr Robinson. ‘That's because she's Greek,’ he said. It's as good as going back to skool to spend a night with Mr Robinson.

By the way, I hope you got the money. Mr Robinson told me to send it to the London branch of the Bank of Bangladesh.

We was all very screwed up when Tony Greig dug up the Leeds pitch with a knife and fork. Well, that's what the Australian papers said happened. They said the Poms were trying to blame it on some naked bloke up a tree because they knew they'd get beat.

Funny thing was how all the Australian reporters seemed to be on holiday when we wasn't doing so well at Lord's. But this Oval Test is all over the front pages under headlines like *Tomkins Roasts Puny Poms* and *Greig's Gang Grovel Under Aussie Pace*. I'd send you some cuttings except that Mr Robinson only takes *The Sheep-grazer and Shearer's Quarterly.*

And also some Danish magazines without any words in them.

Anyway, you're very famous now and we're very proud. Mr Whitlam mentioned you in a party political broadcast the other night and said that if the whole population showed your spirit we'd all soon be back to the good old days of inflation.

What's gone wrong with the Poms? Mr Robinson says that due to the Welfare State over there they now get paid more to stand in a dole queue than bat for England. 'Where's the incentive?' he keeps saying, just like Dad on visiting days.

Myself, I think it's because the Poms eat all the wrong food. You've only got to look at that Greig and that Knott to know that they're half starved. Mr Robinson says they eat only snails and drink Noilly Prat now that they've gone European.

What happened to Amiss and Fletcher and Hampshire and Denness and Gooch? All down with food poisoning, I suppose. By the way, is Geoff Boycott still alive? No sooner do you get to remember some of the Poms than you never see them again. It's a bit like Dad really.

You'll be glad to know that our Shirl has been allowed back in skool after her little naughty. No harm done, touch wood, but of course she'll never be quite the same again. They grow up so quickly nowadays.

I'm only thankful the Pommie Press never got to hear about it because Mr Robinson says they can be very spiteful when England are losing. I even heard they'd been steaming open some of your letters to me and printing what you writ.

Well, the tour's nearly over now and I expect you'll be looking forward to some good, solid, home cooking and putting your feet up for a year or two. Gloreen's been working very hard at the slimming and is now nearly down to 16 stone. She's asked me to remind you about not stopping over in Bangkok on the way home, but I don't know what that means.

By the way, could you bring back about a dozen Cashmere sweaters? I don't normally like Pom things but Mr Robinson says they're made from good Aussie wool and only made up by Indians in Bradford.

Are there any Englishmen left in England? Mr Robinson says that, in the end, that's probably the whole thing that's gone wrong with their cricket.

Your loving mother,
Signed Mrs Tomkins.

ONE OF THE PLEASURES *down the years has been to work with Monty Fresco, Daily Mail photographer. Pictured left, chatting up an old friend, Fresco's Cockney—Jewish humour and resource have opened frontiers, let alone doors.*

A FRESCO—EYE VIEW *of John Curry, skater. "I dunno' about art," said Fresco, "but since there's a mirror on the wall I might as well use it." Curry was intrigued.*

UNDERSTANDABLY *Fresco's picture of Princess Anne at the opening ceremony of the Montreal Olympics won him awards throughout the world. It is the most beautiful off-beat sports picture I have ever seen. Rivals accused him of luck. It was the luck of a man*

who had the nerve to ignore the massive panoply of an Olympic opening ceremony and focus a 600-mm Nikon lens on a single face for more than an hour from a range of 180 yards. The picture was shot at 1/125th of a second at 5.6.

SURREPTITIOUSLY, *while President Dr Adi Amin Dada wasn't looking, Monty Fresco snapped this picture of the Ugandan Head of State's Guard of Honour during our visit to Semliki. The trumpeter demonstrated his loyalty by playing throughout much of Amin's impassioned speech to his peoples.*

‘There’s only one word for Pom sportwriters and that’s bleedin scorpions’

London. — The award of the Nobel Prize for Literature to Mr Terror Tomkins, Australian fast bowler, raconteur and belles lettrist, will surprise few Sportsmail readers since it was in these columns during the cricket season that the titanic array of his talent was first unveiled in an anthology of letters to his mother, Mrs Ada Bradman-Tomkins. ‘What sublimity,’ Mr Kenneth Tynan now writes in the current issue of *Signalman and Shunter*, ‘to have exhumed from the antipodes a talent so catholic that the man not only bowls like Henry Miller but writes like Keith Miller.’

Currently unwinding in his sixth-floor menage-a-treize in Sydney's Latin Quarter in preparation for the imminent Test series against West Indies, Mr Tomkins is still writing. His latest letter, published exclusively here, is in the nature of advice to Mr John Hipwell, captain of the Australian Wallabies Rugby Union team, which recently arrived in London for what most critics assume to be a 25-round boxing tour of Great Britain.

Dear John,

Please exkuse the handriting but my sekretry went off for a check-up and must be grabbin a sicky. Anyway, Mum said you'd phoned for some tips about how to root the Poms so here goes and I'll start by passing on some telephone numbers the boys might like.

The Earls Court ones are definitely okay but if a man's voice answers when you try the Hampstead one say it's Colin Cowdrey calling and ring off quick.

Not much has happened in Oz since you left except that they've given me this bleedin riting prize and now they want me to go to some place called Norway to pick up the Cup. It's in Russia, I think. Also Princess Margrit lobbed up. What a sheila. Said she wanted to go to the pictures so when those Melbourne gingers took her to an art gallery she pulled off her shoes and sat on the floor.

You'll find that in Britain. It's the old ones what have got the real spirit. The younger ones are too tired because they spend all their time beatin one another up in football grounds.

The old ones wear ties and still think they own us despite slaggin us off and going into the European Frenetic Community. When you arsk 'Why are so many Poms emirgrating to Australia then?' they say things like 'How else are we going to win the Ashes back.'

Beating the Poms is really all about gettin on their nerves first. Chew gum at cocktail parties, don't wear ties to banquets and always ask money for autographs. Mostly Poms are sensitive blokes who want to be liked so don't talk to them except in the scrums. Then say something like 'I hear they're fitting high-speed gas in your home today' and they'll start missing passes.

Naturally, being cricketers, we didn't meet many rugger people but they're much the same as the Lord's lot except that they wear second-hand clothes and frayed ties with crests instead of stripes. At Twickenham they always meet in the car-park first and after they've eaten one piece of game pie and drunk nine bottles of claret they pull on sheepskins and fall into their seats and shout things like 'Haw, haw, I thought REAL Orstralians was black.'

Afterwards they all go to Thames-side pubs, ask who won the match, pour half-pints of keg beer down one another's trousers and cut off their best friend's tie just below the knot with a nail-file. Then they drive home, give the baby sitter 50p and complain that the trades unions are holding the country to ransom.

Most of their wives are pretty randy because when it comes to handling wimmin the average British rugger man is still like Bulldog Drummond. But if you take my advice you'll play safe and ring the Earls Court numbers instead.

It's a bit different when you get up north because they talk German or something and leave their wives at home and only have cowheel pie on the menu and wear mayors' chains to be trendy.

Lancashire's okay, but only when compared with Yorkshire. Be very careful you don't mention Eddie Waring or Rugby League. Rugby League is like leprocy. Eddie's a real good bloke but the Rugby League people reckon he's brought the north into disrepute because he treats Australians like gents and only talks Latvian. Obviously you'll get lots of offers to turn pro but don't tell the Press. There's only one word for Pom sportwriters and that's bleedin scorpions.

Scotland I don't know about because cricket to them is like wot ballet is to Australia. They can't stand the English who pinched all their sheep and are now pinching their oil so you'll probably have a good time.

I also see from your itinerarily that you've got to play Wails. Well, that's the big one. They're Rugby crazy. Everyone gets so stoned on the morning of the match that the only way they can tell whether it's Saturday in Cardiff Arms Park or Sunday in chapel is to see whether the seats tip up or not. Even then they spend the whole match singing hymns in case they've got it wrong.

It's a bit like a Grand Final in Melbourne. Famous Welshers like Richard Burton and Tom Jones always come back to fall down a few valleys, see the big games and drink a few toasts to St David Lloyd George. When they lose a few usually drive into the outback and blow up a few electricity pythons.

The big difference you're going to find everywhere is that the Poms have got this snide way of saying that sport is only a game and may the best man win. Secretly they're training like kamikaze pilots and trying like hell. Poms is devious. Against us last summer they shaved all the grass off the wickets so we couldn't bowl fast.

Anyway, it gave me time to work on me riting and now the Australians are hailing me as the new F. Scott Hemingway. Can you find out if this Sobell Prize thing has got any money attached to it?

I gotter stop now because they want me to go out an knock down a few wild West Indians.

Yours in Aussie sport,
Terror Tomkins

P.S. Almost forgot to put in the Earls Court numbers. Try Gloreen first. She's a good sort. As a matter of fact, she probably won the Ashes.

If you like hotels you can actually live in you will enjoy the Palace in Madrid, the Windsor in Melbourne, the Plaza in Buenos Aires, the small Astor in Paris and, above all, the Algonquin, New York. The staff there never parrot banalities like 'Have a good day' on the strict assumption that you'd never planned to have anything else. There are many legendary tales about the Algonquin but my favourite concerns the businessman who simply said 'I've been staying in this hotel for 25 years, 17 of them waiting for the lift.' I only include this piece because it was written in a corner room high up in the Algonquin and reminds me of a good weekend in the friendliest of all newspaper towns with Dermot and Jane and Phillip and Allison. Also, I liked Chuck Wepner very much, even after he'd been duly flattened by Muhammad Ali.

'We shot the traffic lights but my whimpers were drowned by Sounds Elegant on Mr Wepner's stereo'

New York. — As a concession to the magnitude of his next fight, which happens to be against Muhammad Ali for the world heavyweight title, Mr Charles 'Chuck' Wepner has made a radical revision to his life-style.

He has switched from vodka to beer.

He savoured another mouthful of Miller's High Life straight from the bottle and philosophised that moderation in all things, particularly self-denial, is the secret of happiness. 'Even this stuff,' he said, 'can give you a bit of a lift.'

As he tilted the bottle with his right hand, Chuck Wepner was using his left to pilot his primrose-yellow Cadillac down the New Jersey Turnpike at just over 70. We shot a couple of traffic lights on very late orange, but my whimpers of anxiety were drowned by a multi-decibel track called *Sounds Elegant* on Mr Wepner's auto stereo.

'S'okay,' reassured the world title challenger, 'I know all the cops, I do a lot of stuff for their charities.'

Anyway, you wouldn't readily pick an argument with Wepner. Cast from a Hammer Productions mould, he stands 6ft. 5in., weighs 16 stone, has a nose which appears to have been remodelled by a vigorously swung baseball bat, eyebrows which have been rebuilt into cliff-overhangs by extensive plastic surgery, hands the size of batwing doors and an official fight record which diplomatically makes no mention of several bare-fist engagements in bars, all comprehensively won.

We were on our way to a TV show in New York City and were very late, mostly due to a longer-than-scheduled refreshment stop at Johnny D's Lounge back in Mr Wepner's native Bayonne.

On the show he was articulate and unabashed. He said he planned to become a woild heavyweight champeen in the Cleveland Coliseum on the night of March 24 by putting Muhammad Ali flat on his ass somewhere between rounds nine and thirteen.

Asked to justify so confident a prediction, Chuck said: 'Good living has caught up with that guy. He caint run no more. If he uses the ropes against me like he did with George Foreman, he's dead. Ropes is for hangin' people with.'

Asked whether accession to the world title would fundamentally change his mode of life Chuck leaned forward to see if he were being interviewed by a certifiable lunatic and said: 'Are you kidding?'

There is, indeed, much that Chuck Wepner, half-German, half-Polish, ex-U.S. Marine, grandson of a soldier in the Kaiser's Army, wants to change about his life. He wants a Rolls-Royce, a home with a garden for his second wife and new baby, and famous people to come up to him on the beach at Acapulco and say: 'Hi, Champ, howya doin'?'

At the moment, all that Muhammad Ali's next and carefully selected opponent has got is a £22-a-week rented apartment with a peeling front door which his wife has to help pay for working as a post office clerk.

The yellow Cadillac, he confesses, is to impress the 85 bartenders to whom he daily delivers cases of booze in the service of Majestic Wine and Spirits Inc. (motto: 'By Appointment to His Majesty the American Public'). This paid him more last year than he's ever made from a fight.

The worst thing of all is that he knows only too well that America hides its mirth when his name is mentioned. He's known as Superbum of the Month, Human Sacrifice and the Bayonne Bleeder, a reference to his proclivity for such reckless advance in the ring that his face tends to get cut to ribbons.

'Crap,' he said, 'all crap. I'm in there fighting Ali because I can beat the guy. I'm a roughhouse fighter of the type Ali don't like. Ever notice how he don't like havin' his face hit? That's what I'm after. I'm going in there to rearrange his features.'

What about the bleeding? 'That's crap, too,' he said. 'I've only been cut once in my last nine fights. I had a 1,500-dollar operation on my eyes. They took away all the scar tissue and sewed me up neat and strong.

'If anybody's going to get cut in there it's Ali because I know how to use the lace of the gloves.'

We had a final beer with the boys in Johnny D's and Chuck insisted on having his photograph taken with his arms round the neck of a black taxi driver — 'to prove I ain't prejudiced against spooks'. Then he said: 'He's the only spook we let in here. We've indicated to the others that they're not welcome, if you know what I mean. Otherwise they'd be dancin' with white women and that'd cause trouble.'

Chuck Wepner, the man upon whom fame has been thrust so suddenly, seemed unaware of the indiscretion. His opponent, apart from being heavyweight champion of the whole planet earth is Black America's most famous spokesman.

If he ever needed a motive for this highly-paid training fight he might just have found it against the man from the back of Bayonne.

There appears to have been a stage when football-watching became so intolerable that anything was preferable. I fear that this anti-soccer prejudice is evident in many of the pieces in this book. In fact I was brought up on the game and wrote about it, minimally three times weekly, for half a dozen years. Overnight, almost, I failed either to understand it or enjoy it any more. The great players were required to conform, genius was stifled by the system, the avoidance of defeat superceded the joy of winning. Style meant nothing. One may accuse Dublin and the Dublin Horse Show of many things but one can never suggest that it lacks style.

'More booze was shifted in Dublin last week than in Chicago during the whole of Prohibition'

Dublin. — Acting on the principle of why get yourself insulted at Wembley when you can enjoy yourself practically anywhere else, I skipped the Charity Shield and went to the Dublin Horse Show instead.

It was definitely the right decision. Horses are so much better mannered than footballers. So are their riders. Even Harvey Smith has got the message that the public are bored to absenteeism by V-signs and tantrums.

The other shibboleth that went for a burton was the belief that spectator hooliganism is invariably inspired by the demon drink.

More booze was shifted in Dublin at the back end of last week than was dispensed in the Chicago speakeasies during the whole of Prohibition.

There were men there to whom half a bottle of gin before breakfast was a mere aperitif. There were others who regarded a bottle of Scotch after dinner as almost total abstention.

Yet with 30,000 spectators passing through the palladian columns into the Royal Dublin Society's show grounds every day, there was not a single recorded incident of window-smashing, widow-bashing or insulting behaviour.

The only hard luck story I ran across in three days concerned a man who had received severe lacerations of the left leg while attempting to separate two quarrelling Alsations.

Pouring his tenth pre-lunch vodka into the same bloodstream as his recent anti-rabies injection, he actually said: 'Bejasus, I bought a horse from a woman in here last night for £500. I can't even remember who I made the cheque out to, what the woman looks like or where I am supposed to collect the horse.'

The jumping was brilliant. Apart from Bayi's stupendous run in breaking the human 1,500 metres record in New Zealand, I have seen nothing more thrilling this year than Britain's victory in the Aga Khan Challenge Trophy.

The Germans put such pressure on in hitting only one fence in six rounds that nothing short of complete perfection, achieved at high speed, could win the day when Peter Robeson entered the arena for the very last ride.

He was as composed as the Queen riding side-saddle to Horse Guards. He rode faultlessly round the relentless course and, when he cleared the last fence, his only acknowledgement of the huge strain he had been under was to give his mount a gentle slap on the neck. Nobody kissed him.

Ireland finished last, a position they now accept with fortitude since the horse is to the Irish economy what the motor car, until recently, was to the British. They breed them and sell them.

Most of the TV stars of the last decade, like Stroller, Mattie Brown, Ballywillwill, Mr Banbury, Manhattan, Buttevant Boy, Pennwood Forge Mill and Sportsman, were Irish-bred and are now jumping in foreign colours.

In fact the Dublin Horse Show is far more about trade than performance, which accounted for the gloom that enveloped a circle of twelve dealers, in from places like Galway and Cork, who stood up to their ankles in mud and cursed the approaching collapse of the world's monetary system.

'Hisself over there brought 12 animals and hasn't sold one of them,' said a man whose cheek-veins reminded one of a small-scale road map of a built-up area. 'The bottom will fall out of show jumping if this goes on.'

His colleagues squelched about in assent. They blame VAT. 'We sell a horse, say, for £400 and then the Customers and Exercises officer at the other end says "No, this horse is worth £1,000" and charges them £100 tax. How would a man in a bloody blue uniform with gold ribbon all over it know anything about horses?'

By common consent the man who knows more about horses than anyone else at the show is Ned 'Deal-a-Day' Cash, Sen., whose age is an Irish State secret. He's probably 65 and has never looked back since his first livestock deal at the age of 12 when he bought a donkey for ten bob, towed it for six miles and sold it for a pound the same day.

His rivals reckon that's been his average profit ratio ever since, though Ned modestly concedes to have been done down in four deals in roughly 16,000 in the past 50 years or so.

Ned doesn't stand around in the mud any more. The d'Inzeos and the Schockemohles come to him.

He'd been up dancing until 6.30 on Saturday morning but four hours later was looking a million dollars in the ring. Incidentally, he still can't read or write.

I had heard that the Dublin Horse Show was frightfully Tatler but is isn't at all. You'll meet guys there with accents like Bertie Wooster and faces that appear to have been polished by batmen, but after a few dozen crates of champagne it all calms down and nobody cares very much.

James Joyce got it right in *Finnegan's Wake* when he looked out of a bar window and noted among the crowds flooding to the Show shoeblacks and redshanks and plebeians, confusionaries and authorities, Noord Amrikaans and Suid Aferican cattleraiders.

They were all there again this year, riding and laughing, selling and drinking, buying and dancing, hatching engagements or discussing quite calmly last year's divorce.

Meanwhile at Wembley Messrs Bremner and Keegan were squabbling like urchins and tearing their shirts off as though renouncing white slavery for the rest of their days.

Maybe it would be just as well if they did. The Dublin Horse Show is only one of a thousand increasingly attractive sporting alternatives to paying to watch nonsense like that.

British sporting life has been much enriched over two decades by the mere existence of Mr Robert Lord, whose secondary hobby during this period has been banning successive generations of Daily Mail *sportswriters from the Press box at Burnley Football Ground. In fact, not to have been banished by Bob Lord is a disgrace not easily lived down in the newspaper trade since it implies mealy-mouthed sycophancy. I fear I have never been banned by Burnley, though it has not been for the want of trying. I attribute my survival to the fact that in the days when my bride-to-be attended football matches I once took her into the Burnley boardroom at the end of a match where she distinguished herself with the following remarks: "Who won?" and "What were those heavenly little sidesmen waving their flags for?"*

'Who is effectively known as The Butcher of Burnley?'

Burnley. — You could always tell a football director in the good old days by his waistcoat, his watch-chain, his bowler, his black Armstrong-Siddeley and his browbeaten wife.

Times have changed. Today's archetypal director has his hair blow-dried by Henri, his steak rare-to-blue at the Connaught, his wife brainwashed by *Which?* and *Nova* magazines, his Ferrari parked at an angle of 30 degrees to the pavement outside the Playboy Club and his boardroom stocked by Bollinger instead of Haig.

Mr Bob Lord spans both these generations of sporting administrators.

He is chairman of Burnley Football Club, which lies in a black valley between two even smaller Lancashire towns called Ramsbottom and Foulridge, and is by profession a butcher.

From time to time he confirms this by charging into china shops with a meat cleaver raised above his head. He did it again, metaphorically, at the weekend in a remarkable interview with Mr Karl Kershaw of the *Sunday People*.

Demonstrating once more that Britain remains the last bastion of really free speech, he laid about the new generation of soccer club directors with such vehemence that even his victims must be moved to admiration by the thoroughness of his attack.

Some 'hardly know the first thing about the game'. Others 'are just in it for the glory'. Still more 'are in it to make business contacts'.

In short, our national game is in the hands of a bunch of trendy amateurs whose most noble thought for its survival, let alone heritage, is to fill their boardrooms with cronies and curry favour with business associates by distributing largesse in the form of tip-up seats in the directors' box, half-time refreshments and such seasonal perks as free Cup Final tickets.

As one who last agreed with any of Mr Lord's major policy announcements in 1957, I do, of course, know what he's driving at.

All manner of people have latched on to soccer for all kinds of motives. Some have been millionaires in pursuit of publicity and New Year's Honours, others have done it because it's the only way to get TV crews rushing to their doors so that they can appear in tinted glasses and murmur 'No comment,' which rates a gold star in the suburban mouse-race.

The financial background of several would not bear intensive investigation and it is quite right that Mr Lord should have drawn this not unimportant matter to our attention.

However — a word which tends to crop up frequently whenever one feels like pouring approbation over Mr Lord's latest proclamation — one is forced to ask whether Your Average New Director is actually any worse for the game than Your Average Old Director?

There is a rich anthology of soccer and social gaffes committed by Old Directors and my favourite concerns the one who was entrusted to visit another club to complete the signing of a Very Important Player.

The fee was £30,000 (then no trivial sum) and he duly returned to his club to report that X had had an excellent game and that the whole deal was signed and sealed.

'Thanks very much' said his manager. 'X may have had an excellent game but you've just been and signed the wrong player.'

Another very famous Old Director distinguished himself almost as greatly in my own hearing. On an overseas soccer tour, at which he was an England selector, he was present at the meeting at which Y was dropped from the international team.

Four days and some 800 miles later England played well and won. 'I must say' declared the very famous Old Director that evening, 'that Y had a much better game today.'

What made it even more hilarious was that Y had been sitting not 20 yards from the selector throughout the whole of the match.

It was about this time, towards the end of the 50's, that the brilliant and irreverent Len Shackleton published his celebrated autobiography. What caused the sensation of the day, of course, was his much-discussed chapter headed 'What the average football director knows about football.'

The remainder of the page was left totally blank.

This is not to say that the unique Mr Lord is not fully entitled to question the competence of some of today's soccer directors. It is simply to suggest that it is surprising he has left it till now.

To be fair to Mr Lord, he came up with one practical suggestion which was that all prospective soccer directors from now on should be subjected to written examination to test their fitness to serve.

The appended questionnaire was found in a handbag on Paddington Station and there was some speculation in London last night about whether or not it was the genuine article.

ALL *questions* MUST *be answered. Time allowed: 15 seconds. Candidates with nine correct answers or fewer will be rejected. Particular attention should be paid to spelling.*

1. Who is effectively known as The Butcher of Burnley?
2. What is the most famous cricket ground in the world?
3. DROL (anagram)
4. What were the titles of the famous heroes who
   (a) won the Battle of Trafalgar.
   (b) led the Charge of the Light Brigade.
   (c) said 'Pray God no professional will ever captain England?'
5. What is the second word of the 23rd Psalm?
6. Insert the missing four-letter word: 'Praise the **** and pass the ammunition.'
7. To which institution was Mr George Brown elevated after his distinguished career in the Commons?
8. Which fearless football club chairman has banned more journalists from his ground than any other?
9. What was the sacrilegious codename given to the Allied invasion of Europe in 1944?
10. Who is unanimously regarded as the wisest, most perceptive most popular football administrator in the world?

Answers: 1. Bob Lord. 2. Lord's 3. Lord. 4. (a) Lord. (b) Lord. (c) Lord. 5. Lord. 6. Lord. 7. Lords 8. Bob Lord. 9. Overlord. 10. Bob Lord.

Those experienced in pugilistic matters did not deign to leave their offices in London to attend the most bizarre ring contest in recent years, the Tokio meeting between Muhammad Ali, boxer, and Antonio Inoki, wrestler. Apart from the curiosity interest I had some inexplicable presentiment that Ali was about to be seriously or even mortally injured. The presentiment proved to be wrong and those experienced in pugilistic matters right. For 15 rounds Inoki flung himself on the canvas and kept Ali at bay by kicking him behind the knees. This ludicrous exhibition was eventually declared a draw. The only compensation was spending a week in the Ali camp, an opportunity never to be missed.

'Ali always brings his handlers, his friends, his handlers' friends and his handlers' friends' kids. They total 51'

Tokio. — Riding downtown with the Muhammad Ali Cats was really good fun.

There was Angie, Quiet Jim, Bundini, Big Trev, Piranha Fred — so called because he once bit a piece of flesh the size of a filet mignon out of another man's shoulder — a dozen laughing, finger-snapping, gum-chewing black ladies, and two very pretty white girls with Press Photographer badges and no cameras.

There was also Mr Gene LeBell, but we'll come to him later.

Angie, of course, is Angelo Dundee, Ali's trainer since he turned professional in 1960. Quiet Jim is Jimmy Ellis, formerly world heavyweight champion, now Ali's senior sparring partner and conceivably the most modest chap ever to make it to the top.

Big Trev is another sparring partner, coincidentally built exactly in the shape of a punch bag.

Bundini's real name is Drew Brown. You've probably seen him in Ali's corner. He has a face like Stan Laurel, only black, which registers absolute anguish when Ali gets hit, absolute joy when Ali hits anybody and absolute ecstasy when Ali wins.

Ali fires him, absolutely, every fight and always re-engages him within the hour.

Piranha Fred, a newcomer to the entourage, is actually Fred Blassie, an ageing American professional wrestler who used to have the eccentric habit of fitting needle-sharp caps to his incisors to facilitate biting lumps off his opponent.

Mr Blassie is along in a consultancy capacity due to certain unusual aspects about Muhammad Ali's Saturday morning fight with Antonio Inoki of Japan.

Some of the black ladies I know to be the lawfully wedded wives of some of the above and there were others to whom I have never been formally introduced.

Anyway, they filled the morning with joyous decibels as did the two girl photographers, despite looking utterly blank when I inquired whether F11 at 1/125th would be suitable since the day was slightly overcast.

Thus we rode from Ali's hotel, where his suite is costing him £240 a day, down to Tokio's Central Gym, which is five floors above a meat shop and measures a cricket pitch by a Wimbledon baseline. The great man had gone ahead, of course, in a limousine, but times are as hard in Tokio as anywhere else and the rest of us had to follow in a bus driven by a gentleman seemingly intent on making the record books as Japan's only two-time kamikaze hero.

Ali always brings his handlers, his friends, his handlers' friends and his handlers' friends' kids along on these junkets — they total 51 here — so the man who stood out on the journey downtown was the previously mentioned, but until now unexplained, Mr Gene LeBell.

Mr LeBell you have met all over the place.

You have met him refereeing at Wembley, presiding over rate tribunals, umpiring at Lord's, chairing licensing magistrates, line-judging at Wimbledon, running courts martial, touch-judging at Twickenham, adjudicating over 'marrow of the year' at village fetes and insisting, in a frenetic off-hand sort of way, that you spell his name right.

'It's a bit complicated,' said Mr LeBell. 'The Gene is spelt with a *G*, you see, and after the Le in the surname the next *b* is a capital. Now, do you think you can get that right? Anyway, I'd be obliged if you'd airmail a copy of your newspaper to the following address . . .'

Mr Gene LeBell then gave me the address of an extremely well-known sporting location in Los Angeles, at which his mother was a boxing promoter and his brother a wrestling promoter, and proceeded to explain that Muhammad Ali is the greatest boxer in the world, Antonio Inoki is the greatest wrestler in the Orient, and therefore, etc, etc. . .

Though patient to a fault, I would have found these excruciating exchanges terminally boring were it not for one fact.

Gene LeBell is to referee the bizarre £6 million encounter between boxer Ali and wrestler Inoki in the Tokio Budokan.

Obviously one does not question Mr LeBell's assertion that it's more than his reputation is worth to get up to any monkey tricks. All one *would* question is his wisdom in staying in the same hotel, eating in the same restaurants, and travelling in the same community transport as the Ali caravan.

In short, why identify so closely with only one half of a promotion which, while being the most lucrative fight since Cain and Abel started it all, is also provoking scepticism on such a scale that many people are going round openly saying it is bent?

'Look,' said Gene LeBell, 'people say that about nearly every fight. What I'm saying is that I won't put up with any nonsense. For instance, look at Ali now. He's covered all over in grease. There won't be any of that when he gets in the ring on Saturday.'

Another acid test of a big televised fight is whether, even if there's a vast disparity between the quality of the fighters, it is kept going at all costs so that television companies all over the world can clip in the highly remunerative commercials between rounds.

'That doesn't concern me at all,' said Saturday's referee. 'For all I know it will be over in 30 seconds flat.'

Oddly enough, I believe him implicitly. I merely look forward to this baroque promotion with a combination of nausea, fascination and some alarm because without Muhammad Ali the world, these past dozen years, would have been a much smaller place.

And I am not convinced, despite all the money at stake, that his heart's really in it.

Riding downtown with the Ali Cats might have been fun but watching Ali work out was quite embarrassing.

You never know with this man. He is moody. Quixotic. But for two days now he has given me the impression he would call the whole thing off if he decently could.

As for Inoki, I can tell you nothing more than the bare biographical details that he's the same height, a little heavier and one year younger than Ali, and is married to a Japanese film actress.

'No,' said his manager, 'he's giving no interviews and you can't watch him train.'

It's all a very inscrutable business but at least there was one busload of people yesterday having another hell of a time on Muhammad Ali's meal tickets.

There are three explanations for the following column: an enjoyable party, a blank mind the next morning and being employed by a newspaper which is generous enough to print what you write.

'In a flash we sports riters knew this was a statement from one of the world's foremost interlectuals'

London. — It's not very often us sports riters get invited to interlectual parties because of falling down drunk and that.

Also just when we're explaining Bertie Mee's deployment of the pivotal back-four everybody says things like 'How utterly beguiling' and starts walking away.

So it just goes to show wot a good bloke Mr William Davis, the very famous editor of *Punch* is. 'Come in, chaps,' he shouts as he sees us stubbing out our fags on the doorpost, 'there's plenty of booze.' It's no wonder you sometimes see lorry drivers reading *Punch*.

You could tell it was a very important party because there was only champain and canopies and everybody kept asking whether Michael Parkinson had turned up yet.

Anyway they started without him and there were enough other famous personalities to make up for the disappointment. There was Miss Joan Bakewell who looked much taller than she does on the telly because she was standing up, and Mr A. Coren, the famous funny riter who invented President Amin.

There was Miss Judith Chalmers, who is just as warm and friendly as like what she sounds on the radio. She had this big bloke with her. 'Get rid of him and we'll show you a good time after,' we suggested, but she said 'Well, that's my husband' and sure enough it turned out to be Mr Neil Durden-Smith, the very famous commentator and grand prix milk-float driver.

Also present in sunglasses although it was already lighting-up time was Mr Nigel Dempster, the very famous *Daily Mail* column socialist. 'Good God,' he cries, 'what are they doing letting sports riters in?' He seemed very angry.

Fortunately Mr Davis, the very famous editor of *Punch*, was much more congenital. Suddenly, about an hour after they had broke into the reserve stocks of champain, he shouts 'Gather round, chaps' to show us he'd read all the obituries of Monty.

What with all the champain and his long words we couldn't make sense out of most of what he was talking about and unfortunately Miss Joan Bakewell couldn't explain because she had slipped away just before the speeches. I expect she was going off to interview Alex Solzernitsin or some other famous profit.

It conspired that what Mr Davis was on about was some cartoon competition wot his magerzine is running in confliction with the Montreal Olympic Games. 'Wot I want,' he said, 'is about ten million cartoons from lorry drivers and that,' or words to that effect.

Suddenly and without notice he says: 'That is defnitly what sport needs. What sport defnitly needs more of is culture' and in a blinding flash we sports riters knew that this was no mere social function but a definite policy statement from one of the world's foremost interlectuals.

'Ferinstance,' he exclaims, 'there oughter be art competitions and that and proper music at the Olympic Games so that people like me and my interlectual friends can understand what's going on like.'

Mr Davis, speaking without any notes whatsoever, became very intense about this and you could tell that he was going to use his very famous magerzine to get this culture thing off the ground.

Well, us sports riters present began looking at one another and feeling a bit uncomfortable because of all the free champain we'd drunk. We didn't have the heart to tell him and his very famous friends that they were 2,500 years too late.

Rite from the time the Olympics started in the olden days in Greece they've always had picture-shows and concerts and poetry competitions etc so that the athletes had something to listen to or look at when they was knackered in the evenings.

In fact when the Olympics were restarted in the 1890s it became a rule that any city which puts on the Games has got to promise to cater for people who can't stand the smell of sweat and embrocation. Naturally the Berlin Philharmonic don't get reported because we're usually watching the boxing.

But it really was funny that *Punch* didn't seem to have heard of this. In fact, if they'd looked the records up, they'd have seen that Britain has won almost as many gold medals for Olympic art competitions as they have for running and throwing things.

Mr William Nicholson won one in 1928, Mr John Hughes got one in 1932 and Mr Alfred R. Thomson kept the flag flying in the field of painting and graphic art as recent as 1948.

Anyway, we wish *Punch* and its very famous editor all the best with their drawing competition.

It's a smashing idea and the fact that at the Montreal Olympics it will clash with a Picasso Exhibition should not put them off at all.

For me the second best sensation on earth is getting into an airplane and going somewhere. Almost anywhere, with the exceptions of Uganda and South Africa. I would quite enjoy a protracted stay in New York, I hope to continue going back to Australia as long as our two countries continue to play cricket against one another and, if forced to live abroad, I would like to commute between Crookhaven, a tiny village in the bottom left-hand corner of Ireland, and Madrid. This is because each contains friends with identical interests. Curiously enough I really want to live nowhere except England which, despite certain exasperations, still has a tolerance and an instinctive understanding of personal freedom which I have not found equalled anywhere else. The next two pieces, vaguely connected with two of our annual sporting events, may obliquely explain why.

'He was in deep mourning for his pet falcon which keeled over very dead the week before last'

Putney. — Tomorrow fortnight — which by utter coincidence is All Fools Day — there will be enacted on a snaking reach of the River Thames an ancient initiation rite every bit as sadistic as those dreamed up by the Sioux to turn their sons into card-holding braves.

Over the four miles 374 yards from a pub in Putney to a brewery in Mortlake 16 husky young men, goaded on by a couple of carping midgets, will strain their muscles, blood vessels and lungs beyond all reasonable limits to win a prize of less intrinsic value than a packet of Woodbines.

It is a supreme contest and no end of a spectacle and it grieves me deeply to have to ask: whatever happened to the Boat Race?

In the days of my youth the banks of the Thames were crammed with hundreds of thousands of spectators cheering as though they'd been to both Seats of Learning when, in fact, they had no association with either.

It was all over in a flash. Two arrow-shaped cockleshells, weighed down to the outriggers by men with five initials, hyphened surnames, clipped accents and the aesthetic features of Rupert Brooke, streaked under Hammersmith Bridge and were gone. All you had done was glimpse the hybrid blooms of Young British Manhood but, year in year out, the world stopped for the Boat Race.

Not much will stop tomorrow fortnight. Not even the traffic over Hammersmith Bridge.

'The reason, I suspect,' said M. J. S. Allen (Downside and Exeter), who is reading Turkish and Arabic at Oxford in preparation for a discreet career at the Foreign Office, 'is the whole of the "student thing". For one thing I don't think that students have the sympathy of the public any longer and, for another, there are now so many universities that almost everybody has been to one.

'To be honest, the Boat Race is now a private war between Oxford and Cambridge.'

It was a surprisingly soft-sell from a man who, in addition to being cox of the Isis crew, has been appointed to handle Oxford's publicity.

Press officers tend to be high-pressure men with machine-gun vocabularies, trendy suits and elastic facts. Mark Allen, with whom I spent an extremely civilised hour in the lounge of the London Rowing Club at Putney, does not quite fit the bill.

He wore neither socks nor shoes, could not even remember his own phone number and was in deep mourning for his pet falcon which keeled over very dead the week before last.

'It was not,' he explained 'an indigenous falcon. It was a Damascus falcon and I'm inclined to believe it succumbed to the cold humidity of the English winter. It was an extremely well-mannered falcon and I'm very sorry about it indeed.'

This wasn't getting us very far about the Boat Race so I asked the Oxford Press officer about the deep emotions aroused by competing in an event whose traditions reach back to the reign of George IV.

'Ah, well,' said Mr Allen in the kind of voice that Harold Macmillan might use to describe a disappointing crop of tea roses, 'it is not necessarily the highest standard of rowing and such glory as there is in competing in it is, quite naturally, ephemeral.' Mr Allen is 21.

In an attempt to attract the attention of the popular Press Mr Allen is part-author of a handout.

It lists, among other data, the relaxations of some of the crew: K. Bolshaw (Christ Church), *bus routes and Plasticine;* S. D. Hunt (Keble), *young ladies and photography;* P. J. Marsden (Lincoln), *witchcraft;* E Yalouris (Merton), *chess and Bacchanalia;* the Hon. P. D. E. M. Moncreiffe (Christ Church), *rustic pursuits;* A. R. Nairne (University), *painting pebbles and needlework.*

'How many of these hobbies are genuine?' I asked.

'Forty per cent.,' he replied, 'are totally facetious. The two Presidents phoned one another and decided we really ought to do something about getting publicity.'

Honesty could well be Mark Allen's downfall. As a Press officer he should make a good ambassador.

The simple truth is, of course, that apart from hoping to raise a few extra pounds to defray the staggering expenses of this annual aquatic pilgrimage, the Boat Race crews don't really give a damn whether anyone watches them or not.

So, what DID happen to the Boat Race?

Nothing. The Boat Race is what it always was. It's you, me and the world that's altered.

'Even the Royals made a point of standing to show they were clapping'

Wimbledon. — Students of the British character had a field day at Wimbledon yesterday. Our Way of Life was being threatened and it really did feel like 1940 over again.

We were all there, of course, in a show of solidarity. Group-Captain and Mrs Biggles, Brigadier and Mrs Bulldog Drummond, Lady Metroland and paramour, the executors of the late Rudyard Kipling.

Their conversations, outside the champagne-and-strawberries tent echoed exactly a very real letter which appeared in last Saturday's *Times* from Prebendary G. Hodgshon, of Exeter, whose reaction to the great tennis row was such that I take for granted his permission to repeat it here:

'Sir,' he wrote. 'When taking my wife her morning cup of tea I also took the news that 69, or some such number, of the professionals had announced a boycott of Wimbledon. Her immediate comment was "Oh, good!"'

So it was at Wimbledon yesterday. Large men with nicknames straight out of 'Angels One-Five' were saying things like 'Greater than ever this year' and 'Perhaps we'll now see what *real* championships look like.'

At 1.58 pm precisely it really got emotional as Hans-Joachim Plotz, from Hanover, and Ilie Nastase, from Bucharest, came through the corridor on to the Centre Court to set the tournament in motion.

Plotz was so blond and bronzed that he looked as if he'd just stepped out of one of Miss Riefenstahl's documentaries. Nastase had the sort of haircut you associate with wandering medieval minstrels.

I don't suppose a couple of such obvious foreigners have ever received such a reception in any

British sports arena. Before they'd hit a single shot in their knock-up they got an ovation which would have drowned anything you hear at the last night of the Proms.

Even the Royals, the Duke and Duchess of Kent, made a point of standing to show they were clapping.

But that, naturally, was nothing compared with what happened at 5.11 pm when Roger Taylor made his entrance. He had that grim, determined look you see on the faces of all picket-line breakers on TV.

This time roars reinforced the applause and the Duke of Kent even clapped vigorously with his hands in front of his face in case anyone should have missed seeing where his sympathies lay at 1.58.

There was, incidentally, one other touch of organisational genius. They always recruit Service personnel to act as stewards at Wimbledon and the uniformed lady who showed the world's sportswriters to their seats in the Press box was a rating in the Wrens. Her hatband revealed that she came from HMS Dauntless.

As a display of British stiff upper-lip I can recall nothing like it since the Hun put a stick of incendiaries straight up the High Street of my tiny home town. It wasn't chauvinism this time but total loyalty to the proposition that Wimbledon won't, and never will, bow before blackmail.

That is admirable. It is a principle damned nearly worth dying for. The real tragedy at Wimbledon yesterday, behind all the brave faces and the bogus bonhomie, was that this year's men's championships are as good as dead anyway.

I fear you need powers of self-deception greater than mine to kid yourself you are watching anything other than a brilliantly organised, marvellously staged and totally irrelevant festival of male tennis.

Last year's championships, with John Newcombe sitting it out as a political prisoner, were bad enough. This year's, without virtually anyone who's anyone, will be the beginning of the end if the present uncompromising attitudes are maintained.

The simple, distasteful, disenchanting fact is that the players now hold every ace in the argument.

Sheer resilience of spirit and a blazing June sun held Wimbledon together through its darkest hour yesterday but the moment must come when even the Biggleses and the Drummonds raise an eyebrow at one another in some quiet corner and admit that you cannot hoax all of the people all of the time.

Wimbledon, as we know and love it, cannot survive such pressure.

It will either have to acknowledge that tennis is now all about cheques and not titles or suffer the fate of so many of the great British institutions which felt that their traditions alone guaranteed survival.

The subsequent two columns were meant to be less about golf than contrasting national attitudes to playing games for recreation. The second one, written in the Keio Plaza Hotel in Tokio, reflects all too accurately the mood of a reporter who suddenly finds himself a long way from home with a kidney stone on the march. I fear I probably did my hosts less than justice.

'Being a priest I have time to play golf. All I miss is a girl to go home to'

Mullingar, Ireland. — The headline in the *Irish Independent* was full of promise. 'Archbishop Shot Behind Irish Pair' it proclaimed, so we flew to Dublin and then drove 53 miles west to inspect the eminent blood stains.

What, in fact, we were witness to was the quickest resurrection in ecclesiastical history. 'Hello,' said the Most Rev. Dr John Murphy, Roman Catholic Archbishop of Cardiff, 'I'll have a Guinness.'

The large mauve stone in the ring on the third finger of his right hand glittered brilliantly as he raised the pint glass. For a man of 69 he looked incredibly fit. 'I have never felt better,' he confirmed, 'but I appreciate your concern.'

The explanation for English readers — none being required in Ireland where the improbable is taken for granted — is that His Grace is one of the 70 men of God from all over Britain who have been competing this week in the first ever International Clergy Golf Tournament.

Far from being a calamity his first-round 89, which left him one stroke behind an Irish pair, was an outstanding achievement.

Mullingar's 6,291-yard par-72 course is a tough test for the occasional golfer on a still summer's day, but when a force-six gale is hurling in rain from the Atlantic you really do need some supreme power looking after your interests.

It was in these conditions that Father Anthony Pierce fired successive rounds of 71, 72 and 76 to prove himself the best clerical golfer in Britain and Ireland.

But more of that in a moment. There's more to 70 golfing priests being gathered together than golf. I refer, perhaps indiscreetly, to the £300 which changed hands in a poker school last night and the élan with which four men of the cloth cleaned out the bookies on the last two races at Mullingar dogs the night before that.

It's been quite a week in darkest County Westmeath, and our thanks are due to *The Universe* newspaper for organising this junket and the splendid B. & I. shipping line for sponsoring a unique insight into priests at play.

As a high handicap non-Catholic golfer, I was particularly interested to observe the effect of morning prayers on their game. Each competitor said Mass on his way to the course, the early starters in the Cathedral and the late starters at a nearby convent where the nuns laid on tea.

The only conclusion I could come to was that such inspiration as it gave them was directly in inverse ratio to their rank in the church.

For example, an interesting conversation took place yesterday at the point where the first tee and the ninth green meet.

'Good afternoon, Monsignor,' said Archbishop Murphy, addressing John O'Mahony, now of St Edward's, Scarborough, but once senior Catholic chaplain to the whole British Army. 'How are you going?'

'Not all that well, Your Grace,' replied the Monsignor. 'The light of consistency steadfastly fails to shine upon me.' He was seven over par for the front nine, which put him right out of the hunt, and proceeded to cut his drive down the tenth into the long grass at the foot of a chestnut tree.

Nor did Archbishop Murphy's own game quite match up to his scintillating form of the previous day.

He kindly invited me 'to play a few holes'. This turned out to be a blood match of over three hours which I have to confess to winning when the Archbishop three-putted the 17th green and said: 'I knew I should have gone fishing.'

Meanwhile parish priests were hitting huge drives, rifling marvellous iron shots and sinking phenomenal putts all over the course. The standard of play, to the likes of me, was depressingly high.

But even in this class Father Tony Pierce was out on his own. He's 34, teaches maths and Latin at St Peter's, Wexford, took up golf seriously at 18 and was down to two-handicap by the time he was 20. Now he's scratch and plays to it more often than not.

He's extremely handsome, has a beautiful swing and dresses on course as trendily as Johnny Miller. 'Don't you ever regret,' I asked, 'that with all that talent you didn't take up professional golf instead of going into the priesthood?'

'Not at all,' he said, 'the gulf between the very highest class of amateur golf and even the middle ranks of professional golf is unbridgeable. The professionals would simply eat us every time. If Neil Coles had been playing here you could have handicapped him off plus-five and he would still have murdered the lot of us.'

Then Father Pierce, unprompted, said a curious thing. 'I have a very happy life. Being a priest at a school instead of a priest in a parish, I have a lot of time to play golf. All I miss is a girl to go home to.'

The night became noisier.

The glasses piled up on the tables. Someone suggested a game of cards and in a corner a priest in mufti, almost vertical, sang two verses of Kevin Barry. It was the usual end to every amateur golf tournament everywhere.

'Why is it,' I asked the Very Reverend Joseph Kilmartin, who is 75 and has been playing the game for 60 years, 'that so many priests are such accomplished players?'

He answered: 'Golf might not get you very far in the Church, but it will keep you in the Church. It will keep your mind off other things.'

In Ireland the explanations always confound you.

'Japanese now talk golf like the Greeks talk politics and the Italians sex'

Tokio. — When our old buddy the Emperor Hirohito came to the welcome conclusion that he wasn't exactly God, it left an awful lot of Japanese up the creek without a religion.

This was a pretty unhealthy blow for a nation which does neither its loving not its hating by halves so I feel sure you will join me in giving thanks for the new faith Japan has embraced with total fanaticism. Scottish in origin, adopted by the Americans as a profession, messed around with by the English as an excuse for a long walk followed by ten gin-and-tonics it is, of course, golf.

I hardly joke. In one weekend's golf in Tokio I have seen the fun business of banging a ball into a hole accorded all the ritual of High Catholicism and the kind of intense devotion demanded by Islam. Also I have shelled out enough money to have bought a life subscription to the Mormon Church, which doesn't come cheap.

Times being what they are we headed 17 miles out of the city centre to Tokio's Icu Golf Club which, compared with some, has the social status of the Scunthorpe Screwmakers and Allied Trades Darts and Skittles Society. It was an inspired choice.

Our green fee for 18 holes was a mere £15.20, including hire of trolley, and we hustled round the course in a shade under 5¼ hours, which is the Japanese golfing equivalent of the four-minute mile.

It was worth every yen of it to have witnessed one solemn moment of Oriental golf lore.

Behind us, down the par five, 580-yard third, came four archetypal club members, which is to say they could all have looked Ronnie Corbett straight in the eye, and were playing such an eccentric game that they might just have well been dragging their clubs and hitting the ball with their trolleys.

Unabashed by the audience still waiting to drive off at the fourth, one of their company earnestly prodded the air with a pencil as he checked his score for the hole. It would appear to have been 12 to the green for he certainly took five putts and religiously endorsed a 17 on his scorecard.

With only 15 holes to go he was already 23 over par but, from the eagerness with which he allowed me to see his card, he must have been heading for a personal course record. On the other hand he may have been demonstrating that the only way to get your money's worth here is to hit the ball as often as possible.

Logic, anyway, does not survive the *non sequitur* that one million of Japan's three million golfers have never set foot on a golf course.

The explanation is that the Japs are already so thick on the ground (there are 11,607,790 just in Tokio who literally employ human shoehorns known as 'shovers' to squeeze them into the tube trains at rush hour) that there is no land left to lay out new links.

Hence the phenomenon of the golf-driving range, of which there are almost 500 in Tokio. They extend from wire hutches on the roofs of tall buildings to the Shiba Park Range which is built on a cemetery, has three tiers, can accommodate 155 golfers hitting but mostly mis-hitting balls simultaneously, is fully booked from 6 a.m. to 11 p.m. 365 days a year and must come as close to defining sporting onanism as anything ever has.

Dressed like Johnny Miller, equipped like Jack Nicklaus and as engrossed in dreamland glory as Walter Mitty, these horseless cowboys of the range fire hook after slice into a target area as big as Trafalgar Square quite content and probably relieved that they will never be called upon to apply the pure science of hitting a golf ball to anything so tawdry as whacking a 7-iron out of a muddy divot mark.

To you and me it's a fall-about spectacle but here where club golf is prohibitively expensive for all but those with handsome salaries or unchallenged expense accounts, it is of no importance.

To be associated with the new religion whether as range disciple or club apostle is everything. The ranks are growing daily and the golf industry's profits leap by the minute.

The Icu Club, with its Sahara-coloured fairways and hand-pulled trolleys, is still fairly big deal. To get into a really fashionable club you need little more than to be personally proposed by the prime minister and raise an entry fee of around £60,000. This would not include your annual dues and green fees.

Socially, as everywhere, you are rated less by the length of your drive than the depth of your cheque-book. You can get an excellent graphite-shaft driver for £168 and a really good set of irons for as cheaply as £1,300.

With all that loot invested it stands to reason that you don't dash in, rip off 13 holes and dash out again.

Our match was preceeded by the ritualistic discharge of 50 balls on the practice grounds, suspended for the obligatory meal after nine holes and extended a further hour by soaping oneself in preparation for the communal bath in near-boiling water during which politeness demands that you listen to your opponent recounting all 114 shots of his dreary round.

Japanese now talk golf like the Greeks talk politics and the Italians sex.

After bathing and a couple of drinks your Jap host is quite likely to drive to a golf range for an hour's practice and then go home to watch golf on television. On Sunday night there were nine separate golf programmes on six Tokio TV channels. Then, after an hour or two with the golf magazines and a chapter of a golf instruction manual he might go to bed to dream about a hole in one.

If it rains he can go to an electronic golf academy where he can drive balls off a mat into a screen showing film of the world's famous course.

If he lives another year or two he can drive two hours out of Tokio to what must be the most absurd golfing project yet. In the prefecture of Tochigi a Mr Zenya Hamava is building a club house and course which purport to be exact replicas of those at St Andrews in Scotland.

The curious thing is that 43 hours in Tokio have almost cured me of an incipient madness for golf.

There can be few more ridiculous figures than the man who takes infinite pains over something for which he has wild enthusiasm and no talent, and that, by the minute, is what you see here.

If only they would laugh, or play drunk, or tear up their cards, or wear filthy clothes, or get round in a frivolous three hours it would all be closer to the only conceivable motive the average no-hoper has for playing the game.

But that is not the way of new religions since there's no faith so strong as that of the convert.

After consultations with an out-of-date diary I suspect the following column was written at around that fascinating period of sporting history when Sir Alf Ramsey ceased to be England soccer manager and was replaced by Mr Don Revie.

‘The sherry decanter contained a pale liquid which burned five large holes in the carpet’

London. — My dramatic global search ended in brilliant success late last night when the door creaked open and I became the first British reporter to set eyes on the short, stocky figure who disappeared nine days ago.

He was holding a storm lantern and wearing Paisley pyjamas and a mobile frown.

In that moment in this picture-postcard Suffolk suburb I knew my sleepless quest was over.

‘Sir Alf . . . ?’ I suggested.

‘Hit is I,’ he replied. The voice was flat, resigned. I produced my credentials and a bottle of duty-free gin. ‘Enter,’ he said.

My glance fell on a copy of *Teach Yourself Sheep Shearing* lying open at page seven on the scrubbed-wood table. ‘Surely you're not . . . ?’ I began. ‘Probably,’ he answered, ‘they're so infinitely preferable to members of the human race.’

Exile had not impaired his dignity. He dusted cottage-loaf crumbs from a chair and came straight to business.

He said: ‘My old nanny, McDougal, had this wonderful philosophy. “Alfred,” she used to say— it was before my knighthood, of course — “Alfred, never apologise, never explain.”

‘She was not to know, rest her soul, what my memoirs would be worth one day. Let us not beat about the hedge. I have already rejected offers of £15,000 and £20,000.’ I took the hint and signed a cheque for £25,000.

It is a story of intrigue, pride and treachery.

Sir Alf Ramsbottom, 56, for 11 years manager-supreme of England's volleyball team, knighted by his monarch in 1966 for winning the coveted Entwistle Trophy for Britain, walked up the 86 stairs to his green-carpeted third-floor office in Lorenzo Mews, Shepherd's Market, at 10.38 on Tuesday morning of last week. He was whistling the opening bars of Beethoven's Eroica Symphony in the unusual key of F.

He removed his 48-guinea off-the-peg blue Harris tweed sports jacket by Simpson's of Piccadilly and placed it in the larchwood Danish-designed office tallboy from Heal's of Tottenham Court Road.

It was only then that he noticed the dead parrot in his in-tray.

'Why has that not been placed in the out-tray?' he thought to himself. Then he discovered certain other surprising aspects about the normally Spartan-neat office known throughout sport as the engine-room of world volleyball.

Fifty yards of barbed-wire had been wound round his chromium swivel chair. The desk drawers had been sealed with candle-wax. The sherry decanter now contained a pale liquid which, when spilled on the floor, burned five large holes in the wall-to-wall carpet.

The wall-safe was sagging open and all 17 books of Green Shield Stamps, meticulously saved to procure volleyballs for the 1978 assault on the Entwistle Cup, were gone.

'Most definitely,' recalled Sir Alf to me exclusively late last night, 'I began to suspect something. Indeed, I would go so far as to say that you could have knocked me down with a bleedin' feather. It was the first intimation I had ever received that I might be less than universally revered.'

By 10.43 on that crucial Tuesday morning Sir Alf was beginning to feel that the plot could have been laid *within* the walls of the Volleyball Association itself.

He thought fast and decided to go to lunch.

Over the first course, a 30p avocado with prawns served by 29-year-old Portuguese waiter Costa da Santos in a taverna 72 yards from Moss Bros., it occurred to him what had happened.

'I know who is behind this,' he said to himself. 'It is Machiavellian 86-year-old classic scholar and non-ferrous comptometer research scientist Buffer Bardsley, who has been honoured by many foreign governments and decorated by his monarch for his service as assistant to none other than Dr Barnes Wallis between 1942 and 1945. Yes, that's who it is.'

The end of Ramsbottom's originally nine-inch Romeo y Julieta cigar glowed red as he drew contemplatively upon it and continued to tell me exclusively:

'I never name names but I'm damned sure it was this Bardsley chap who got me the chop.'

For 27 minutes the hideout was filled with the sound of post office nib scratching on a sheet of sea-blue Basildon Bond as Ramsbottom noted down the name of his enemy in case he should forget it again. Somewhere out in the black, reporterless night an owl hooted.

Sir Alf laid aside his pen with a sigh. 'It has happened to greater men than I,' he said, modestly.

'T.E. Lawrence of Arabia, author of the *Nine Pillars of Wisdom* was so badly treated by Britain that he changed his name to Bernard Shaw.

Churchill himself was reviled after his election campaign in Gallipoli. But, of course, *they'd* never won the Entwistle Cup.'

It is this kind of deep, psychological self-analysis, The Anatomy of Removal from Office, that convinced me I was getting full value for our £25,000.

As the first salmon-pink tinges of another flawless dawn rose above the roof of the nearby brewery the one-time Czar of volleyball said:

'Our failure to beat Estonia in the big one in the emotion-filled bowl that was Wembley Stadium was probably the thing that finally stuffed me. Buffer Bardsley was just waiting for that.'

The Solshenitsyn of Sport took up his pen again. I knew he was getting the hang of things.

The second instalment should be an absolute riot.

ITEM: Those who travelled on the 1962-3 MCC cricket tour to Australia have fond memories of the late Duke of Norfolk, then Earl Marshal of England. Dining with us one evening in the middle of the Indian Ocean he warmed to the natural friendliness of all sportswriters and suddenly announced: "Look, I want no formality on this trip. You may call me 'sir'." Apparently the mellowing process had begun.

'Mr Thomas, it seems, didn't take an instant shine to the Duke'

The secret life of the grand old Duke of Norfolk, Earl Marshal and sportsman, was getting an airing up on Merseyside last week.

It came in the *Liverpool Post*, which was running a series of Behind-the-Battlement articles by George Thomas, ex-Secretary of State for Wales, about the investiture of their Prince.

Mr Thomas, it seems, didn't take an instant shine to the duke.

'He kept me standing up while he went on reading a paper,' he wrote. 'Then he said: "I am going to call you George and you will call me Bernard." It was a command.'

I can assure Mr Thomas that he was more honoured than he apparently realises.

Not long ago the duke took a private cricket team to the West Indies. One morning a famous cricketer took a headlong dive into the swimming bath and surfaced right alongside the floating duke.

'Good morning, Your Grace.' said the cricketer.

The duke replied: 'You may call me Bernard . . . in the pool.'

It is hardly a trade secret that 'unconfirmed reports' are generally something the taxi driver lets slip on the way from the airport and that 'usually reliable sources' are, almost invariably, barmen. I therefore remain grateful to the usually reliable source who put me in touch with Herr Christian Rubi and a brief story that echoed back to Hitler's Olympics, surely the greatest sportswriting assignment in history.

'Some froze solid where they clung, unable to move up or back on its pitiless face'

Kleine Scheidegg, Switzerland. — The man who first called this the Playground of Europe was surely standing with his back to the North Face of the Eiger. It towers into the blue sky of the Bernese Oberland like a jagged, mile-high tombstone to the 41 men it has already lured to terrible deaths.

Some froze solid where they clung, unable to move up or back on its pitiless face. Others made one mortal error and fell. Eight men were killed before one succeeded.

Some playground. Some sport.

In July, at about the same time Evonne Goolagong defends her title at Wimbledon and England bare their forearms for the third Test at Nottingham, the Eiger-scaling season opens all over again.

Like tennis and cricket — but unlike any other perilous climb in the world — it will have enormous spectator appeal. You can sit at a cafe table in this Alpine village, armed with powerful binoculars and a bottle of cognac, and watch the whole macabre contest.

It is a ghouls' paradise, the ultimate in vacarious theatre.

I write of mountaineering with all the authority of a man who suffers from vertigo on the top deck of a London bus. Which is why I sought out Christian Rubi, who has witnessed man's fight against the North Face from the first disaster in 1935 till the most recent conquest in 1971.

Herr Rubi, now 75, with gentian-blue eyes and a habit of picking out English phrases with the same precision that he once traversed ice and rocks, was for 40 years a legendary Alpine guide.

As such he was summoned from his home on a July evening in 1936 to attend the appalling last act of the worst tragedy even the Eiger has ever seen. Climbing out to the North Face from the rail tunnel, he found that three men from a party of four were already dead.

One had frozen to death. One had fallen. One had been strangled by his own rope. The fourth, a 23-year-old Bavarian named Toni Kurz, was stranded on an overhang 120ft. above the search party. He did not have enough rope to get down.

'By the time we arrived it was dark and there were avalanches,' said Rubi. 'There was nothing we could do until daylight. We had to leave him. He was crying "I am alone." I still hear his voice today.

'At daybreak we returned. We told him to unpick the rope he had, knot it together and send it down to us so that we could send up another rope. He did this one-handed because his left arm was frozen beyond use.

'On the second rope he lowered himself until he was just above us. We could have touched his feet with an ice-axe. Then a knot jammed in the ring at his waist. He was within two minutes of being saved but as we reached for him his head fell forward and he died.'

Christian Rubi does not believe it was coincidence that this team of four, two Austrians and two Bavarians, all perished at the moment that the athletes of the world were assembling in Berlin for the Hitler Olympics.

'There was a terrible nationalism in the race to conquer the Eiger,' he said. 'The Germans and the Austrians were determined to be first and many died because of it. Some were mad people.'

But what of today? 'Today,' said Christian Rubi, 'that nationalism has gone. The young climbers of Europe are climbers only. I would warn them of the perils of the North Face, but if they were accomplished I would not dissuade them from going.'

At the last official count 256 people had climbed the Eiger. That count is wrong. 'There are men I know,' said Rubi, smiling, 'who have ascended the North Face discreetly. They did it, shall we say, for their own satisfaction.'

When you stare at that vertical mountain it is hard to believe. But Christian Rubi, patently, is a man who does not lie.

Olympic Games are generally reported in a state of panic. I speak only for myself, of course. There are men in Fleet Street who write brilliantly at high speed, the greatest of my time being Geoffrey Green, lately retired from The Times, *who could pick up a telephone without a note or a word written on paper and produce phrases that made your hair stand on end. George Follows, tragically killed in the Manchester United air crash in Munich, had the same enormous gift and his death deprived British readers of a stunning talent.*

Subconsciously this is probably seeking excuses for some extremely bad writing in the next three columns. All are about the Olympics of 1976, the first two from the Winter Games in Innsbruck and the third from Montreal. Because of deadlines each had to be produced in around 30 minutes. I include the John Curry piece because it refers to a remarkable sportsman, the day after his greatest triumph, dominating an unusual Press conference. The second, a report of Franz Klammer's victory in the Downhill, is included because it was among the half dozen greatest spectacles I have ever seen. The third is one of the few really happy stories to come out of the tense and neurotic Montreal Olympics.

'Curry smiled at the room's discomfiture and said 'What other people think of me doesn't matter''

Innsbruck. — The price of gold was written clearly across John Curry's face at lunchtime yesterday. He was deathly pale and the lines induced by remorseless training were almost vertical ravines.

Uncharacteristically, for he is by nature a courteous person, he was nervy, snappy and abrupt.

'Do come on,' he instructed his mother, 'I'm *extremely* hungry.' It was 12.42 p.m.

Mrs Rita Curry, a nice, small lady with the slightly harassed expression of a widow who has continued to run the family's light-engineering firm during the nine years since her husband's death, jumped a little and said: 'Sorry, I've got to go.'

She lunches rarely with John. The last time was in London in December. She does not know when the next time will be. It could be in America. 'I would so like to go and see what he's doing over there.'

They were a small isolated party in the dining room, high up in the Alps above Innsbruck. Mrs Curry had been staying there for 11 days without seeing her son.

'We spoke twice on the telephone,' she said, 'but he concentrates so completely I did not want to interrupt him. I shall not see him again after today. I'm going home on Sunday.'

They had all got to bed at 4 a.m. 'It was lovely,' said Mrs Curry. 'We went back to the Olympic village and drank champagne.'

She is a kindly woman. She would remember to ring her factory back in Birmingham and give everyone the day off.

John Curry, at 26, is her baby, the third of three sons who renounced soccer and rugger at prep and public school and then renounced Birmingham as well.

He was the one who left home at 18 and went to London to take courses in advanced skating and elementary sophistication. He became a £13-a-week receptionist at the National Cash Register offices near Madame Tussaud's.

He was the one who turned to America for the training that brought Britain its only Winter Olympics gold medal for 12 years before an entranced audience in the great ice stadium in Innsbruck on Wednesday evening.

He was the one who turned to his mother after his triumph and simply said: 'Oh mum . . . !'

'That was all he said for a long, long time,' said Mrs Curry. She dashed into lunch.

That was the private face of John Curry yesterday. The public face, squared frankly at a roomful of some of the world's toughest newsmen during an official Press conference seven hours later, was wholly different.

It was the face of the nerveless champion.

An agency report of an interview he had given earlier was already circulating the world. It said John Curry admitted to being a 'gay' champion.

'Gay' is a trendy synonym for a homosexual, and slowly the questioning got around to words like 'virility' and 'masculinity'.

Curry heard them coming and smiled at the room's discomfiture and said simply: 'I don't think I lack virility, and what other people think of me doesn't matter.'

When the official conference was over he was put under private questioning. He crossed spread hands like a referee counting out a boxer and said 'Finish'.

His day of triumph had also been a day of tribulation. I am among 56 million Britons who care not whether John Curry is white, black, Moslem or Greek Orthodox.

All I know is that he skated the world out of the frame at the Olympics and the public face he

THE SECOND MOST GLORIOUS EXPERIENCE IN LIFE:
Flying with the RAF's Red Arrows aerobatic display team over Ely Cathedral in their last public performance of the 1977 season. The author, petrified, is to the right and slightly to the rear of the leader. Mike Phillips was piloting the plane.

JACK LONDON COUNTRY: *Flying low along the Iditarod Trail across Alaska, the loneliest race in the world. After 16 days, Anchorage seemed like the Venice of the North.*

THE LAST WORD: *It must be for the skills of the Red Arrows pilots at play. This picture, taken by Lincoln freelance photographer Bob Reding, tells more than a dozen columns ever could.*

showed yesterday revealed the qualities that had allowed him to to it.

'The two days before going into the arena,' he said, 'were the longest days of my life. It had suddenly hit me that there were a lot of people in England hoping that I'd skate well.

'A lot of people sent letters and telegrams. It weighed pretty heavily on me but I wasn't nervous.

'I'd had a sleep in the afternoon. Before I went to sleep, I concentrated on getting the mood I wanted to wake up in. That was the mood I did wake up in.

'When you start skating you see winning the Olympics as top. Now it's happened it all seems rather easy. There are some major skating competitions that make you feel as though you're pulling a coal wagon uphill. The Olympics weren't like that. They were on the flat.

'After I'd done my last triple I knew the hard part was over. I said "Now just sit back and enjoy yourself." That's what I did.'

The American questioners, knowing well that without American sponsorship and Italian coaching John Curry would probably still be eating lunchtime sandwiches not far from Madame Tussaud's, asked him whether he considered he had really been skating for Britain.

'Of course I was,' smiled Curry. Then he said: 'But I love America. I love the energy of the place. I love the American attitude that before you start, all things are possible.'

There are writers who could sit down for an hour without coming up with half such a perceptive accolade to the United States.

Curry calculated that 'very roughly' his final year's training for the Olympics had cost almost £10,000.

Didn't that come close to making him a professional? He smiled serenely at us all and said very carefully: 'I am an amateur as described by the rule books.'

Then, with a disarming frankness that caused the Olympic officials sitting close to him to drop their eyes to the floor, he confirmed that after next month's world championships in Sweden he will be on the open market.

'I will then know what options are open to me,' he said, 'and I shan't do anything until I've heard all the options.'

If the options are as good as most of the world's skating experts expect them to be, John Curry, of Birmingham, will join Franz Klammer, the Austrian skier, as the second young man to go on from the Olympics to become a millionaire.

What he plans to do is create a Theatre of Skating based in the United States, comprising half a dozen performers who believe, as he does, that skating can be raised from the plains of sport to the mountain peaks of the performing arts.

'There are those,' he said, 'who'd like me to go into some ice show.

They say: "But it's only two years of your life." But that would be two years out of my artistic life, and I reckon I have about 10 years of that left.'

It was John Curry's second stunning performance in 19 hours. He had taken on the world's hard newsmen and beaten them at their own less artistic game.

The private face was of a man as out of place at the Olympics as Harvey Smith in a launderette. The public face looked as imperturbable here as it did to you on television.

He'd won his second gold in two days.

'Immortality is when those who watched you win will never forget it'

Innsbruck. — Champions are men who deliver on the day. Great champions are men who face crushing odds and still deliver on the day.

And then there are immortal champions. They are men who face crushing odds and conquer with such brilliance and style that unconsciously you hold your breath till your ears sing merely watching it.

Such a champion is Franz Klammer, who yesterday hurled himself down 3,000 yards of solid ice on the upper flanks of Austria's Mount Patscherkofel in 1min. 45.73sec. to win what Alpine aficionados proclaim the greatest Olympic downhill ever.

One measure of his achievement was that not one of his 74 rivals begrudged his triumph by so much as a covetous glance. They wrung his hand and conceded that only one skier in the world could have done it . . . Klammer.

The crushing odds against him were threefold.

Overnight, to a corporate groan across his native Austria, Klammer was drawn to come 15th out of the starting gate: the last and worst possible position for the seeded fast men.

Then, with the Blue Riband event of the Winter Games less than six minutes old, it became clear that the Swiss were prepared to fling their bodies down the Patscherkofel with the doomed philosophy of kamikaze men in a bid to stop him.

Their Bernard Russi, defending champion and third man down on the fastest ice, flashed over the finish line in a time which caused experts to believe the computers had blown. His 1min. 46.6sec. had slashed nine seconds off Klammer's official course record. It was the Alpine equivalent of the three-and-a-half-minute mile.

Klammer's half-hour wait at the summit must have seemed like the Stone Age. Eventually the digital clock began to spin hundredths of seconds against his number and he was on his way, bouncing, twisting, lifting one ski, then the other, at times totally airborne.

The third crushing blow was to come. At the halfway mark with the swiftest runs of the piste behind him, he was only third fastest. Even loyal Austria, whose idolised son he is, gave him not a chance.

Their Anton Steiner had already crashed, losing a ski which drove into a hut like a spear, in frenetic pursuit of Russi.

From the halfway mark you could plot Klammer's descent by the sound. The roars grew and grew as he leaned into turn after turn — until suddenly there he was, a tiny, double-bent figure in vivid yellow streaking wide from the left-hander which takes them into the last 300 yards to the finish.

He came on, crouching, at more than 80 miles an hour, until he suddenly threw his hand up. It was over. The clock had stopped at 1min. 45.73sec.

It is hard to say how long it was before Klammer knew he was champion, that he had just raced the race of five lifetimes, that he had come as close as the human can to achieving the impossible and that in less than two minutes with the commercial contracts now open to him he had won himself £1 million as well as an Olympic gold.

Two seconds, perhaps.

Again he threw up his arms in ecstasy, skied gently down to his colleagues and was lost from sight.

With brilliance and style, against massive odds, in the face of supreme, courageous and at times reckless opposition, he had confirmed a coveted definition of sport. Immortality is when those who watched you win will never forget it.

He did not, incidentally, wear those revolutionary new skis with the holes in the front. That, it may now be revealed, was a publicity stunt. He did not wear the gold-and-black gear of the Austrian team. His vivid yellow outfit, not at any great financial loss to Klammer himself one presumes, will now be mass-produced and publicly marketed whereever two or more skiers are gathered together.

It would be wrong, though, to carp at the commercialisation of it all. Klammer was worth every penny he didn't officially earn.

'Several times I nearly lost it and fell,' he said. 'It was terrible on the corners. I don't mind confessing now that I never thought I could do it, just as I'm sure Bernard Russi was convinced he could never lose.'

Austria stopped for the race. It was just as well. They may never see another like it.

‘Lord, how the Olympics need the Cayman Islands and another dozen teams like them’

Montreal. — As Britain’s athletes get swept from the track and Australia lament their worst Games ever and East Germany pile gold upon gold to the glory of Karl Marx and the Fatherland, one team here is having its own private ball.

I refer to Joel and Doug and Peter and Jerry and two wives, both called Debbie, who represent the 132nd and youngest of the Olympic nations, the Cayman Islands.

The story of their emergence as a premier sporting country began some while ago over a late-night bottle of brandy.

Joel and Doug were discussing holiday plans for the summer of 1976 when Doug said: ‘Why don’t we go up to Canada and watch the Olympics?’ Joel said: ‘I’ve got a better idea. Let’s go up there and compete in them.’

On April 8 this year they received a letter officially welcoming them into the Olympic brotherhood. On July 17, with the two Debbies tripping along with their handbags, they marched in the opening ceremony. Since Red China, representing 800 million of the earth’s population, did neither, that in itself is an achievement which should not pass unnoticed.

Since then Joel Bonn, prosperous proprietor of a speed-reading school, and Douglas Calder, a 35-year-old attorney who once rowed for Cambridge, have been having a few drinks and the two Debbies have been shopping, sightseeing and watching the Games.

Meanwhile, down at Kingston, their team of Peter Milburn, a 25-year-old professional diver, and Jerry Kirkconnell, who left school only last month, have been competing in the 470 class of the yachting events.

Their results include a last and two 18th places. ‘This,’ said Joel Bonn, Secretary-General of the Cayman Islands Olympic Association, ‘is considerably better than we expected.’

Well, here’s to the Cayman Islands, which, if you didn’t know, are three specks of land 140 miles west of Jamaica famous for turtles, tax refugees and one soccer pitch with ankle length grass and a concrete cricket wicket in the centre circle.

‘We are,’ said Joel in the sort of accent you hear all over Tel Aviv, ‘proudly British. We play a lot of rugby and we're most grateful to George III for issuing the edict that still exonerates us from taxation. Apparently some Cayman Islanders once saved one of his kids from a shipwreck and that was his way of saying thanks.'

How the Caymans achieved Olympic status scarcely bears investigation since you have to have five of the 22 Olympic sports in a flourishing condition.

That they were two short presented no problems for Joel. 'We built a basketball court out of scaffolding and plywood and started a National Basketball Association,' he said. 'Then, because I needed the exercise, I became president of the Cayman Islands Weight-lifting Association.

'As it happened I was the only weight-lifter we had, but the Olympic people were very nice about that. We had to fill in a form and then in April we got this letter from Switzerland telling us we were members.'

They were the first team to arrive at the Games, bearing a national flag borrowed from a local police station. And since they are paying their own expenses and don't give a damn whether they win, lose or get simply annihilated they have spread laughter and friendliness all over the place.

In the case of Peter Milburn, their Olympic helmsman, national soccer goalkeeper and best all-round cricketer, this is hardly surprising. He was born in County Durham and is a cousin of Colin Milburn, who played such robust cricket for England before losing an eye.

Lord, how these Olympics need the Cayman Islands and another dozen teams like them.

Joyless East Germans, solemn Soviets, Australians haggard with their lack of success, Britons searching dark corners for feeble excuses, have brought to this city such pervading gloom that you almost suspect Sunday's closing ceremony will be a prelude to the end of the world.

'Well,' said Joel Bonn. 'We may be many things but certainly not joyless, solemn, haggard or feeble. We just thought we'd start with the Olympics and work backwards.

'We've learned a lot. Do you know that the entire population of the Caymans would fill only one fifth of the Olympic Stadium? Do you know that what they've spent on the Montreal Games would keep the whole economy of the Caymans going for 1,000 years?'

Mr Bonn didn't actually say it all added up to ultimate losing, mainly because he doesn't want to offend an Olympic movement which is taking care of his holiday problems, but he came up with an attractive proposition. 'I think we'll make a bid to stage the Olympics in 1984,' he said. 'They will be restricted to athletes who don't mind changing behind a hedge because we haven't got any dressing rooms.

'All competitors will have to sign a form saying they intend to enjoy themselves. And just to let the world know what a hell of a party we're having we shall invite two newspaper reporters, two radio commentators and two television cameras.

'We ought to be able to do the whole thing for about 1,000 quid.'

As he spoke the £700 million Montreal Olympics rambled on outside, and the Australian athletes were muttering angrily about their fall from their accustomed gold-strewn path.

Suddenly a Cayman Olympics seemed an irresistible idea. They sounded precisely what the old baron had in mind when he started it all.

Quite often those who complain about Press intrusion into privacy are accomplished publicity seekers, either merely gratified by seeing their names in print or anxious to remain in the public eye for commercial reasons. Surprisingly, Malcolm Allison, itinerant football manager, is not one of them. He is one of the most likeable men in the game. His life is generally in a muddle but to suggest this in print is to receive from him an invitation to listen to his philosophy, an enriching and entertaining experience if not a wholly logical one. An invitation to attend the launching party for his ghost-written memoirs was too good to refuse.

'What heights could Graham Greene reach if he stayed up all night with Dorothy Squires?'

London. — Mr Malcolm Allison arrived looking like death and announced he'd been up most of the night with Dorothy Squires, a statement which demands precise syntax at the best of times but even more so when you are crippled by hangover.

A glass or three of Lanson Black Label brought the colour back to his interesting face and at the hour about six million factory workers were knocking off for lunch he borrowed a match and lit his first Havana of the day.

Then they wheeled in the obligatory blonde, a nice lady whose mum and dad apparently forgot to christen her because she's known as just Flanagan and comes from the

East End and models things and has written three books, all of which, I gather, lean heavily on sexual intercourse for the plot.

Flanagan must have had some sort of accident on the way because her lovely white ball gown had a big hole in the front which left her navel exposed to photographers, free-loaders, hangers-on and anyone else who felt disposed to press past in the crush.

After a while they rounded up Mr Allison, Flanagan and four other pretty girls and took them into the room next door where Flanagan hitched up her gown so that it wouldn't get crushed when she sat on Mr Allison. Coincidentally it revealed her knees and a disturbing acreage of thigh to the photographers, who'd also been invited.

About £300-worth of champagne later Mr Allison felt strong enough to answer probing questions about his autobiography, published Tuesday, at this Literary Event of the Year.

In introducing Mr Allison, Mr Robin McGibbon, publisher, stated that Mr Allison was one of the most respected figures in the world of Association Football.

''Ere,' shrieked Flanagan, with that instant repartee for which the East End is renowned, 'Oi fought that was Georgie Best.'

Mr McGibbon, who had also been up most of the night with Dorothy Squires in connection with another literary project, showed pain at the interjection (Mr Best's autobiography having been brought out by the rival publishing concern of Stanley Paul Ltd.) and invited the rest of us to put to Mr Allison questions concerning his philosophies about life, death, and the off-side law, etc.

'Hey, Mal,' inquired a gentleman I presumed to be the literary editor of a distinguished British newspaper, 'ow much are yer goin' to bid for Rodney Marsh?'

Mr Allison cleverly parried this query and concentrated his full attention to the next which was:

Had he not, in a manner unbecoming to a gentleman and manager of Crystal Palace Football Club, knowingly subjected three ladies, to wit his wife Beth, Miss Serena Williams of the Playboy Club, and a Miss Christine Keeler, to considerable embarrassment by publicly revealing his emotional involvements with all of them in order to boost the sales of *Malcolm Allison: Colours of My Life (Everest, £3.25)*.

Mr Allison, whose shirt mysteriously had the words Mercedes and Fine Old Columbus Rum printed all over it, and was open down to the fourth button, replied: 'I have never tried to avoid anything. That's how it happened. It is now a controllable factor.'

In reply to my appeal for clarification, he said that when a man gets married he often tends to protect his wife so much that she doesn't know what the world is all about. In short, he implied that philandery is a fairly masculine trait but that, while some men tried to conceal it from their wives, he didn't.

By now Flanagan was displaying her boredom at the way the day was going by chatting up a handsome young reporter. Allison ignored her and announced his earnest intention to become a gentleman.

First he plans to spend seven years making Crystal Palace great again. Then he intends to set up as a freelance international soccer consultant, travelling to places like America and Australia and showing them how to manage and coach. 'I've seen them round the world and I laugh at them,' he said. 'They're crap.'

All this forward planning, I gathered, featured his wife as well as himself so now, maybe, we can all get some sleep.

Anyway, the need for further personal publicity hardly existed by the time the party reached its Hogarthian heights, which coincided with about six million factory workers heading for home. After only two days on sale the book has gone into a second reprint, as much a tribute to the perceptive way Mr James Lawton has written it as to Flanagan's much-photographed navel.

It just makes you wonder what heights Graham Greene could reach if he had the sense to stay up most of the night with Dorothy Squires?

The Trinidad dateline requires some small explanation since the following column is about a private cricket ground in New Zealand. In fact it was written in the air in the middle of an orgy of sportswatching. We were in transit from the Commonwealth Games in Christchurch, New Zealand, to a West Indies-England Test series in the Caribbean. This proved to be a journey of some 43 hours and was made tolerable only by the companionship of Bryan Cowgill and David Coleman, of the BBC, and their willingness to join me in an interesting experiment confirming that one dry martini every 500 miles is the only known antidote for jet-lag. It does little for the powers of speech, but you can't have everything.

'They intend to go on discriminating against anyone they please, particularly women'

Port-of-Spain, Trinidad. — Acting on the assumption that you don't want to read another word about throbbing steel bands, calypso carnivals or Test match disasters I propose to order a treble Daiquiri and change the subject completely.

Last Sunday, 11,868 travelling miles back in New Zealand, this chap picked me up in his car and drove me out to the Valley of Peace.

Well, we've seen some rum places in our time, such as the Winkelstrasse in Hamburg, Harry's Bar in Barbados, and the National Liberal Club on The Embankment, but the Valley of Peace is out on its own.

It is flat and green, measures 100 yards by 80, is concealed from prying eyes by a fringe of commanding oaks and heartbroken willow trees and is probably the loveliest, definitely the quietest, and quite certainly the most exclusive mini-cricket ground in the world.

It is so exclusive that half the human race may go there only by private invitation while the other half may never go at all.

Since the ground was opened in 1926 no woman has passed through its gates and according to its present rules if you don't like the sound of it the members of the Valley of Peace Cricket Club Incorporated don't give a damn. That's why they're incorporated.

They own every blade of grass on the ground and intend to go on discriminating against anyone they please, particularly women.

Last Sunday Princess Anne and Captain Mark Phillips were touring the vicinity.

I asked: 'What would happen if they arrived here and requested to have a look? Presumably only Mark Phillips would be allowed inside?

A middle-aged member replied: 'That is quite correct, but I would certainly go out and talk to her in the car.'

To be fair they're not as queer as they sound. They're mostly successful business and professional men who are so obsessed with correctness that even their purple, black, and gold cricket caps come 12,000 miles from Fosters of Clifford Street, London.

Their roots are English because Harry Waters, who laid down both the pitch and the no-women rule 48 years ago, came from Winchmore Hill near London. His son, John, is now president.

I asked: 'Was your father a misogynist?'

He replied with what may be described as an enigmatic smile: 'Far from it. For one thing I would hardly be here if he had been. For another he happened to love women very much. Just one day a week he wanted some peace, that's all.'

Nothing has changed. Today's members do not fear Miss Germaine Greer. She doesn't exist.

Their lavish catering is handled by two elderly, respectful male retainers. They refuse to have a telephone on the ground so that they cannot be troubled by such matters as blown fuses, pestering mistresses, or accelerating labour pains.

Although their president gave me permission to write about his club for English readers no local publicity is tolerated.

The Valley of Peace were playing a strong Christchurch team when I was there but no report of the match will ever appear in the Press.

John Waters said: 'We have an arrangement with the local newspapers that they ignore us completely.'

It is effective complicity. At a party that evening I spoke to five local residents about the Valley of Peace. Four of them had never heard of it, yet it lies only six miles south-west of the great Christchurch stadium which staged the Commonwealth Games.

There are no road signs to point the way and the metalled road runs out two miles short of the ground. The rest is a dusty wagon-track down which only the curious, the adventurous or the hopelessly lost would venture.

Paradoxically it is internationally famous among the close fraternity of great cricketers. Although only 40 pages of their visitors' book have been filled in almost half a century the names there add up to a roll-call of genius: Bill O'Reilly, Maurice Tate, Clyde Walcott, Bill Bowes, Richie Benaud, His Royal Highness K. S. Duleepsinhji and

Brian Statham to name but a handful of my own special heroes.

Herbert Sutcliffe played there in 1932 and scored two separate centuries in the match. He made the first for the visiting team and everyone was so entranced by his artistry that they asked him to bat for the home side as well. He did, and scored his second hundred of the afternoon.

As you would expect the Valley of Peace Cricket Club Inc. has its exclusive rules. A boundary counts only two and you get four instead of six if you strike the ball clean out of the ground.

In 1948 a visitor who shall remain unidentified wrote the following comment after his signature: 'Wot no women, thank the Lord.'

The hand trembles when trying to contemplate how he would have felt here in Port of Spain as the Caribbean celebrated its tumultuous victory. Eighteen-stone-ladies danced in the rain and younger ladies were more enthusiastic.

A man has just passed in front of me inadvertently carrying his bicycle over his head. He was not wearing the colours of the Valley of Peace Cricket Club.

It is just as well that the world is not full of Larry Simpsons. I fear I am still not at liberty, nor ever will be, to explain how the trick works. All I will say is that it is so astoundingly simple that few people would ever think of it.

'By some oversight, Larry Simpson didn't have his personal armchair on the penalty spot'

London. — The official attendance at Crystal Palace when Malcolm Allison walked into the centre circle last Saturday, and raised both arms in what looked suspiciously like a Papal Blessing, was 39,325.

This figure, I can categorically inform you, was wrong. The actual attendance was 39,325 plus one, Larry Simpson, whose curious hobby is getting into big football grounds without paying.

It was 17 years ago last September that Mr Simpson came to the conclusion that only mugs actually hand over money at the turnstiles. Since then he has watched, on average, between 90 and 100 League and Cup games per season for free.

Like you, I did not believe this was possible — which is why I turned up in the saloon bar of a north London pub last Saturday, wearing sun-glasses and a disreputable overcoat, and challenged him to get not only himself but me into one of the day's biggest games free of charge.

Precisely 96 minutes later both Mr Simpson and I were inside Selhurst Park and in such close proximity to the action that we could have touched Mr Allison as he walked off the field. Additionally, our car was safely in the VIP car-park and at no point had a penny changed hands.

At this point I went off to see the Crystal Palace secretary Alan Leather, who was kind enough to avoid pressing too many questions and gave me, instead, a ticket for a legitimate seat in Block F in the stands.

By the time I got there Mr Simpson was sun-bathing on the grass behind the Crystal Palace goal.

For my own convenience, such as not running the risk of a punch on the nose, I agreed not to reveal Mr Simpson's methods of entry. Nor, in view of my own complicity, is this the place to come to any profound moral conclusions.

The simple fact is that since 1955 Larry Simpson, who is 39 and a football-crazed bachelor who lives with his brother in Islington and only reads soccer magazines, has been slipping in and out of football grounds like the Invisible Man.

To keep his body-swerve in trim in the off-season he occasionally glides into speedway or greyhound meetings and indeed rates among his more virtuoso performances free entry into Highbury Stadium the night Henry Cooper fought Muhammad Ali and to the Miss World fracas the last time it was staged in the Albert Hall.

'But mostly I stick to football and the London clubs,' he said. 'Orient is the easiest and West Ham the hardest. Wembley's a piece of cake. Outside London, Watford, Luton, Villa Park and Coventry are no bother.'

Irritatingly, he refused me permission to record his most staggering coup at Wembley, where he has never missed, yet never paid to see, a Cup Final in 17 years.

But he did authorise publication of a considerably lesser feat which occurred only last month when he slipped not only himself but his bank manager and his bank manager's son into the old grey fortress to witness the League Cup Final.

It is absolutely killing me not to be able to go into intimate details about his methods of entry but certainly part of his stock-in-trade as the supreme infiltrator, is undoubtedly, his appearance.

Larry Simpson is neither fat nor thin. He is neither tall or short. He is neither handsome nor ugly. He is neither well-dressed nor shabby. He is neither voluble nor is he ever lost for a word.

He is, if it is not the ultimate contradiction in terms, classically average. He is the kind of man who defies a second glance, and by my rough calculations his averageness, up to Saturday night, had saved him something between £1,200 and £1,800 in recent years.

'It is not,' he said, 'that I can't afford to pay. It's just that there wouldn't be much of a thrill going to a football match in the ordinary way.

'There are really two secrets. Never get cheeky with people. And never, never stop walking. The moment you hesitate, you're dead.'

My cheque for £1.40 is already on its way to Crystal Palace Football Club. This represents £1 for my seat in the stands and 40p for Larry Simpson, who, by some extraordinary oversight, didn't actually have his personal armchair on the penalty spot.

It was less by choice than editorial decree that I ever came around to watching Grand Prix motor-racing. The instructions were to go and find Niki Lauda, somewhere in the vicinity of Monza, and interview a man just back from the dead. It was neither a difficult nor happy task since I am immensely conscious of the moral fallacy of the first of the three succeeding pieces. I was, if anything, much guiltier of intrusion than any of the Italian villagers who came to stand and stare.

Monza, however, was also an introduction to a new world. After half a lifetime of absolute indifference I found Grand Prix pits a thrilling place and the drivers a race of such courtesy and modesty that I cursed the films that had established a prejudice with such a wrong impression. The second piece merely sets the scene in which James Hunt drove to a remarkable world championship victory in Japan and the third, from South America a few weeks later, was by courtesy of Hunt, who opened all the doors.

'Word of his presence spread and they came to gaze for minutes on end at one man back from the dead'

Monza. — The rain was smashing vertically into the Monza circuit yesterday as the third car out in practice threw up a fantail of solid water, slewed sideways, spun twice and hit the fence.

Watching unblinkingly from the Ferrari pits not 100 yards distant was Niki Lauda. We expect him, as world motor racing champion, to remain emotionally unmoved by a minor spill, but there was another reason for his gaunt, unblinking stare.

He has virtually no eyelids. They were scorched off 40 days ago.

So was much of his left ear, the top layers of skin on his upper face and all the skin around the right wrist left unprotected by fireproof covering when his last car exploded in a sheet of flame on the sadistic German track at Nurburgring.

They got him out in 32 seconds. Had they been 20, even 15, seconds slower we would be requested to stand here tomorrow afternoon in the brief traditional tribute to a dead motor sports hero.

Instead, if his Formula One engine can match his nerveless ambition, we shall witness him gearing down from around 190 mph on the Monza straights to something like 85 on the most treacherous bends.

He will once again be sitting astride what amounts to an incendiary bomb, and changing gear between 1,300 and 1,500 times with a right hand which could easily have been amputated as recently as the same day that the Olympic Games ended in Montreal.

Is it courage, or madness? Is it bravery, or obsession?

Is it one man, aged 27, so unwilling to concede an earthly title that he is prepared to wager life against death when most men would be hiding their desperate injuries in a darkened room in a clinic?

And, if so, what is the psychologist's definition for that?

Perhaps our own James Hunt, the driver closest to wresting the world title from Lauda, comes nearest with the explanation.

'Niki,' he said, not permitting the close camaraderie of the Grand Prix circuit to cloud reality, 'is a single-minded chap. If he found you lying on the ground, he would sooner walk over than round you.'

This is the man who will drive the Italian Grand Prix tomorrow in a flame red Ferrari emitting a sound like tearing calico.

Someone once called him the Red Baron equating him in outlook with Baron Manfred von Richthofen, the First World War air ace who refused to camouflage his scarlet fighter so that his mortal-combat opponents should always know who they were up against.

The allusion was very perceptive. Lauda, proud, abrupt, formal and scrupulously polite, strikes you as more Prussian than Austrian.

Even to the point where he fixes your eyes with his, challenging you to allow your gaze to roam over the terrible facial geography left by first-degree burns and, at the moment, first-operation plastic surgery.

God willing, Dr Rudolf Zelmer, Germany's leading cosmetic surgeon, will rebuild the features over which, at the moment, he has only had time either to lay pink, shiny skin removed from Lauda's left thigh or cover with a skull cap specially constructed to avoid pressure on what remains of the left ear.

Lauda's attitude to his disfigurement is to ignore it. It is his friends in the close knit Ferrari team who are left to protect him from his own apparent indifference.

He flew into Milan by private plane on Thursday, checked into an hotel with good food but no glamour 25 miles from the city and, presumably, expected some peace.

In fact, his temporary face stared back at him from the front page of the many Italian newspapers scattered around the bars and restaurants, and his dinner was transformed into a grotesque public peep-show.

Word of his presence had spread and they came, in twos and then tens, to gaze for minutes on end at one man back from the dead.

At shortly before 9 p.m., declaring himself utterly relaxed but in a condition for which the modern parlance is extremely uptight, Niki Lauda went to bed.

Yesterday it rained so hard across the Plain of Lombardy that Monza practice was suspended.

It was still pouring when proceedings resumed three hours later, and Lauda lay in his car, pulled the oxygen feed in under his helmet, steered left out of the pits, drove gingerly round one lap, and then rammed the accelerator to the floor.

He drove two laps extremely fast, stepped out of the Ferrari and announced to a large audience that he was totally fit and not returning to the track a moment too soon.

To an Ealing ratepayer with a mortgage and three kids, and a mild ambition to see minimally 50 if at all possible, it confirmed that such men, if not actually dangerous, are certainly different.

Lauda's obsession with speed started ten years ago when, at 17, he informed his wealthy grandmother that he had crashed a friend's car and would be in great trouble if he didn't replace it.

This was not strictly true, but it put him on wheels and set him on the course that brings him to Monza this weekend via the very portals of the next world.

Once the doctors had pronounced him capable of driving, there was no one to stop him.

Marlene, Lauda's wife of four months, had no chance. 'She doesn't drive the car,' said Lauda, 'I do. And we're both fine.'

There is no room for argument. 'I do not live as other men do,' said Lauda. 'While I can walk and drive, why live in a clinic? This is my world.

'I remember nothing of the crash at Nurburgring except the impact. I knew nothing for four days after that, but what I did know when I recovered consciousness was that I had to get better every day, and never slip back.'

Niki Lauda crashed at 180 m.p.h., and just one of the consequences is that for at least the next year he will spend more time under an anaesthetic than he will behind the steering wheel of a Grand Prix car.

Several of his closest friends did not share his luck. The fatality statistics of his sport are such that there are others with whom he will not share old age.

More than 100,000 Italians will occupy vicariously safe positions around this track tomorrow to see him ride again, and what is in their minds bemuses me almost as much, even now, as what is passing through his.

‘There are chilling factors beyond wondering whether two obsessed Europeans will affront other men’s gods’

Mount Fuji, Japan. — In the long history of man’s inhumanity to man there may have been more beautiful battlefields. But, if so, I cannot imagine them.

Towering over you, 11,000-feet tall, pink snow-capped in the setting rice-harvest sun, symmetrical as a lampshade and combining the mysteries of a semi-retired volcano and one of the Orient’s holiest shrines, stands Mount Fuji.

Below you, shimmering with lakes and tinted by autumn, lie what could easily be the foothills to the Western Highlands of Scotland.

The incongruous bit is at eye level: a harsh, dark, snaking circuit of metalled road, almost three and three-quarter miles long, totally flat, and as clinically terrifying as an operating theatre.

It is here, where the souls of those who believe in the Shinto religion are said to come, at an hour on Sunday when even those who have remembered to put their clocks back in Britain will be still sleeping soundly, that an English Anglican named Hunt and an Austrian Catholic called Lauda will fight for the Formula One racing drivers’ championship of the world and, coincidentally, more money than you or I could ever earn in three lifetimes.

Niki Lauda, a millionaire already, does not need the cash. James Hunt, whose parental home in Surrey symbolises exactly what they mean by the stockbroker belt, could take it or leave it.

But no. Separated by three points — Lauda’s 68 in the red Ferrari to Hunt’s 65 in the orange Marlboro-McLaren — they intend to drive to the bitter end of a 10-month personal duel that has already seen Lauda come back from a priest’s last rites and contributed in no small way to Hunt losing his extremely photogenic wife to an ex-rugby playing actor named Richard Burton.

You get nine points for winning, six for coming second. If Lauda wins here, he wins everything. If Hunt wins with Lauda second he takes the title by virtue of more outright Grand Prix victories. No other driver matters a damn unless he hoists Lauda off the track or zigzags in front of Hunt to stop him getting through.

It is the ultimate in mano-a-mano contests and the only irony is that it is taking place in a venue so beautiful and mystical that, on a clear day, you could sit here without the remotest counter attraction from sunrise to nightfall.

There has never been a climax to a motor-racing season quite like it and there are chilling factors beyond wondering whether two obsessed Europeans will be affronting other men's gods.

James Hunt has instructed his parents, both of whom wanted to come, to stay away. And Niki Lauda's wife, a lovely girl with swept up hair, looked 89 years old with concern when she came down in the lift yesterday.

It would be wholly libellous to call these men mad, but they are certainly not like the rest of us. It is a private war accentuated by the intense politeness each separately accorded the other yesterday.

Hunt, the eternal English public schoolboy, said: 'We're perfectly good friends. At the American Grand Prix we had neighbouring rooms with a connecting door. This allowed us to annoy one another.'

Lauda, still horrendously scarred by his Nurburgring crash which brought him to within 15 seconds of being burned to death, said: 'James and I don't see a great deal of one another, but don't forget it was the British who started cheating this year at the Spanish Grand Prix. There's no sport left in motor sport.'

On Sunday they will settle it, if their respective cars stand up to the strain at around 175 m.p.h. 'It is not a dangerous course because it only has four real bends,' said Hunt, 'but only the Italian and Austrian courses are faster. You can even come out of the bend into the pit straight at around 130.'

Today they go into two days of qualifying drives to establish preferential, and possibly critical, positions on Sunday's starting grid. Yesterday, pottering around their pits 60 miles outside Tokio, they were merely watched by hundreds of bemused Japanese, who had not the remotest idea what to make of them.

This is Japan's first international Grand Prix and while Japan turns out cars like shirt buttons it has yet to produce a driver who can keep his foot to the floor when all around him are easing theirs.

They even missed the glorious irony of Lauda, Austrian star of the Italian Ferrari team, being driven to the track in a cobalt blue British Rolls Royce.

Classically European, each gave the other the better chance. Hunt said: 'Niki has only got to race me while I've got to race the field.' Lauda said: 'My car was getting slower and slower in the last two races. I can't improve on a car if the engineers don't give me a chance.'

Lauda, upper face crenellated by stage-one plastic surgery and top half of the left ear charred out of existence, declared himself perfectly fit. 'If you are not perfectly fit you make mistakes and mistakes is hospital,' said the man only recently back from an intensive-care unit.

Hunt, five years younger than Lauda, has spent the past five days beating up all Japanese opposition on a Tokio squash court. He looked as Corinthian as C. B. Fry, but the tension showed in the myriad gestures he made to prove how relaxed he was.

One thing genuinely pleased him: that at least an edited version of the race is to be transmitted by BBC television, whose sudden aversion to motor racing allegedly had something to do with the advertisements scrawled all over racing cars just as they are now scrawled all over Lord's, The Oval and Twickenham.

'That's very flattering to me and I believe it's just about the best thing to have come out of this whole season,' said Hunt.

Lauda, 50 yards down the pits, took still greater pains to inform British readers that even in the darkest days of his semi-consciousness it had never occurred to him to quit motor-racing.

'I won the championship last year and I intend to win it next year,' he said. 'In fact I plan to make it three in a row.'

This implies that Niki Lauda intends to drive very, very fast on the world's third fastest race track on Sunday. Our own Mr Hunt is unlikely to be sluggardly.

The amazing thing is that neither of these modern matadors remarked on the breathtaking scenery. Mount Fuji could have been Fort Knox or the nearest Woolworths. Its tinted lowlands might have been Wormwood Scrubs or the Atlantic Ocean.

We can only hope that Mount Fuji's gods took no offence and accept that that's what separates the boys from world champion drivers.

‘There is only a filthy, fly-blown room where the drivers sprawl and sweat out their ordeal’

Sao Paulo, Brazil. — In contrast to the almost Gothic ritual involved in preparing a matador for the bull-ring, the countdown hours for a Grand Prix driver are callously uncomplicated.

There are no gaunt minions skilfully consuming time by the ceremonial adjustment of intricate medieval dress. There are no flickering candles in cool side-chapels. There are no priests or prayers or pale next-of-kin murmuring invocations to the family saints.

There is only a filthy fly-blown room, harsh with sunlight, where the drivers sprawl and sweat out their ordeal.

After an eternity, you learn not to put your watch to your ear again to discover whether it has stopped.

Mostly they are nearly naked against the furnace heat which will generate in their cockpits during the coming two-hour race. And therefore you notice that each man is wearing a steel medallion or a bracelet which is neither talisman nor adornment.

It is boldly engraved with the hieroglyphics of his blood group.

It is different in Europe where the drivers can come to terms with their nerves in the privacy of personal caravans.

Here for the Brazilian Grand Prix on Sunday, as in Argentina a fortnight ago, no such discreet waiting rooms exist.

Like bullfighters, they are enormously paid, though not proportionately, in terms of the ultimate risk. In recent years, three drivers have died at the wheel for every matador who perished under the horns. Thus I am indebted to James Hunt for permitting me, back in Buenos Aires, to share the long, dragging wait.

I am equally grateful to Jody Scheckter (South Africa), Mario Andretti (United States), Ronnie Peterson (Sweden), Jochen Mass (Germany) and Jacques Lafitte (France) for tolerating my presence.

I would have detested an outsider there in the hours immediately prior to being harnessed into what is less a car than a grotesque and highly combustible test-bed which you are expected to weave through chicanes, fling round hairpins and smash down straights at speeds flickering on 200 m.p.h.

Not that the tiny, drawn, low-flashpoint Lafitte knew much about it.

He had started the day with a shouting match with a woman at the hotel breakfast table and now, from somewhere, he had hijacked one of those expanding deckchairs as advertised every summer Sunday afternoon on British middle-class lawns.

This he flung into a corner, unfolded, threw himself upon it with his face to the wall and either slept or feigned sleep throughout.

At the end of a table dishevelled with plastic cups and scarred with cigarette burns, Andretti was propped on his elbows and staring into the palms of his hands like a man who's just drawn the Queen of Spades. Only he didn't have any cards.

In practice the previous day, a fire extinguisher had exploded and blown his best car to pieces.

Tanned, heavily masculine and with forearms as thick as Arnold Palmer's, he was the only one of the six who looked remotely like any racing driver ever seen in screen fiction.

Someone said: 'Mario, you're going home after the race. Can you bring me some new visors from Brazil?'

'Yeah,' said Andretti. 'Get them flown to my house.'

And that was all.

To his left, Ronnie Peterson leaned on his knee in an upright chair and examined the floor four feet in front of him. He has the plump face of a choirboy who scoffs Mars bars during the sermon and a reputation for driving on the frontiers of recklessness.

Pale from a Scandinavian holiday, he was sunburned only on the tip of his nose. After half an hour of silence, he said: 'Where are the warning lights at the first right-hander?'

Jochen Mass, archetypally German heroic with tight blond curls, blue eyes and stoic composure, already had his outer space driving suit on, as though waiting a sudden command to scramble to a squadron of Messerschmitts. He was wide-awake, sipped Coca-Cola, smiled frequently but said nothing at all.

Against a window overlooking the track, Jody Scheckter leaned his head against the glass and dozed. He is a keep-fit fanatic with a perpetual pallor. He also had a pretty wife out there somewhere and a brother, an initiate to the scene, driving his first Grand Prix. He spoke two sentences, both inconsequential, in an hour.

James Hunt, the world champion, contrived to sit on a chair at an angle of 45 degrees to the wall looking exactly as if he were about to go in to bat for Old Wellingtonians. No hypotenuse in tattered beach shorts has ever been equal to such wildly switching conversation.

'*Private Eye* is absolutely brilliant . . . This saline should be injected — not drunk . . . No, only Britain has anti-rabies laws . . . You must come to Indianapolis . . . What's Richard Ingrams like? . . . So we'd lost them at Moscow Airport . . . Are you insured against libel? . . . Monaco's something else as long as you don't have to drive there . . . I get it sent out from England but I never open it till the evenings . . . We could do with another accountant . . .'

So another three minutes passed. The chief of police entered. No one reacted. Then Hunt said: 'Absolutely ripping band you've got,' referring to the discordant breach of the peace which was marching up and down outside the windows.

'Gracias,' said the chief. 'Many guns, yes?'

'Divinely beautiful,' said Hunt and closed his eyes.

Two more minutes have gone.

As we stamped out the last of a carton of filter-tips, the cleaner knocked and walked in. He was dressed like a Welsh lay preacher.

Could he have the infinite honour of presenting his family to the world champion, the honourable successor to the great Juan Fangio himself and a man whose infinite courage and bravery, etc., etc.?

'Certainly, absolutely, right on, old boy,' said Hunt, and in they came: wife, only son, and three daughters who stared in disbelief at the squalid scene and the sleeping preoccupied men. Andretti, Peterson, Scheckter and Lafitte never moved. Mass had disappeared.

The family shook hands with Hunt with infinite grace and Hunt instantly dropped the cynicism and charmed them into a lifetime's memory.

Five more minutes had been destroyed.

Then Hunt, too, fell silent, and eventually a man came and requested the drivers to proceed to the pits and when you next saw them they were men from Mars, helmeted against instant death and anonymous inside asbestos suits which hopefully give a Grand Prix racer fully 15 seconds before he's burned alive.

Ten minutes later they were accelerating, slip-streaming and braking like mortal enemies.

Of this, I have no first-hand knowledge but I know that the waiting was awful.

It will all happen again this weekend, between tea and dinner British time on Sunday, and it will happen for the fortunate another 15 times this year before the season is done.

Curiously, almost to a man, they are the most modest, undemonstrative and equable of professional sportsmen and such qualities may well come from short contracts and futures indefinite.

One of the curious facts about Joe Bugner's second fight with Muhammad Ali was that he received more injuries from the British critics than he did from the world champion. I do not claim to be a critic. They were probably right but the terrible hitting, seen very close from the ringside, tempers such judgement as I have. If Bugner's performance really was more cynical than suggested here I still don't really care. This heretical view is based on the belief that too many have made too much money out of boxing without ever getting punched at all.

'Try going into the greenhouse and stoking it up to 118 degrees and see how it feels'

Kuala Lumpur. — This time there was no glow of triumph in the old champion's eyes, only purple weals beneath them and even they hadn't been pasted there by Joe Bugner's gloves.

They stood for exhaustion and the knowledge that it had been a fight without magic and Muhammad Ali, above all, has pride.

It had been a tradesman's world heavyweight championship and Ali, tired beyond measure, could not even rouse himself to roar out his usual commercial for the Moslem faith.

The general view here, among critic and layman, is that, at best, the fight was a flop and, at worst, a cynical performance by two men lining their wardrobes with vicuna and mink at the expense of a deeply disappointed world audience.

This is harsh condemnation, particularly when you learn that the temperature within the four ropes of that canopied ring was actually 118 Fahrenheit.

No athlete should be required to perform in such conditions, no vicarious spectator should complain at the outcome, and no great boxing championship should be decided in any venue, at any hour, where sheer human endurance counts for more than the beautiful skills.

For me, Joe Bugner fought bravely for eight rounds until the scorching sun and the stifling humidity sapped his strength. And then, what small chance he had of slipping a lethal or lucky blow into Ali, had gone.

For me, Ali's performance at 33 years of age, compounded though it was of artifice and strength-saving evasions as well as much artistry, remained a masterpiece of athleticism.

It is easy to sit in an air-conditioned room in Asia or a cool drawing-room in Surrey and condemn two fighters, but try going into the greenhouse and stoking it up to 118 degrees and see how it feels.

The real condemnation should be directed at the promotional-electronic-financial monster which now decrees that our major fights be staged in exotic or esoteric capitals, whose ambitious Governments are prepared to go broke to stage them, for world-wide live television showing all geared to dinner-time in New York.

Money, of course, is the motive. Bugner, while less distressed than Ali after 15 rounds yesterday, was the first to agree that 'the conditions were not fair to either of us'.

Ali, who now plans return fights against Foreman and Ken Norton as well as Frazier before he executes his repeated threat to retire, said nothing. He cut his post-fight monologue from the usual hour to under four minutes and went off to get his head down behind a 'Don't Disturb' notice.

Before leaving, he paid handsome, even fulsome, tribute to Bugner's courageous if not over-inspired or adventurous performance.

'I may appear to have been victorious,' he said, 'but I feel worse than he does.' The modesty was matched only by the magnitude of his parting-shot prediction. 'I am leaving you,' he said, turning to Bugner, 'with the next world heavyweight champion.'

Bugner said firmly: 'Well, gentlemen, we tried.' He shed 11lb in the ring and, apart from the sunset complexion and the facial puffiness which are the trademarks of fighting, he was unscarred and uncut.

He did not dispute the unanimous verdict against him, only the margin of the marking. The referee and one judge credited him with winning two rounds, the other judge with three. There was no doubt that he won the second and the 12th, but there was equally no doubt that he was shocked out of his wits when Ali sprang from his corner at the opening bell as though he'd decided to end it then and there and get back to bed.

Ali flayed his way through that first round with about as much sweet science as George Foreman might expend on a street mugger. Having failed to achieve the *coup de grace* while the national anthems were still echoing round the stadium, he proceeded to work and rest in alternate rounds.

He acted and he talked, he danced and described the occasional mocking circle around Bugner. Once, mid-interval, he strolled across the ring and engaged in earnest conversation with Frazier, a VIP ringsider who was sitting in his braces.

But it was all done without the malice or deep insult he has shown to so many opponents in the past.

His liking for Bugner is genuine, though that should not be interpreted as meaning that he gave him a comfortable ride. Twice later in the fight he came forward to end it all swiftly, but Bugner slid away.

In the last third of the fight Andy Smith, Bugner's manager, was pleading repeatedly for the million-dollar punch that would have brought Britain its first world heavyweight title this century.

But Bugner sheerly did not have the reserves of strength. When at last he went for it, desperate for hit-or-bust glory in the 15th, it almost proved fatal. His defence was wide open and the Ali of three years ago would have almost certainly sent him spinning and out.

At Wembley or in Madison Square Garden, Bugner's lack of gambling instinct might have been culpable but, for me, his performance ranked above that of that familiar figure, the gallant British loser. It is worth adding that his conduct in the ring was as exemplary as his conduct throughout his long stay in Malaysia, where not all Britons are remembered for their quiet, appealing charm.

Where now? we ask. A fight with Foreman on some Arctic iceberg? A meeting with Norton on a Pacific atoll? We shall see. Anyway, Bugner is not too modest to disagree with Ali's insistence that some day he'll come back with the title for Britain.

There was a period when George Best's name was hardly ever out of the newspapers. Indeed such was his fame that it became an amusing exercise one morning to attempt to write a whole column about him without actually mentioning it.

'Image Making is our business and we're projecting a Five-Star Prodigal Son'

London. — Well, boss, I fink we can definitely say the show's on the road again.

They was all there, BBC, ITN, CBS, 67 scribes and 86 photographers including one bird from *Paris Match* who hid herself in the showers so I smashed her camera.

Excellent, Morrie, excellent. Did you remember the flowers?

Biggest bleedin' bouquet you've ever seen, boss, in red and white naturally. Wrote the card myself. 'Undying love from 2,000 Salford schoolgirls.' I also sent a cake with 'From four Mosside Pensioners' wrote on it in red icing in a shaky hand. Just to bridge the generation gap, like. The photographers really went for that.

Astute, Morrie, astute. Do you think everyone got the message that this time it's for real, that this time there's going to be no meandering with girls or night club punch-ups and that?

Well, boss, he did turn up half an hour late for training.

Late, Morrie? Is my hearing suddenly defective or did I hear you say he turned up LATE? I suppose you're going to tell me next that he DROVE there in his Jag?

Well as a matter of fact, boss, yes, but it wasn't really like that, see, because first of all he had to go to have a medical che . . .

I don't like it, Morrie, I don't like it at all. I promised the PedalFit people that he'd be riding there on their latest model and the chairman of Slimslax that he'd be wearing their new skinfit track suit. What is more I specifically ordered that he had to be there half an hour before the team, literally pawing at the doors to get in.

I know boss, but Tommy Docherty is . . .

We all know Mr Docherty is a very excellent football manager,

Morrie, but Image Making happens to be our line of business. I repeat, the new image we're projecting is Five-Star Prodigal Son, mortgage-holding, mother-loving, stop-at-zebra-crossing-for-senior-citizens, open-the-door-for-ladies, kindly, intelligent lad. And punctual.

It's all very confusing, boss. This time last year it was hell-raising, actress-hunting, mixed-up Marbella commuter. Now it's like the guy had just been to a Billy Graham concert or something. Do you think they're going to fall for it?

There's no question for falling for it, if I may use your phrase. Our client, Morrie, is utterly sincere. We tell him what to do and he does it. What other footballer can demand such Press attention merely by turning up at a training ground? Manchester United need him. Football needs him. Do I have to spell it out?

Sorry, boss, I thought we were doing a promotional for this book.

Book, Morrie? Are we on the same wavelength? To which literary work are you referring?

Pardon me lowering my voice, boss, but I meant the book that Michael Parkinson is writing on behalf of our client. You know, the seering, tell-us-how-it-was exposé tearing the lid off the iniquities of British football, the Ulster political situation and a number of ladies' reputations. The word is that it's going to be the hottest seller since *Lolita.*

Despicable, Morrie, despicable, degrading, monstrous and extremely disturbing is the only word I have for that observation. It implies that we are less than utterly determined to see our client denounce commercialism and an erratic existence and dedicate himself to his comeback to football. Who, pray, is propagating this rumour?

Since you ask, boss, everyone in Fleet Street, television and radio. In fact they are making a book on it.

Indeed. And what are the conclusions of these self-appointed prophets?

Well, 33-1 against him emigrating to King's Road, Chelsea, by the end of October; 12-1 against him being back in Marbella by Armistice Day; 8-1 that he won't be playing at Christmas; evens against him seeing the season out and 5-1 on that he is about to become the best-selling author in the English language since Ernest Hemingway.

An extremely cynical state of affairs, if I may say so. Upon what do these people make their statements, Morrie?

Perhaps observation, boss. Or his track record. Or that Manchester United stated quite uncategorically that he'd never play for them again. Or the fact that he had to go back and train to square up matters legally. Or maybe they suspect that people like us are drumming up all this publicity to get him back in the headlines so that his book will sell like *Gone with the Wind.*

Has it ever occurred to you, Morrie, that you may not be utterly suited to the high-calling of this publicity and personal-management business?

Indeed it has, sir. This very morning, at the training ground of Manchester United, it crossed my mind that it is becoming increasingly difficult to delude most of the people most of the time. I even considered resigning.

Perceptive, Morrie. You took the words right out of my mouth.

In the vernacular of the 1970's the Red Arrows are something else. Before you may fly with the RAF's aerobatic display team you are 'invited' to take a medical which, far from being the cursory check on heart and blood pressure I had imagined, is a two-hour-plus physical and psychological examination of one's capacity to withstand the rigours of high performance flying. Only afterwards does one understand the reason why. To fly with them is a unique experience, encompassing the horrific and the euphoric. I hope I shall be asked again, for I have never enjoyed anything more in my life, but in the meantime I would like to record my thanks to Mike Phillips, who flew me in rehearsal and on the real thing; Frank Hoare, who led his team with Celtic panache; and Mike Whitehouse, player-manager of this incomparably disciplined bunch of nerveless cowboys.

'From 500 yards out my eyes were closed by an irresistible force called cowardice'

London. — It simply isn't true that your whole life flashes in front of you, even when you fear that one-and-a-half seconds from now you're going to finish up liquidised in the font of Ely Cathedral.

For one thing you don't really care, because of the raging pain in both ears.

For another, the terror is so absolute that your brain has hardly functioned at all since they explained what happens when you fire an ejector-seat.

Around now, which is to say at the bottom of a near-vertical 400 mph dive straight at the roof of the finest example of Norman architecture in the whole of the Fens, a voice as calm as a cruising Concorde pilot's crackles inside your helmet.

'The next bit may be a bit uncomfortable,' says Mike Phillips, aged 33, a native of Horsham, a graduate of the University of

London and an RAF flight lieutenant at this moment piloting his plane in alarmingly close proximity to eight others in his 287th and final performance with the Red Arrows.

He does not exaggerate.

Suddenly, with a roller-coaster lurch that leaves your stomach in Ely High Street, you have somehow avoided the cathedral roof and begin to streak upwards.

It is then that a medium blow from a rubber cosh hits you across the nape of the neck, and some invisible stream-press begins forcing your head into your chest. You are incapable of lifting your arms and, momentarily, darkness surges in from all sides as you cling on to a keyhole of brilliant light somewhere in the middle distance.

This is what aerobatic pilots call 'pulling g', which is technical shorthand for their constant defiance of the earth's gravitational forces.

In that particular evolution over Ely, Mike Phillips, flying 12 feet from the wing-tip of Flt.-Lieut. Mel Cornwell to his left and 18 feet and fractionally below the tail of Flt.-Lieut. Dudley Carvell's scarlet plane immediately ahead, pulled 5½g. The effect, during the few seconds it lasts, is to make a 12-stone man weigh 66 stone.

At the zenith of that climb, as you collect your stomach and your wits and begin to enjoy it, there is one further small surprise.

You glance upwards through the perspex cockpit canopy to offer thanks to heaven and there, 4,000 feet above you, are the green and ochre fields and small neat villages of Cambridgeshire in early autumn.

You are flying upside down without the slightest discomfort until a quick command from Frank Hoare, the Welsh squadron leader who runs the Red Arrows with autocratic democracy, pitches you into a violent right-hand roll and sends you splaying out into an empty sky.

This year, the RAF's Red Arrows have performed to live audiences totalling more than three million, including one crowd of 600,000 over an airfield in Germany. Their 102nd and final show over the Fens was to commemorate the granting of the Freedom of the City of Ely to the local RAF hospital.

Their display lasted 17½ minutes and, certainly to one layman privileged to fly with them, amounted to the next-but-ultimate thrill.

In their final act, mundanely called Piccadilly Circus, all nine planes streak in from nine different points of the compass at closing speeds of 800 m.p.h. and miss one another by narrow yet rigidly predetermined margins of air-space over a carfax about the size of Wembley Stadium.

I would like to be able to describe this denouement in greater detail, but am unable to do so.

From 500 yards out my eyes were closed by an irresistible force called cowardice, and they didn't open again until Mike Phillips said: 'Okay, that's it. We go home now.'

On landing, he slapped his tiny turbojet on its nose in a small show of sentiment and walked out of his three-year career with the Red Arrows. He rode home from the airfield on a 90 c.c. Honda motorbike.

Three years is the most an RAF pilot can serve with the Arrows unless, like Frank Hoare, he is brought back as leader. During their tour with the most lionised aerobatic team in the world, they receive precisely the same pay as every other officer, deskbound or otherwise, of their rank. A flight-lieutenant gets £5,716 a year, and the leader £6,100.

These are the air aces of our day. They have comfortable middle-class Christian names like Mike and Richard and Martin and Nigel and Tim, and they fly, brilliantly and modestly, without attempting to perpetuate the laconic, wizard-prang, polka-dot neckscarf attitudes of their subsonic forerunners of the Battle of Britain.

'Élite?' questions Mike Phillips, 'No, we're not élite as individuals, but we're probably élite as a team.'

They are, in fact, so élite that an extraordinary chance came the way of the Red Arrows and their manager, Mike Whitehouse, earlier this year.

They were approached by an American entrepreneur, a kind of Kerry Packer of aviation, who wanted to buy them out of the RAF and promote them as the greatest flying circus ever seen, on salaries immensely greater than those they draw under the stringent restrictions of Britain's defence budget.

There weren't any takers.

There are those in Parliament who would deem it a political triumph to disband the Red Arrows, but to fly with them is to be reassured that there are still areas in British life where perfection, for perfection's sake, still exists.

Certainly to this layman, having retched and blacked out during rehearsal and been unashamedly petrified throughout 17½ minutes of actuality over Ely, quite how nine pilots fly in such perilously close formation under the enormous stresses of gravity remains a closed book.

To the newcomer there are many imaginative comparisons, but it cannot be altogether unlike being thrown over the edge of Niagara in a sealed barrel and then hurled back up to do it all over again.

It is a brutal assault on the brain and the nerves and the digestive system, but when, disoriented and upside down, you glance sideways and see the same wing-tip precisely the same distance from yours as it was 3,000ft. lower a few seconds ago, you begin to relax and believe in the infallibility of the Sons of the Few.

It was Tom Clarke, my Daily Mail *sports editor, who uncovered the Iditarod Trail. In April 1976 he read two lines of small type in the American magazine,* Sports Illustrated, *merely recording the result of a marathon sled-dog race across the outer wilderness of Alaska. In February 1977 he made further inquiries and telephoned me at home late on a Sunday evening.*

"Listen, baby, I think we've found something interesting. How are you feeling?" When Clarke addresses you as 'baby' and inquires after your health in a solicitous manner, you generally reckon you can cancel every appointment in your diary for around the next fortnight. In this instance it was almost a month.

The following are four of the 11 pieces the Daily Mail *published in a series called The Last Great Race. At the age of 45 and increasingly becoming devoted to comfort I found merely reporting it unusual to the degree that, when it was over, Anchorage felt like an amalgam of London, Rome and Rio. I resolved then and there that when the wild called again, I'd be out.*

'The mushers just slid away silently, faces set hard and eyes already concentrated on the western horizon'

Anchorage, Alaska. — It was the great Jack London, mixing metaphors with another four fingers of whisky, who captured this God-forsaken wilderness in exactly two sentences.

'The Almighty,' he said, 'was pretty tired by the evening of the sixth day so he just tipped his barrow sideways and slung out what was left. Thus was born Alaska.'

He wrote that 70 years ago but nothing was different yesterday as Serge Amundson, bush pilot, revved his tiny Piper ski-plane across the frozen lake, banked steeply westwards and flew us low along the first 60 miles of the Iditarod Trail.

Ahead towered the smashed molars of the Alaska Range. Behind lay jagged ice-floes. To the left and Canada, to the right and the Pole, there was only blinding whiteness.

Outside it was petrifyingly cold.

Thirty miles out we caught the backmarkers. Twenty miles on we were abreast with the leaders. The mushers waved, the dogs ignored us and pulled on demoniacally. There were just over 1,050 miles to go.

In all there were 47 humans and 604 huskies down there engaged in the last great endurance race on the face of the earth.

By daylight and darkness, across terrain of some danger and unrelieved desolation, in temperatures that have been known to plunge to 100F below, sleeping rough and eating rougher and in the constant proximity of very wild animals, they are retracing the Gold Rush Trail of the 1890s.

They started in Anchorage, the bleak staging post for the big polar jets. They will finish at Nome, which is engagingly known as the Sodom of the North and stands out there on the Bering Strait staring at the blunt end of the Soviet Union.

Their route, which crosses two mountain ranges and winds 150 miles along the banks of the Yukon River at its chilliest point, is exactly 1,110 miles long. This is roughly the distance from London to Naples.

It is a sled dog race of unimaginable hardship and no one can remotely guess how long it will take. In the record year it was won in 14 days, 14 hours, 43 minutes, 45 seconds. Mostly the winning time is nearer three weeks. Backmarker finishers have been known to take 29 days.

There is only one intractable rule. No fresh dogs may be harnessed en route. The same huskies must run every yard of the way and if they die in the effort, you must quit when you are down to five to save imposing intolerable strain on the survivors. Most mushers start with ten to 18 dogs and lose none.

This year as every year, the United States Humane Society has sent outraged telegrams demanding that the Iditarod Trail be cancelled. If the huskies could read, they would fall about laughing. They are half-wolf and wild-eyed and run until their hearts give out, which is usually about a dozen years later around the age of 18.

They are heroically mad, as are most of the 47 humans they pulled off the starting line in bright sunshine and at a temperature of 12 below. This, around here, is a balmy spring day.

There were no flags or fanfares or mayoral send-offs. The mushers just slid away silently, faces set hard and eyes already concentrated on the western horizon.

There was only one hitch. Before one muffled figure was even 100 yards down the trail, a distraught female voice screamed: 'Hey you've still got the car keys,' and her husband reached down into a pocket and threw them back into the snow without stopping.

Thus, with much modesty, and no emotion, the huge ordeal started.

The passing faces were fascinating. There were narrowed Asiastic eyes and flat expressionless features and cheeks as creased as old boot leather, for slightly more than half the entrants come from long, proud lines of Eskimo and Indian hunters and trappers. They are shy, and as fumbling with the social graces as you or I would be catching a salmon down a hole bored through two feet of ice.

The rest are compulsive adventurers. Local businessmen who dog-sled for sport, all-American Hemingway fans up from Texas and Wyoming, one Norwegian who made his name ski-jumping, one U.S. Army officer, a wealthy veterinary surgeon, and, unbelievably, two women.

One, Varona Thompson, will celebrate her 23rd birthday behind 12 huskies on the trail. She is 5ft, weighs just over 9st, is very pretty, Alaskan-born and more than a match for most lone Metropolitan muggers.

The other, Dinah Knight, is probably the last member of the human race you would identify with mushing sled dogs across the tundra beyond the last frontier. Aged 38, and with the honey-blonde looks of a late 1940s movie star, she is a consultant psychiatrist at the University of Minnesota and is spending 4,000 dollars to compete.

She took up dog-sledding five years ago, as a change from horse riding. 'I've saved up for four years to come here,' she said. 'It's a massive compulsion. I can't hope to win but I've got to go the distance. I'm not afraid of getting lost or of freezing to death. I'm simply terrified of falling through the ice and drowning.'

Two long stretches of the race are across ice, but north and west of Anchorage there is little fear of it cracking. By last night the temperature was down to 20 below, and as they move westward it will sink progressively lower. Over the plane radio we learned that in McGrath, less than 400 miles ahead, it was 49 below.

This is not quite the whole story. Vicious winds combine with the cold to produce a chill factor equivalent to 70 and 80 below, a condition which frostbites any exposed flesh in around 30 seconds. In the 1974 race a chill factor of minus 120 was recorded. That year 15 dogs died.

The ultimate danger is a white-out, when swirling snow blocks out the vision so completely that a hand stretched in front of the face is invisible. Then you stop and, if so inclined, pray.

Along the way there are checkpoints, mostly a single wooden hut where the mushers can stretch out on the floor in sleeping bags. Occasionally, there is a small clump of homes where they can rest.

There are places proudly marked on the map as townships and these include Iditarod, from which the race derives its name. It thrived in the Gold Rush. It is now believed to have a population of two, but no one can be sure until we get there.

Few of the competitors stay in any of the checkpoints. They drive on, guided at night only by the sixth sense of their lead dog, moonlight when available, or otherwise a thin torchbeam from a miner's-type helmet. When exhausted, they scoop out revetments in the snow and sleep on their sleds, under down-lined bags and six layers of clothes, surrounded by their huskies.

It is hard to convey such privation to a British readership, which regards a roof over the head as a legal right. One way may be to point out that there are stretches further than from London to Edinburgh without so much as the crudest version of an end-of-the-garden lavatory.

Along the 1,100 or so miles of the trail there are only 4,000 inhabitants, and most of these are congregated in two small towns which, in the coming days, will doubtless assume an allure somewhat greater than the Savoy or Claridges.

Tomorrow, after one final night in the best rooms of Anchorage's finest hotel, we shall join the trail. In Serge Amundson's 31-year-old Piper PA14, which can take off in 20 yards of snow and land in 80, we shall stage-hop the race and hopefully send back reports.

These may be periodic, for Jack London's Alaska still lives. The only conspicuous change is that desperate men are now tearing at its entrails for oil instead of gold. Their pay is enormous but so is the risk, for the environment can literally kill you.

Quite how a 1st. overweight, 45-year-old reporter dedicated to urban comfort, with a life-long aversion to cold, no Boy Scout experience, a paranoid hatred of camping, a dislike of baked beans, an immense suspicion of portable stoves, and no affinity with dogs, is to fare during this unusual sporting event is a matter of considerably greater interest to me than any *Daily Mail* reader.

As another Englishman said on another occasion: 'I am just going outside and may be some time.' On the other hand, if Miss Varona Thompson can do it we must stand a chance.

‘If you make a mistake around here you can finish up dead’

Rainy Pass, Alaska. — All day the huskies have been toiling up the terrible gradient that gashes through the Alaska Range like a white-walled Khyber Pass.

Men and dogs rested overnight at Ann Budzynski's sprucewood lodge eating moose steaks, 12 to a table, and sleeping 29 to a single fetid room. By dawn they were gone, crawling 30 miles upwards and westwards at four miles an hour.

The first 217 miles of the 1,110-mile Iditarod Trail have been accomplished at a near-record sprint. The hard men like to storm through here before the weather closes in.

In past races whole teams have been snowed in for up to five days by blizzards. This time they faced the ordeal in brilliant sunshine and a temperature of minus 19 Fahrenheit. By nightfall 29 of the 47 man-and-dog sled teams were through one of the world's most cruelly beautiful corridors.

The remaining 18 teams are strung out over 75 miles to the rear. They include three teams who took a wrong turning in darkness and headed up a dead-end canyon. They lost 15 hours before swinging back into the race.

The leaders, with a mere 850-odd miles to go, now accept that Alaska's Riviera is behind them. As you top the ridge in Rainy Pass, the scenery changes from Christmas-card pretty to labour-camp grim.

The mountains have been scoured of snow by vicious winds off Siberia, and from here on the chill factor brings the temperature down to anything from 20 to 110 below.

Any European who cares to challenge the contention that the Iditarod Trail is the toughest flat race still open to men is welcome to get here and change his mind. It is not a new world he will be entering but an old one.

Across this same wilderness at the turn of the century came the Gold Rushers, fighting, pillaging, robbing and sometimes murdering their way in pursuit of the identical motive that now inspires millions to post off brown envelopes to Littlewoods.

In their wake came mailmen dedicated to getting letters through in two months, missionaries on the hapless self-appointed task of saving souls, and ladies with big hearts, decoratively protected. They died like flies. Seventy years later, it is still no place to bring your aunt.

Coming contentedly up the trail

from Happy River to here yesterday, between high walls of snow, Al Crane and his huskies were suddenly leapt upon by a moose, a huge ill-shapen example of Arctic wildlife, which weighs anything up to a ton, stands 6ft to the shoulder and kicks its victims to death.

Crane was ill-prepared. His gun was laced into his kit on the sled. 'All I could do,' he said, 'was to yell in the hope of distracting him from trampling my dogs to death'.

By good chance and nothing more, Warner Vent, runner-up in last year's race, was coming up hard on Crane's heels. He removed his Mohawk 600 243-calibre from its zip-up cover and killed the moose with a single shot that tore its head open above the right eye.

Earlier yesterday, at the Finger Lake checkpoint, Gene and June Leonard invited us into a cabin barely visible above eight feet of snow to take tea.

Leonard, New York-born and now a trapper, learned all about British tea addiction while serving with the Eighth Army in Africa.

His fame here, where your next-door neighbour can be 70 miles distant and these impressions are being dictated to London over the only telephone in exactly 347 miles, is that in last year's race he was the man who found Colonel Norman Vaughan.

At 21 Vaughan was in charge of all 97 huskies on Admiral Byrd's 1928 expedition to the Antarctic. At 69 he was the oldest competitor in the 1976 Iditarod.

They told him he was mad to go but he went just the same. Less than 200 miles from Anchorage he took a wrong turning and disappeared.

Three days of concentrated air search failed to locate him. On the afternoon of the fourth day Leonard found him.

He was out of food and in the mid-stages of hypothermia, a physical condition that smashes the human will into terminal submission. His starving dogs were eating their own harness.

'When I found him' said Leonard, 'he was just wandering around. He had so little idea what he was doing that he didn't even care he'd been found. Sure as hell, he'd have died that night.'

There was no bravado in Leonard's remark. He received no medals. There are different rules and values here.

Tom Mathias, a 38-year-old Michigan man up to compete in the last dog sled race of his life, said: 'You want to listen to these guys. These are the real experts in Arctic survival. If you make a mistake around here, you can finish up dead.'

Certainly knowing your way around the world's finest hotels, opera houses and tailors is of little value. You can throw privacy, hygiene, books, baths, menus, President Amin's latest outrage and

President Carter's latest public gesture straight out of the window. This place is about staying warm and staying alive, and they are largely synonomous.

Ann Budzynski's home, for example, would hardly win Egon Ronay approval, but it takes ten stars for hospitality.

For wall decorations, it has an original Springfield 73 and a picture of two redskins plotting bad medicine. All night, dog mushers arrived, jowls festooned with icicles, to be met with hot meals. Some stayed, some immediately moved on. On a floor shining with melted snow under light from a red lantern, those who stayed slept shoulder-to-shoulder in sleeping bags.

Over a stove in one corner, they heated up fearsome stews of meat, fish and tallow to recharge the dogs who are running from Anchorage to Nome on the Bering Strait. In another corner, Marty Hoffman, a young U.S. Army officer vet, prepared antibiotic pads for the dogs with ravaged feet. It was like trying to sleep on Euston Station concourse in the rush-hour.

So far, about 30 huskies of the original 604 have been detached from the race. They are immediately flown back to kennel base in Anchorage, for there are do-gooders who would stop this race on grounds of cruelty if they could establish evidence.

Such altruism is somewhat misplaced. Given half a chance, the Iditarod dogs would eat any year's entire entry at Cruft's as a mere snack between breakfast and lunch.

It is hard to determine which are tougher, the dogs or the men. It is an academic argument, for if you fancy either your chance or your pet's, there is an opportunity to prove yourself here in conditions which may modestly be described as alien.

‘Against a soft European face the wind feels like frozen steel wool scouring right down to the nerve ends’

Unalakleet, Alaska. — Nothing moved yesterday except the brushwood, bending double beneath the murderous wind, and the dog teams coming onward, ever onward, at a resolute six miles an hour. Their heads are down now and at each halt they keel over and sleep where they fall.

Of the 604 huskies which left Anchorage 800 miles ago, four have died and some 160 have been unharnessed and airlifted out.

Mostly those relieved of heavy duties are suffering cut or bruised feet, hardly surprising when you calculate that there are around 5,000 canine strides to the mile. Five United States Army vets fly back and forth along the trail, administering treatment and drugs.

The terrain has changed from powdery snow to hard Christmas cake icing, honed skating-rink fast by the wind. Against a soft European face the wind feels like frozen steel wool scouring right down to the nerve ends. That and the indescribable desolation explain why the mushers now jerk and mumble and stare like automatons.

On the 90-mile leg up through Old Woman Pass and down to this Eskimo village on the Bering Strait, there was only one indication that you weren’t flying across the far side of the moon. High on a mountain promontory stood four objects that looked like gigantic electric fires.

These are the early warning radar screens of America’s North-West Frontier, for directly ahead, across 250 miles of frozen sea and the international dateline, lies the Union of Soviet Socialist Republics. Indeed, I have just worked out that if you go due west from here the next bar where a man can get a respectable drink is almost certainly in Moscow.

The thought was inspired by the fact that Unalakleet is another of Alaska’s Native Territory ‘dry’ towns, which probably explains its high proportion of staggering drunks.

From here the racers turn north along the Norton Sound and then west to Nome and the finish line. It is 260 miles of the fastest conditions they ever encounter and it is here that the real contenders fight it out.

They strip their 10ft. sleds of everything but iron rations and a gun, abandon sleep, urge one last effort from their dogs and sprint for it.

The experts say it will be won in two-and-a-half days from now, with the also-rans and stragglers coming in up to ten days later.

It was here, just after noon yesterday, that Joe Redington played his ace. He arrived after 15 hours on the trail from Kaltag, fed his dogs and gave every indication that he was going to join his rivals in an eight-hour sleep before the final assault.

While they bedded down, Redington discreetly harnessed his dogs and slipped out of town.

A Redington victory would be acclaimed across Alaska, whose every radio network is now carrying hourly progress reports, as emotionally as Stanley Matthews's eventual triumph in a Wembley Cup Final.

He is a tiny, soft-spoken man of great courtesy and gargantuan modesty and he is at an age when most European men are negotiating pension rights, watering tomatoes in their carpet slippers, and complaining that the new generation has lost its drive.

Joe Redington is, in fact, 59 and when he sledded out of here he had not slept for more than 22 hours and had spent all but four of the preceding 16 nights out of doors in temperatures ranging from 20 to 55 degrees Fahrenheit below freezing.

When his rivals were woken and told of his departure, they dragged themselves out of sleeping bags and prepared for pursuit.

But getting a sled dog team back on the trail is not like refuelling a Grand Prix racing car in the pits. Dog food has to be prepared and heated and at least partly digested and that takes two hours.

As I write, there are eleven teams trying to catch him between Shaktoolik and Koyuk and they include Warner Vent, twice runner-up in the Iditarod Trail, Jerry Riley and Emmitt Peters, both former winners, Dick Mackey, a close friend of Redington's and The Big Swede, Rick Swenson.

The feeling is that Redington can't get away with the one big prize he's never won. 'Son of a gun' said a non-contender. 'They ought to let the old guy win it. If they don't, he's going to keep at it until they find him out there frozen dead one of these years.'

Back down the trail by almost 300 miles, the woman to whom this race has been a four-year obsession has quit.

Dinah Knight, who wrecked her marriage and spent 4,000 dollars preparing, is the victim of near-starvation, total exhaustion and good manners. Held up by blizzards in open country for three days, she eventually arrived in Iditarod and said: 'I can't be a burden to this race any longer.'

Some time today, weather permitting, she and her dogs will be flown out from a nearby airstrip.

Aged 36, a psychiatrist from Minnesota and impelled to tackle an ordeal in which she stood out like a gym mistress against Muhammad Ali, she has earned nothing but admiration from menfolk in a country where a woman's place is at the sink.

The other woman entrant, 23-year-old Varona Thompson, survives. Also snowed up in a trapper's cabin for almost three days, she is on the move again and was last sighted at Anvik.

'If you survive this one there are few things on earth that will ever concern you again'

Nome, Alaska. — Ten yards from the finish line, Rick Swenson made a lovely gesture.

He halted his team, stumbled alongside them and almost hugged the remaining daylights out of his lead dogs, Old Buddy and Andy.

'Here,' said the gesture 'are the real heroes.' But no words came, for the Big Swede's lips were sealed by his own frozen breath. Icicles hung down like stalactites from his thin moustache and the upper reaches of his face were sand-papered scarlet by the awful winds.

He then re-mounted his sled, gently eased his huskies through the archway that dominates Nome's filmset Front Street, and thus won The Last Great Race on Earth.

It was a sensational finish to the Iditarod Trail. After 1,110 miles across mountain ranges, ocean, dangerous thin ice in canyon beds, and passes where the cry of the wolf carries five miles, Swenson won by 800 yards from Jerry Riley, a musher of half-Indian, half-European blood.

This, over a distance almost exactly that of London to Naples, was somewhat less than the length of The Mall which separates Trafalgar Square from Buckingham Palace.

Swenson completed the journey in 16 days 16 hours 27 minutes 13 seconds. Riley's time was 16 days 16 hours 32 minutes and 1 second. Warner Vent, an Indian who renounced alcohol for the whole of the race, was third, 12½ minutes later.

The reason Vent went on the wagon was that in two previous races he had finished second, each time admitting getting staggeringly drunk during the mandatory 24-hour stop that all mushers have to make at some point in the race to rest their dogs.

Mr Vent, understandably, has been taking the occasional drink today. There is no shortage of it here in the old Gold Rush town at the end of the trail.

When Rick Swenson asked for a glass of milk over lunch, a waitress with lipstick which appeared to have been applied by a billposter, snapped: 'You can have either beer or Scotch.'

So Rick Swenson, the Big Swede, returned to civilisation. He is 26 and third generation American with a frontier Alaskan's contempt for politicians, welfare systems, fast-talking businessmen in suits, those trying to outlaw guns up here, and animal protectionists who conduct their campaigns from the pet spaniel and dachshund territory alongside New York's Central Park.

He met them in high school and university, which he quit after two years. 'I studied draft evasion and gin,' he said.

'And then I went to work on the Alaska oil pipeline, where they paid me $1,400 (around £800) a week to do nothing. We sat around in buses and ate huge meals. I don't need their money and I don't want to live like that.'

Swenson typifies the men taking part in this race. He won £5,400, which just covered his expenses of raising and entering a team.

Every other entrant will suffer a loss and, as I write, 11 are into Nome, 20 are still out in the wilds up to 300 miles distant, and 16 have retired because of tired dogs, personal injury or illness.

It is almost impossible to convey the toughness of these men or of Varona Thompson, the only woman survivor, who will receive a heroine's welcome here about six days from now if she can endure the head winds that cut through to the soul on this side of Alaska.

Swenson does not have the technique to survive at Chris Bonington's shoulder on Everest. He probably wouldn't last a single round with Muhammad Ali. He couldn't stay two laps of an athletic circuit with Lasse Viren.

But he has dimensions of hardness and endurance and a capacity for survival long lost to those of us now cradled from birth certificate to early retirement by government acts, central heating or union vigilantes.

It may not make these men better but it certainly makes them different.

'What,' I asked Joe Redington, aged 59, who arrived here in fifth position nine hours after Swenson, 'would you say to a European daily commuter whose world would end if he woke up one morning to find there was no hot water for shaving?'

'Well,' said Redington, whose sleep has averaged three hours in 24 over the past 17 days, most of it outdoors in temperatures of up to 70 below freezing, 'I wouldn't say anything unless asked.

'But if I were asked, I would suggest that you only get one shot at this life and you might as well make the most of it.

'I don't think we're here to take things for granted. A race like this reminds you that the world doesn't necessarily owe you a living.'

Mr Redington, who could own villas in the Caribbean and on the Riviera and a flat or two in Paris and New York if the fancy took him, will be competing on the Iditarod Trail again next year.

Apart from prize money, the Iditarod competitors receive nothing apart from a belt with a metal hasp which bears the words 'Iditarod Finisher'.

They get one of those, irrespective of the position they come in under the arch in Nome.

'That belt,' said Swenson, 'means more to me than any amount of money. It is one of the few objects that a man can no longer buy. To get one you have to come here and do it.'

All manner of people come here to do it for all manner of reasons, including Dr Terry Adkins of the Lower Forty-Eight, which is what Alaska somewhat deprecatingly calls the remaining parts of the United States.

Along the trail, Adkins has been a charismatic figure, amusing, highly intelligent, roughing the roughest conditions with a supreme defiance.

Awaiting his arrival here his wife said: 'When he first took part in this race he came home a very different man. It was all of six months before we could get on the same wavelength again.

'He had seen things and understood things and when I asked stupid questions he said nothing at all. Now I understand a little more and I shall be up here for every race until he decides not to do it again.'

If it sounds like male chauvinism in excelsis that is probably the case.

The point is, of course, that if you can survive this one, there are few things on earth that will ever concern you again.

The Pamplona Feria, in the Basque region of Spain, is an immovable feast. It starts on July 7 each year, lasts seven days and attracts writers, drunks, drunk writers and some 100,000 others. It is all things to all men and completely addictive. I hope to continue going there annually until the Great Matador in the Sky decrees otherwise.

'Hemingway's idea that the Estafeta is the last peace-time proving ground is unjustifiably romantic'

Pamplona, Spain. — At the risk of outraging genteel opinion I must confess that the Pamplona Fiesta seemed an adequate alternative this year to that other piece of naked butchery known as the Birmingham Test Match.

At least it bore some semblance to a contest. The bulls only lost 42-1 this time. Well, 42-2 if you count the Australian who mistook a high balcony with a very low parapet for the bathroom.

Such elemental errors in navigation are not uncommon in Pamplona where the Basques, the Sons of Jake Barnes, phoneys, remittance men, Swedish madmen, American bores, Australian dentists, some virgins, a large number of international inebriates and not very many animal lovers congregate each July in the common belief that since Armageddon is scheduled for August, what the hell?

Mostly they drink and watch the bullfights, but some run. 'Run' in this context means they commit themselves to hurtling down a narrow cobbled street through the dusty morning sunbeams in front of seven half-ton fighting bulls who've never heard of the Marquess of Queensberry.

It has been brought to my attention that certain sequences from one of this year's 'runs' were shown on BBC and ITV, which is much to be regretted.

It caused great anguish to some of my loved ones and all of my Income Tax inspectors, who were under the impression that my insurance policies were about to mature all of a sudden. Fourteen men were gored by Don Pablo Romero's animals, including Gregorio Gorriz, ironically a celebrated 10,000 metres athlete, for whom, regrettably, the sun will never rise again.

Actually, I was 50 yards away at the time, leaning against the bronzed bust of Papa Hemingway, drinking Carlos III and wondering what all the fuss was about. In fact, it was the most murderous run in 40 years, but the following morning the bulls came through with the dreary discipline of sheep and there would have been much more danger crossing Regent Street in the rush hour.

The TV pictures, however, have aroused some interest in this esoteric activity and I have been asked to compare the relative dangers of having your back to the bulls or your front to Lillee and Thomson.

There is no question about it. Having run with the bulls, off and on for 14 years at Pamplona, I would rather run with them for a further 14 than face two consecutive overs from Australia's opening bowlers.

For one thing, it is advisable to face Lillee and Thomson wholly sober. For another they give you no respite, whereas there is a well-charted coward's route down the street called the Estafeta and I am acquainted with every buttress, recess, concavity and gutter of it.

There is even a doorway of a ladies' hairdressers half way down, where you can squeeze almost two-thirds of your body out of sight, only this is normally requisitioned long before you get there by about 430 Italians.

The run, in short, is what you make it. You can get yourself killed if you insist but, if you don't, it is an amusing and occasionally exhilarating way to round off a night's drinking.

Pile-ups, bruises and grazes are frequent but fatalities, in view of the ratio of nasty bulls to nice runners, are rare. Three men have been killed in the past four years. One of those gored this year was 71 years old and had been running for 60 years without mishap.

Hemingway's idea that the Estafeta is the last peace-time proving ground for men of courage is, I fear, unjustifiably romantic. Whatever it looked like on the box, Pamplona is a piece of cake compared with the next three Tests.

The only real qualities demanded of those who are drawn back there year after year are a high tolerance to strong drink, the ability to work a 48-hour shift and a total acceptance of behaviour so eccentric that it would not be tolerated elsewhere or, indeed, in Pamplona itself during the other 51 weeks of the year.

There was a moment this year, for example, when 14 diners continued to eat well and convivially while two of their company slid off their chairs beneath the table of a crowded restaurant.

One was a European lady of great elegance and the other an American journalist of much enterprise. They returned for coffee and brandy with the detente between our two great Continents visibly strengthened.

The final piece was written for Sportsworld *magazine and the* New York Times. Sportsworld *died a few months later, a reminder, perhaps, that prophecy is a dangerous business.*

'The public rose up against tawdry little starlets who sold their boring non-life stories to newspapers'

London, January 1, 2000. – By some miracle we survive to see the 21st century. For millions it is sheerly due to Red China's anti-cancer vaccine discovery back in 1985. In my trade of sportswriting, where excess in all things was once an industrial hazard, there are other reasons. With whisky at £73 a bottle who can afford alcoholism? And the 1993 Act of Parliament at least forced fresh air back into our lungs by banning the manufacture of all tobacco products.

So, mostly, the Doomwatch patrol got it all wrong. The false premise of their pessimism was that our children and grandchildren would be as greedy, indolent, covetous and self-indulgent as we were back in the hooligan days of George Best and Geoff Boycott and a capitalist-Communist Rumanian gypsy named, if I recall it correctly, Nastase.

As the venerable Lord Bannister told the United Nations Assembly in Kampala only last week: "For almost two decades in the 60's and 70's sport contributed nothing to world health, culture or contentment. Avarice reigned as sport was raped by its promoters and practitioners. We must be grateful to a responsible new generation for a true Restoration." Lord Bannister, of course, will be remembered by many as the world's first four-minute miler. He smiles now when he recalls that achievement. Today the world mile-record stands at 2 minutes 57.8 seconds.

How off-beam we were in those days is only apparent in retrospect.

The politicians of the Eastern bloc were using sport as a blunt instrument of propaganda. The religious fanatics of the Black Muslim movement were using Muhammad Ali as a spokesman for racism and damned nearly started a revolution. The sportsmen of the capitalist west rose up in anarchy against the reactionary and ill-visioned rulers of sports like tennis, athletics and even cricket. They formed their own unions and roamed the world like circus troupes, caring nothing that the world would soon tire of synthetic sensation.

It was inevitable that the faltering Olympic movement could not survive the riotous shambles of the Teheran Games of 1984. It has taken a dozen years to revive them under new management and we are entitled to take pride in the fact that this year's Olympiana will attract athletes from 204 nations to oil-rich Aberdeen. There will be no national flags and no national anthems and we confidently expect the 10-foot barrier in the men's high-jump to be broken.

* * *

It is not without humour that we may now look back and see what the prophets and soothsayers of 1975 were envisaging for sport in this year 2000. Satiated by sex, bored with promiscuity, tired of wife-swapping but convinced that degeneracy was there to stay, they assumed — to relapse into the smart argot of that absurd and semi-literate era — that we'd all be into the violence kick.

Pimpled youths, seeking diversions other than smashing up Continental towns after football matches or using frail widows for their kung-fu and karate practice, were attracted back to the cinema by two films purporting to portray the Ultimate Sport.

One was called *Rollerball* and the other *Death Race 2000* and the spurious messages of both were that future generations, bereft of the thrill of world war by a lasting if somewhat tenuous peace, would need vicarious relief in the form of gladiatorial combat in which some of the players bought it as bloodily and conclusively as those groovy old Christians in the Rome Coliseum.

Death by deliberate collision, death by injuries received while roller-skating crammed them into the movies. But that was just before the days of the Jenkins-Heath Coalition which won a spectacular points victory over inflation and the Moral Revival Movement of 1978. *Rollerball*, which you can still catch these days in the old Classic cinemas, is now a laugh a minute.

* * *

British domestic soccer was in such an advanced state of decay by the mid-70s that what has happened in the intervening 25 years was wholly predictable. Moribund tactics, unintelligent planning and ill-mannered fans so undermined the game that as soon as the banks called in their overdrafts the monolithic 92-club English League was a goner.

Our 12-club League (average crowds 120,000) is adequate and the success of our two leading clubs, Arsenal Hotspurs and Merseyside United, in the World Club League is proof that we can still hold our own globally. Merseyside's recent victories over the Sydney Rangers and the San Fransisco Quakers, away from home, were sufficient to rouse even the acerbic critic of the *Times-Express-Sun* to comment that the 4-4-2 tactics of the old days were about as intelligent in concept as Field Marshal Haig's deployment of cannon-fodder almost a century ago on the Somme.

Naturally none of these global Leagues would have been possible without today's inter-continental rocket travel. We can now watch Arsenal-Spurs play in Paris on a Saturday and England struggling to save the Ashes in Melbourne on Sunday and still catch Muhammad Ali's 215th defence of his world heavyweight title in Johannesburg on the Monday evening.

* * *

That Ali is fighting in Johannesburg at all is a miracle which younger readers may not appreciate. The Mao Stadium there is one of sport's high temples these days but I well recall the time when coloured athletes of any description were *persona non grata* in South Africa. The government of the day was warned what would happen but since they only paid lip-service to putting their miserable house in order, the inevitable happened.

South Africa's full readmission to world sporting circles has been one of the bloodless triumphs of the past 20 years. Ngbanga Odole now must rank with Christopher Cowdrey as one of the two finest No 4 batsmen in the world and South Africa's successes in the mixed doubles at Wimbledon last year was not without ironic humour for those who know family trees. When Felicity Vorster announced her engagement to Jimkomo Masambula in the euphoric moments after they'd carried off the title it took the *Daily Mail's* wicked old society columnist, Nigel Dempster, to point out in public whose great-grand-daughter she is.

* * *

We always knew that once the United States took off at soccer they'd annexe the World Cup, as they did in 1994 and 1998. We always knew that once Lester Piggott felt the financial draughts of retirement he'd leap back in the saddle again and win the Derby, as he did in 1987, 1989 and 1992. We always knew that once Edward Heath got the bit between his teeth he'd capture the America's Cup, as he did in Evening Cloud in 1994. We always knew that once the world came to its senses and stopped playing war games and started diverting its wealth into science and medical research, some very simple and long overdue things would happen in sport.

Aged linesmen have at last been replaced at Wimbledon by an

electronic device which simply flashes 'In' or 'Out'. It is infallible and has put the actor-players right out of business. Test match umpires now carry mini-TV's to adjudicate leg-before-wicket verdicts. They no longer have to read where they went wrong in tomorrow's paper. Personality-defect detectors now eliminate all candidates to become gatemen, turnstile operators or security guards at our great sports stadiums before they spread misery throughout the occasion. Blatant-lie detectors are at last in use to keep from Press boxes hangers-on, representatives of wholly mythical newspapers and distant relatives of small-time officials.

These are major advances.

* * *

In short, a 20th century which started with bloody fools ordering the poor of one nation to go and blow the heads of the poor of another nation ended with lots of healthy people from lots of nations competing, without too much rancour, in most of the traditional sports.

The optimism was always justified after, say, 1980 when the public rose up against tawdry little starlets who sold their boring non-life stories to newspapers and failed to give a damn whether Charlie Ficklebum was wanting away from Allbranchester United again or not.

It was justified the moment we started educating our kids and teaching them to differentiate between class performance and dross and, above all, that to identify with a team or a sportsman to such a degree that you get depressed when they or he loses is perhaps the most idiotic form of masochism the human race has ever inflicted upon itself.

Mind you, my six-foot nine-inch sepia grandson who's an archery professional with Harlow New Town doesn't believe a word of it. 'If it was a Jenkins-Heath Coalition,' he asks, 'whatever happened to Peter Wilson?'